# English Provincial Silver

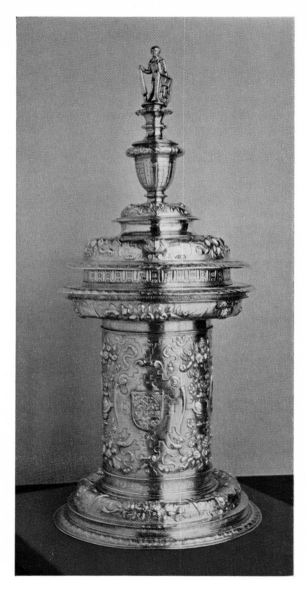

The Reade Salt by William Cobbold
Norwich, 1568. (Corporation of Norwich)

# English Provincial Silver

An Account of Old Country Silver with Sections
on Ireland, Scotland and Wales

*Margaret Holland*

Arco Publishing Company Inc
New York

Published by ARCO PUBLISHING COMPANY, Inc.
219 Park Avenue South, New York, N.Y. 10003

Library of Congress Catalog Card Number 79–160142

ISBN 0–668–02492–5

Printed in Great Britain

# Contents

# List of Illustrations

7

*Simplified Outlines of Silver Marks in the Text*

# One

# The General Picture

Silver has mirrored an important part of history through the ages, and where it has been made in the country districts of England a local slant is often added to the story. The type of things that were made, and the fashions they followed, did not just happen. On the wider scale they show national needs and reflect major events: the coming of Christianity and the desire to beautify the church; the Norman invasion and the creation of great households, all requiring domestic plate; the dissolution of the monasteries and virtually a fresh start; times of national riches, with grand silver; wars, and other times of need, with simple, unadorned objects, often dual-purposed.

Provincial silver mainly followed the national trends and, in most cases, differences that point positively to a given area are only in detail. Naturally the standard of work varied between individual craftsmen, but some places had a higher overall reputation than others. Rarity adds value to a piece that is not necessarily better than its fellows; historical interest or a known story, such as the standish by the American Philip Syng, from which the Declaration of Independence was signed in Philadelphia, has a similar effect. In England the system of hallmarking stamps certain basic facts on each piece and knowing the background story of these marks helps to bring the subject to life. These marks were not really a code; properly and legally punched they were the result of laws made to protect the craft and prevent bad or dishonest workmen from disgracing it. They were also designed to ensure invariable quality, and almost invariably they did.

Throughout early history, London complained that frauds were practised in the provinces, but when the subject came to thorough examination at the great enquiry of 1773, stories emerged showing that even London goldsmiths had not been above buying a drink for the man who would punch their plate. The master craftsman had a pride in his work and would not have wasted time and skill on sub-standard metal; nevertheless, he did not always bother to send the piece for assay, for this was often difficult and time-consuming when far removed from London.

Marks are very important, and a great deal of the history of silver must be told through them. The expert can read them at a glance, but he will also know the approximate date of manufacture from the general style, and the probable maker from the workmanship and detail of decoration. Marks were never intended to be read by the student of silver and were, in fact, a closed book until about a century ago. They are still no substitute for knowledge, and the more silver is handled and studied, the more pleasure and information it will give. This may, at times, be further increased by learning the story of a piece and tying it up with local or personal history, and it is hoped that this book, mainly about actual silver, will help to show the fascination to be found in its background.

The story of the provincial assay offices is, in the main, that of one long fight with London and, except in the beginning, the marks they used were mostly tied up with it. This complex subject will be easier to understand if first taken as a whole, for so much history was common to all. Ninety per cent of all silver made in England was marked in the capital anyway, for London was the headquarters of the English gold-smith, a term which includes the silversmith, and most of the greatest craftsmen worked there, wherever they may have been born. But Goldsmiths' Hall was jealous of its good name and anxious to be the sole custodian of standards all over England—and of the revenue to be derived from it. There were times when silver could be marked legally nowhere else, and some of the countrymen may then have sent work to London, as required, although the majority preferred to deliver goods to their customers unmarked.

In any trade there are good men anxious to produce honest work, and it was not very long before these banded themselves together in unofficial guilds for mutual protection against the charlatans who did not care what they did. Earliest history is mostly lost, but clues suggest that Chester, a mint city since AD 925, had probably organised itself early; goldsmiths, in the plural, are recorded as working in Lincoln in 1155, at Newcastle in 1248, Norwich in 1285, York in 1313 and Exeter in 1327, all of which are likely to have had unofficial guilds even earlier.

The first date we know for sure is 1180, when a London 'guild' was fined for being 'irregularly established' without the king's licence. The use of silver, of course, was already centuries old, and when King Offa cut 240 pennies from a Saxon pound of silver in AD 790, it was sterling silver that was used. This was eleven ounces and two pennyweights of pure silver to eighteen pennyweights of copper, which was needed to make the soft silver durable.

King Henry III was the first monarch to realise that some sort of protection was necessary for so fine a craft, and in 1238 he decreed that six of the most dependable goldsmiths of London should be appointed to superintend the work of all. This was the true beginning of the assay, and every piece of silver was supposed to be tried by them before being sold, although it was not until 1300 that the mark of the leopard's head,

Leopard's head

punched to prove that it had been done, was first mentioned.

The provisions of this Act were specified in much greater detail in the royal charter of 1327, which became the foundation of the Worshipful Company of Goldsmiths. By it, London was given the privilege of marking all silver made anywhere within the King's Dominions with the leopard's head, after proving that the metal was of the 'sterling standard', as in coin. The Germans, who lived to the east of Britain, were called Esterlings by the English, and one presumes that the word 'sterling' derived from this.

In most of the provincial towns where silver was made, the standard of work had been controlled by unofficial inspectors who lacked only authority to enforce their rules. They were as concerned as anyone else that standards should not be degraded by the few who covered base metal with silver and sold it for solid worth, or practised other forms of fraud. Now it was decreed that one man should carry the work of all, from any silver-making town, to London for marking, and that failure to do so would be punished by imprisonment.

The fight was on, and uncomfortable though life might be made by failure to comply, it was as nothing to the possible hazards in obedience. The country was still largely covered by forests, through which roads, or tracks, wound their way, giving ample cover to highwaymen, who had plenty of time to lie in wait. From Exeter, Chester, or York, men were solemnly expected to run this gauntlet, their saddlebags crammed with silver which they and their colleagues had spent weeks in fashioning. Apart from its worth, it was work they were anxious to deliver promptly to customers who had ordered it, and to collect payment, safely and quickly. Had all craftsmen moved to London, as some did, customers in the far corners of the country would have found it difficult to obtain silver at all. There was, in fact, a real need for the provincial goldsmith.

So they carried on as before, with no legal protection against those who worked silver that was 'less fine than it ought to be'. Parliament, recognising the situation, then relented, and in 1378 decreed that each goldsmith should have his own mark, by which his work should be known, and that this should be punched on every object he made. The mayors and governors of all cities and boroughs, or the master of the mint where there was one, were required to examine the piece and to stamp it with the mark of their own city arms.

Almost nothing survives from this period, but it does appear that the provincial goldsmith was happy with the arrangement, and makers' marks begin to appear thereafter, even though a large number have never been deciphered. But Parliament was not satisfied, perhaps finding it impossible to collect revenue from such scores of little places, many of which used virtually the same mark—or no mark at all—as before.

So, in 1423, an Act appointed seven towns to control the provinces: York, Newcastle-upon-Tyne, Norwich, Lincoln, Bristol, Salisbury and Coventry, and it is from this point that provincial history is recognised. But history is inclined to skim over men's feelings, and one has to read between the lines to realise that this Act was unpopular with the workers. There was no rush to set up offices; in fact, the first three towns named were the only ones that ever did so. Nor was there compliance in the outlying districts, where even the shorter journey was still found dangerous and unnecessary. No great care seems to have been taken in choosing these towns either, and the arbitrary selection gave good grounds for resentment. The West Country, where the craft flourished, was particularly badly served. Bristol was undoubtedly a more important city than Exeter, but even Exeter, whose goldsmiths were keen and hardworking, was inconveniently far removed from the workshops scattered all over Devon and Cornwall. Yet Bristol was their appointed guardian.

The extent to which Bristol may have made silver is not really known. A spoon brought up from the river there bore the mark of BR conjoined, as used by the Bristol mint in 1643–5, and other similarly marked spoons, mostly with the addition of a device, are known. This is presumed to be the Bristol mark, but all are of roughly the same date, c 1640, leaving many puzzles unsolved. Although Bristol was

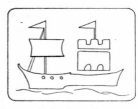

Bristol mark

again appointed in 1701, the earliest piece of silver that bears the arms of the city, a ship issuing from a castle, one of five marks in all, is a straining spoon dated 1730. Then, in 1964, a beautiful, plain, pear-shaped jug turned up in a London saleroom, with a moulded lip and double scroll handle, engraved with a crest, its only ornament. This bears the rare ship and castle mark among the usual five, and was the work of an unidentified maker, 'EM', in 1740. There is a similar jug in Bristol City Art Gallery, probably by Stephen Curtis, and it would appear that this fascinating puzzle is at last about to be unravelled.

The appointment of Salisbury also seems to have been without reason for, so far as we know, only a few goldsmiths were ever registered there and her guild was without importance. Yet Salisbury was the only town south of London to be appointed. Nor were the western midlands well served, although here the circumstances were different, for Chester, a great silver city, was under the jurisdiction of her own earl and did not come under the Crown.

Although Coventry never set up an office, a guild of goldsmiths flourished there in the middle ages and evidently produced fine, and even prolific plate. All has vanished without trace. A few names appear later in history, between 1544 and 1651, but nothing has yet been published to suggest a Coventry mark.

Of the seven towns, there remains only Lincoln, which also failed to take up her appointment though goldsmiths had worked there from the twelfth century. Nevertheless, the little that is assumed to have been made there has had its continuing survival assured, for Lincoln Cathedral has set up a treasury where the ancient ecclesiastical plate of the whole diocese is both safeguarded and displayed. Other cathedrals will soon be copying this fine idea.

York, Newcastle and Norwich, all broadly on the eastern side of the country, had long and fascinating histories which will be told in separate chapters, but in 1423 their appointment had little effect on the status quo.

The general picture now becomes somewhat clouded, but one date to note is 1478, when the leopard's head became crowned. It is generally assumed that any piece bearing this head uncrowned was, therefore, made prior to 1478, in London, but it also happened to be the mark of Shrewsbury. Silversmiths worked in this Shropshire town from the twelfth century, but the greater part of their known work, mostly spoons, was made in Elizabethan times. Spoons so marked may, therefore, have been made in Shrewsbury in the sixteenth century, rather than London before 1478.

It is also possible that date letters were first introduced about that time, although no Act approving such a device has been traced. It is first mentioned as an established fact in 1597, over one hundred years after such letters had appeared on London's silver. Date letters are undoubtedly the most complicated mark to be found on plate, and most of us need a reference book to read them correctly. In London they consist of a series of twenty letters of the alphabet, changed annually from A to B etc, in May; at first this change took place on 19 May, St Dunstan's Day, but was later altered to 29 May, in commemoration of the return of Charles II. This is why, when a piece is dated, a choice of two years is given—eg 1701-2—each date letter, in fact, covered part of two years. Every cycle of letters is also stamped in a different type, Roman, Lombardic, italic etc, and in a different shape of shield, so that an identical style of letter represents an entirely different date if the shield is not the same. The object of this was to identify the assay master-warden responsible if the plate was later found to be sub-standard, not to help the collectors who now find it so useful.

Each provincial office also ran its own date cycle, and where other marks are missing or rubbed, this can place the origin of the piece;

although the same date stamp may have been used elsewhere at an entirely different period, the style should make the difference obvious. Deciphering these tables in the provinces originally was made easier by inscriptions, but some of these can be misleading, for the date on which a piece was presented to a church or person is not necessarily the date on which it was made. However, Exeter's first known date letter, a Roman 'A', is found on a communion cup which also bears the date, 1575, pricked out, and other inscriptions and later letters tally with it.

History had a great bearing on the laws governing the marking of silver in the centuries leading up to 1697. The extravagance of Henry VIII led him to debase the value of coin several times in order to mint more for himself from the same amount of silver. This was the probable reason for the introduction of the lion passant as a standard mark, which

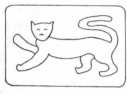

first appeared in 1544. Whether all trace of the legislation concerning this has simply been lost, as with the date letter, is unknown, but the chances are that Goldsmiths' Hall, in pride, wished to dissociate the craft from the royal Mint, and so set this stamp itself. The sterling standard, although once raised, was never lowered on plate, and the lion passant was set upon it in London to show

Lion passant

full value. Later, it was also used in most provincial centres.

Queen Elizabeth, more concerned for her country, boldly restored the value of coin and, except during the period of the 'higher', or 'Britannia' standard, 1697–1720, the standard for silver coin and plate remained identical. This could sometimes have unfortunate results. A goldsmith, short of silver, could melt down coin for his use, and plate could equally be thrown into the melting pot for the manufacture of coin. Despite the magnificent work that had so frequently gone into it, plate appears to have had no added value. When silver was wanted as such, it was taken. When the monasteries were dissolved and their glorious adornments lost their use, some of the finest ecclesiastical plate ever known was lost to posterity through the greed of Henry VIII.

During the reign of Charles I plate was demanded, and confiscated where it was not freely given. The goldsmiths were in for a very lean period, for the king, it appeared, would stop at nothing to obtain money. The Mint in the Tower of London had always been used by merchants as a safe deposit; now the king threatened to commandeer their savings, and the goldsmiths, equipped for safe-keeping in Lombard Street but with very little bullion in hand, turned to taking in deposits from their fellows at 5 per cent interest and lending it out again at 8 per cent. Banking was born, but the true craftsman is an artist, not a financier, and many of the foreigners among them returned to the Continent.

But Englishmen also went away, and those who emigrated to America largely set up their workshops in Massachusetts, where they took in American apprentices and made American colonial silver. Robert Sanderson, one of the first to go, in 1634, had served a nine-year apprenticeship in London. John Hull, who became his partner, was trained in America by his brother who had been apprenticed in London, but Hull himself is responsible for the first all-American goldsmith, Jeremiah Dummer, who was apprenticed to him in 1659. Irishmen also went to America a little later, some of them settling in Maryland; Philip Syng, trained in Ireland, settled in Philadelphia in 1714. William Hughes, also born in Dublin where he gained his freedom in 1767, settled in Baltimore, Maryland, in 1771.

In England things went from bad to worse, and during the Civil War plate was needed by both sides. A large proportion of all that survived this, the second great onslaught on the goldsmith's wares within a hundred years, did so because it was either hidden or buried. Little new plate was required, and although trade picked up somewhat during the Commonwealth, most of what was made was severely plain. Tumbler cups, glorious in their simplicity, were born of this age. But when the country did finally recover from its troubles, there was a reaction against the austere life it had known, and silver plate entered one of its greatest periods. Now the cry was for more and more silver, not only in noble houses, palaces and churches, as previously, but in very much more modest homes, and even inns. The period was expansive, and spending lavish. A new, or at least much wider, class now had money, which led, as always, to trouble. Two separate factions wanted quantities of silver, the Mint and the goldsmiths, and there was not enough to go round. Coin went illegally into the melting-pot to provide silver for plate, and where it escaped this it became ridiculous and debased through clipping. Drunkenness was rife, leading to burglaries and murder, possibly through inebriated tempers but also because silver was there and meant money to buy more drink. In 1695, because of the 'inconvenience' to the public caused by the crime wave, an Act was passed preventing the use of silver, other than spoons, in public houses, which had previously been quite happy with pewter. All the silver thus rendered useless was to be taken to the Mint, for conversion to bullion.

Yet there was no question of mass-producing plate for this hungry public; the domestic silver of the period, particularly in drinking-vessels, was among the loveliest of all time. Nevertheless the prevailing mood may have been responsible for a certain slackness concerning marks, for a lot of silver of the period, both London and provincial, was stamped with the maker's mark only. It is easy to understand the craftsman with an over-full order book finishing a piece, pressing his stamp upon it to show that he had made it, and then getting on with the next, without bothering overmuch about assay. Nor had Parliament, with difficulties enough of its own, concerned itself with the silversmith for over one hundred years, but had left them free to get on with their job. No Act had been passed regarding their work since 1576, and as that had failed to reiterate the standing regulations regarding assay marks, it could well have been interpreted as a relaxation of them. Looking for loopholes in the law has ever been a national pastime in England, and the phrasing of this particular Act appears to have been well suited to the purpose, for it stipulated that the maker's mark should be stamped on a piece before it was set for sale. Work made to the order of a customer, as a large proportion was, was not put up for sale publicly, so that marking, some obviously thought, could legally be by-passed.

But the happy days came to an abrupt end. The coin situation was out of hand, and debasing the value of the currency would not be tried again. Countless laws and desperate punishment had failed to prevent the loss of coin to the country. Arthur Mangy, for instance, who made the Leeds town mace in 1694, was hanged for clipping and forging coin in 1696, and he was no extreme example. So, in March 1697, the standard for plate was increased from 11oz, 2dwt, to 11oz, 10dwt, which effectively ensured that coin could not be melted down, or clipped for other uses. It was dire remedy, and a clean sweep was made of the whole business. Marks were changed radically, so that silver of this new and higher standard would be readily distinguishable from the old, and provincial offices, as a separate entity, were abolished.

London had been complaining, as usual, about the standards of silver worked in the provinces, but it is impossible to say with what measure of justification. Members of both London and provincial guilds had been by-passing the assay, and undoubtedly some had taken advantage of the easy times. Be that as it may, London had won another round, and the only legal marks on the new standard silver were now to be punched in the capital.

The leopard's head crowned was to be replaced by the figure of a seated woman known as 'Britannia', and the lion passant as standard mark by a lion's head erased. The variable date letter was all that remained of the old marking system, but only the letter of London's cycle was legal, and no provincial craftsman dared stamp that. Another change was that all maker's marks, which had previously been either a device or initials, were now to be the first two letters of the worker's surname, an unsatisfactory arrangement which did not last because of the number of surnames beginning with the same two letters.

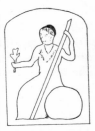

Britannia

All this led to extreme hardship for the provincial goldsmiths and their assay offices, who were entirely deprived of work—and revenue. It appears to have been legal to make silver to the order of a customer and to deliver it unmarked except for the maker's own stamp. This was usually, but not always, in the new form, and the words 'sterling' or 'Britannia', or variations of either, were sometimes added in Plymouth. Very little so marked survives. Craftsmen in the provinces carried on as best they could, and work of that time is less rare than was once thought. Where the maker is known, so is the place of origin, but silver stamped with provincial marks during the next three years is rare, and usually odd in form; more

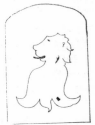

Lion's head erased

often it was individual and independent, without town marks at all.

Change was less marked in the minor guilds, for the simple reason that their marks were not officially recognised at the best of times.

Hull was a case in point. Tucked away in her inaccessible corner of England, she had long made a certain amount of silver, and names of her goldsmiths are recorded from 1427. From the seventeenth century

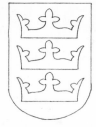

Hull mark

these pieces had been marked with the arms of the town—three ducal coronets in pale—the maker's mark and, very occasionally, a date letter. There is not a great deal of this silver to be seen, but the proportion during this close period remains unaltered.

Obviously, the situation could not continue, and in 1700 the goldsmiths of Chester, Norwich and Exeter explained their plight to Parliament, and petitioned redress for the provinces generally. Even though Chester had only been established in 1686 by royal charter, and Exeter had never been given office, all three had excellent reputations, and they put their case well. The result was the re-establishment of assay offices in York, Exeter, Bristol, Chester and Norwich. By an oversight, Newcastle was omitted, but won its renewed place a year later. Of these six, Bristol continued to take no interest, and Norwich virtually did no more.

The provisions of this new Act of 1700 were much more clear-cut and workable, and the cities concerned, all with established mints, immediately set about organising themselves to fulfil them. They were required to incorporate freemen of their cities who had served apprenticeships to the trade, provided that these worked no silver below the new standard and entered their names and addresses, with a picture of their own mark beside it, in a register kept by the wardens, two of whom were to be appointed annually. There had also to be an assay master, who was to mark all silver already bearing the maker's mark with the lion's head erased, the figure of Britannia, the arms of the city concerned, and a variable date letter. There was also a lot about fines and forfeits and things they should not do, but these clearly defined rules gave new heart to the provincial worker, his office and Goldsmiths' Hall alike; moreover, they ensured revenue to all. Assay was an expensive business, but obligatory. This was now accepted.

By 1719, the coinage had been largely stabilised and as the higher standard of silver was too soft to be altogether satisfactory for silverware, goldsmiths were allowed to go back to the old if they wished. Both standards were acceptable from then onwards, but while the majority reverted to sterling, a few, such as Paul de Lamerie, continued with the higher standard, marking it with Britannia and the lion's head erased in addition to the other marks then required.

23

Plate of sterling silver now reverted to London's old marks: the leopard's head crowned, the lion passant, the date letter, the maker's mark (which was now to be his initials) and, in the provinces, the addition of the registered town mark. This made four stamps in London, and five for the provinces.

An additional mark was imposed in 1784, proving that duty of 6d an ounce had been paid. This mark was the sovereign's head, and forging it was punishable by death. London's sterling silver marks were thus increased to five and the provinces to six, with the exception of Exeter which had previously dropped the leopard's head in 1778. The duty mark was discontinued in 1890.

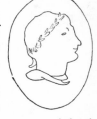

The goldsmith's was the most protected of all crafts, and London never lost sight of her aim to be the sole custodian of standards in the country. The last

Sovereign's head

great showdown took place in 1773, when Birmingham and Sheffield requested of Parliament the privilege of marking their own wares. Sending work to Chester or London had always been a great inconvenience. Now, with the rise of Sheffield plating, which was not so controlled, they felt at a great disadvantage with other provincial offices who neither had this rival in their midst, nor the expense of sending work away for assay.

Silver wrought in Sheffield was not, of course, the same thing as Sheffield plate, nor does the word 'plate', when applied to silver, mean plated wares. Sheffield plating was a process, discovered in 1743 by Thomas Boulsover, of fusing a layer of silver on to copper, first on one side of the copper ingot, later on both sides, then passing the sandwich through rollers before working it, the result being a highly satisfactory work of art that looked very much like real silver. By 1773, the demand for it was increasing rapidly, largely because a new class of people emerging from the industrial revolution wanted to live as the rich were doing, with tea-tables set with silver, but could not quite afford to do so.

This fine work, itself a subject for collectors, declined in the 1840s, when electro-plating, still with us, took over. This process, and the age of the machine generally, marked the beginning of the end for the provincial craftsman. The demand for fine handwork inevitably lessened, and as travelling became less difficult so the need for regional offices diminished.

But, in 1773, Sheffield had petitioned Parliament in much the same terms as other cities had done in 1700. Considerable silver was being made in Sheffield, and her goldsmiths were being put to unnecessary expense, delay and inconvenience by having to send their wares away for assay.

The very next day Birmingham put in a like petition, and Matthew Boulton, who worked in both mediums of silver as well as in other crafts, put the case for both cities in a manner worthy of the efficient business man that he was.

Sheffield did not plead that her plate workers were impressing silver hallmarks on their wares. That was London's charge and Goldsmiths' Hall, taking strong exception to the establishment of new provincial offices, seized this fresh opportunity to have them all closed. Protesting, as always, that frauds were being practised in the provinces generally and, particularly, that workers of Sheffield plate were setting their goods for sale under silver hallmarks, or as near to it as made no difference, Goldsmiths' Hall asked Parliament not only to turn down this petition, but to allow London to resume the sole guardianship of silver standards throughout England.

Parliament decided to look into these allegations thoroughly, and the enquiry instigated into the procedures of all assay offices was full and revealing. Much dirty linen was washed publicly, and London herself did not emerge unscathed. The result was that no office was closed, and a new Act was promulgated giving both Birmingham and Sheffield the right to stamp their own silverwares. Another result of this Act was the prohibition of stamping any letters on any object that was not made entirely of silver. The early plate workers had stamped their goods with initials, often placed in such a way as to look suspiciously like silver hallmarks, and this practice now ceased.

A large proportion of the silver that is bought and sold today was made after this period. The days of massive melting down were over, and what was made, some of it superb, some of it quite ordinary, is mostly still in existence. The collector's age of silver really began in about 1660; Queen Anne and early Georgian is frequently bought and sold—to those with a long purse—but 1773 was the start of the period of the average collector, and from then on quantity *may* be greater than quality.

The very old has romance and value simply because of age, whereas the collector of late Georgian silver needs to be both knowledgeable and discerning. Much that is really elegant and pleasant to live with was, at least in part, made with the aid of machines, and while such silver can never really achieve the patina of the old, hand-raised work, a great deal of it is still very well worth collecting. Fakes have, of course, to be guarded against, and decoration that has been added later, or inscriptions which have been obliterated, are other faults to look for, but these are matters strictly outside the province of this book.

Knowing something of the events which led up to the heyday of provincial silver helps to deepen our interest in the subject generally, but it is only by seeing and studying the best that judgement is formed. For those who cannot afford to buy, and perhaps a large proportion of those that can, the greatest pleasure lies in seeing fine, rare old work, and knowing not only the history of an individual piece, but also something of the conditions that led to its having been made at all.

London is still the best place in the world in which to find silver, but bargains—difficult enough to find anywhere—are less likely to be discovered in London than elsewhere. Provincial silver can also be found in London, and the greater part of all silver to be seen in the provinces will bear the capital's mark. But the finest old provincial work is most likely to be seen in provincial museums and churches, and the later, more collectable items, in the shops or private homes of the region.

# Two

# Exeter and the West Country

Men settled in Cornwall at about the time the use of metals became known, and travellers from Ireland later gave them their first creative inspirations, showing them what could be done with gold. The later discovery that silver was more malleable than gold, and could be extracted from the minerals they had in their own ground—lead, antimony and arsenic—was a natural process in the evolution of the art. Certainly, the Romans worked the silver-lead mines clustered up the Tamar Valley north of Plymouth, and by the time of the Conquest (AD 1066) they were well organised, as were the mines in north Devon. Where silver was smelted it must have been used, but the first record of a silversmith refers to a Plymouth worker in 1281.

By that time great care was being taken over the refining of the metal itself, and an ordinance issued by King Edward I in 1298 regarding the Tamar mines clearly laid down the manner in which it should be done, as well as the duties of the wardens and assayers, surely the first mention of such officers.

This is a fascinating glimpse at untold history, for to reach such a standard centuries of trial and error must have gone before. Even the rules regarding the miners, who were not to loiter in the market town on pay day 'on pretence of purchasing meat', show experience of men and their ways.

English-mined silver was never of great consequence, but at that time it was obviously the country's sole source of supply, and almost all the very early plate, most of which can only be guessed at, must have been made from silver taken from local mines. For domestic purposes natural implements, such as horns and shells, served adequately, but the church needed beautifying.

27

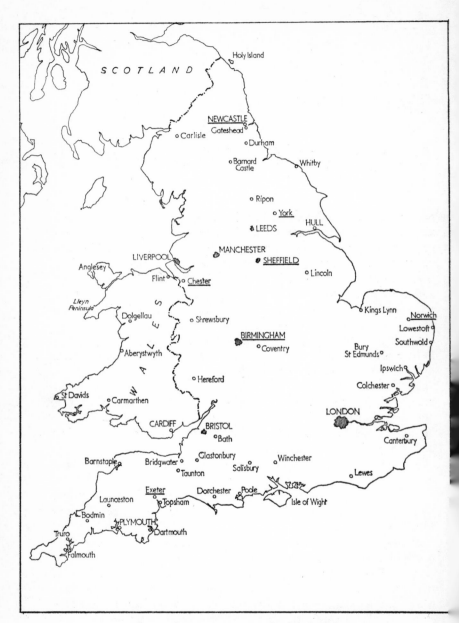

Silver-making centres in England and Wales

Whether or not St Joseph of Arimathea landed at Glastonbury, in Somerset, as is claimed, Christianity certainly spread through the west early. The oldest known chalice in England, made about AD 875, was found under seventeen feet of soil at Trewhiddle, in Cornwall, where it had been hidden from the marauding Danes, along with other gold and silver objects, and coins which help to fix the date. The probability is that the chalice was locally made.

St Dunstan, patron saint of goldsmiths, was born in Glastonbury in AD 909, and should really be considered a West Country man. The work he produced must be typical of that which adorned the monasteries in the tenth century, and although none remains to confirm it, the period he spent in Blandinium Abbey, near Ghent, and which so influenced his religious life, must have also had a bearing on the plate he made. He is also said to have made the crown used at the coronation of King Edgar at Bath in 973, when most of the ceremony we still know, including the singing of 'Zadok the Priest', was used.

It is hard to say exactly when Exeter formed the unofficial guild that was ignored in 1423, but the name of John de Wewlingworth is recorded as a goldsmith there in 1327, after which the names of goldsmiths are fairly constant, both in the city and in many parts of Devon and Cornwall.

Inscriptions have helped to date the oldest known pieces, and it is fortunate that the communion cup which bears the first date letter, a Roman 'A' in a shield, made by John Ions in 1575, also bears the inscription 'The Parish of Trinitye in the yeare of our Lorde 1575'. Another communion cup by the same maker is dated 1576 and marked with a 'B', while pricked out dates later help to fill out the first date-letter cycle.

The inscriptions are often of the greatest interest, and one of the oldest known West Country pieces could not otherwise have even been placed with certainty, for no town mark was used before 1571. This piece is a maplewood mazer, mounted in silver gilt and inscribed on the boss, 'A gift to the Parish of St Petroc'. It is believed to date from about 1480.

That so many mazers have survived from a period that can show little else is probably due to their silver mountings, which protect the wood while being insufficient to warrant melting down. As drinking-cups, mazers were very popular, especially in monasteries and among yeoman classes, but only those of the rich were mounted in silver; gilding, which was early found to prevent tarnishing, was an added refinement. Decoration was usually around the silver lip, the base, or on the boss print, a raised disc within the bowl.

The melting down, or otherwise destroying everything connected with the old faith, which virtually meant all things beautiful, was on the grand scale. Destruction got into the blood, and everything from stained glass windows and fine, illuminated books to the lead on the abbey roof was fair game. Yet enough silver, mostly from parish churches, managed to survive to satisfy the greed of Edward VI, who demanded all, except for one or two chalices in every parish.

This is why chalices form the bulk of pre-Reformation ecclesiastical plate, although a certain number of patens which were successfully hidden still survive. For a while many early chalices continued to be used during the Reformation period, providing they bore no images and conformed in other ways, but most of them were not really large enough for the altered church services in which the laity also used them. Some churches, therefore, melted down their silver and used the metal to make cups of a more practical size, and this practice of replenishing and refashioning generally accounts for the loss of much early work, not only ecclesiastical, through the ages.

Communion cups, particularly in Elizabethan times, were made all over the country, and the new church's trend towards uniformity led to the majority, both in London and the provinces, being made to much the same pattern, with a slightly domed cover and a flattened knop that became a foot when the cover was reversed and used as a paten.

But many cups made in Exeter and the West were distinctive in pattern, having a conical bowl with straight, tapering sides, reminiscent of a wineglass. John Ions was undoubtedly the greatest Elizabethan to use the old Exeter mark, basically a Roman 'X', and his cups appear in churches all over Devon, Cornwall and Somerset. His most frequently illustrated piece, also c 1575, can be seen in the Victoria and Albert Museum, London. This has a conical bowl, with slightly everted lip, but otherwise conforms to the accepted style and is

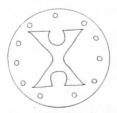

Exeter mark before
1701

30

a perfect example of graceful symmetry and proportion. Another of his cups, in the Glasgow Art Gallery and Museum, is very similar, but without the lip which undoubtedly adds elegance to the majority of his cups. In Chanter's inventory of church plate, there is frequent reference to 'the usual Exeter lip'.

Ions, who can be translated to 'Jones', worked to a pattern which, if not invariable, was quite distinctive, and the following extract from Chanter shows that more decoration was used than was strictly necessary. This 'Exeter type' cup, 7¼in high, from Sidmouth church, is marked with the date letter 'B' for 1576; its conical bowl is engraved with 'a band of interlacing strapwork and arabesque foliation ¾in wide, with pendants around centre, and tongue ornamentation at base; stem with knop and fillets, ornamented with hatching at top and bottom; foot domical, 3⅝in diameter, with tongue ornamentation round base'.

Another variation on the normal is in decoration. A beautiful cup at Swymbridge, in north Devon, by Thomas Mathew of Barnstaple, conforms in outline, for its trumpet bell-shaped bowl is set on a stem, complete with knop rather above middle. But its decoration, graceful and lovely, does not confine itself to bands; flowing foliage also adorns the cover, which has '1576' boldly expressed in the centre. Around the edge of this paten are three lines of 'hit and miss', a sort of continual Morse code, more usually associated with silver made where no expert engraver was available.

Barnstaple, which is not far from the prolific silver mines at Coombe Martin, had been the virtual capital of the wool trade in the fourteenth and fifteenth centuries. Where trade flourished, so did prosperous people eager to commission gold and silver plate. Goldsmiths of the quality of Thomas Mathew naturally resulted, and in fifty years of working in the town he produced fine spoons, including lion sejant and apostle spoons, in addition to many cups. Barnstaple has a mark adopted from the borough seal—a bird in a circular stamp—but Mathew, whose son Robert was also a goldsmith, never used it, preferring a peculiar flower or fruit, ornamented with leaves.

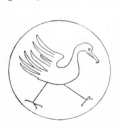

Early Barnstaple
mark

Another Barnstaple goldsmith was John Coton, whose cup for Stoke Rivers church was perhaps the most distinctive example of 'hit and miss' decoration, with three bands of it on an otherwise unadorned, slender, conical bowl, and one on the domed foot. The cover is also dotted, and there is a six-petalled flower on its finial.

These two goldsmiths were the greatest of those known to have been working in Barnstaple at the time, and while it must be ranked below Ions of Exeter, the work of Thomas Mathew was of a very high standard, with Coton only slightly his inferior. These two were inclined to mark their names in full, 'CoToN' alternating small 'o's' with capital letters.

A successful apprentice of Coton's was Peter Quick, sometimes spelt Quyche, who, in addition to spoons, made one of the loveliest cups in north Devon, for Loxhore church. Its conical bowl tapers gracefully and the panels of foliage, rather higher up the bowl than most, are enclosed by interlaced bands; another band of a different pattern is at the base of the bowl. Below this and on the rounded knop of the foot, 'hit and miss' breaks the surface.

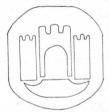

Barnstaple after 1625

Peter Quick and his son John used the town mark so seldom that a search for it might prove fruitless. This town mark was changed in 1625 to the rather common triple-towered castle, arms presented to the borough a few years earlier. John Peard, another Barnstaple man, used this, but his son sometimes varied it with a castle with a BAR above, and VM below.

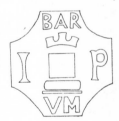

At about this time, roughly 1630–50, the lion rampant was found stamped on some silver in north Devon, notably at Barnstaple and Bideford. Now this was the mark used on Spanish coins at the time and it is reasonable to assume that when trading ships paid their dues in this currency, it was passed on to local silversmiths. After melting it down for use, they then stamped this mark to denote origin. This has been suggested as an explanation for the fleur de lys mark in East Anglia—coin from France.

Throughout England unmarked communion

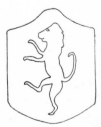

Lion rampant

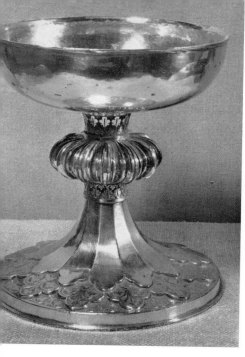

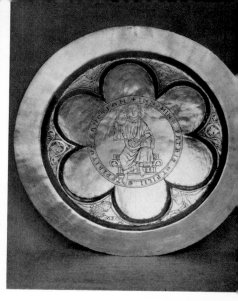

*age* 33 (*above*) The Dolgellau Chalice (*left*) and its paten (*right*), possibly the work of Nicholas 
he Great of Chester, c 1270; (*below*) William Cobbold's lovely cup and cover for St Mary Coslany, 
1567, incorporates most of the features of the Norwich-type communion cup

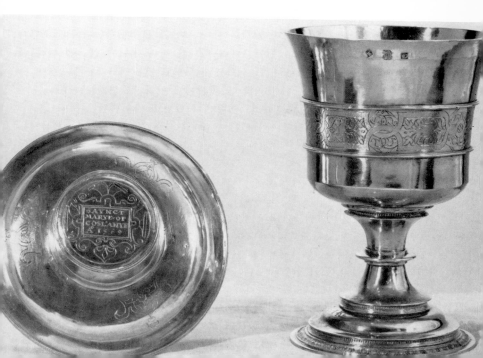

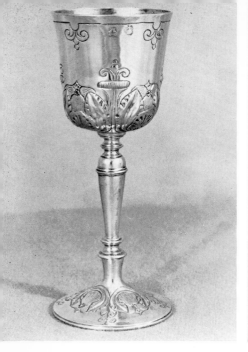
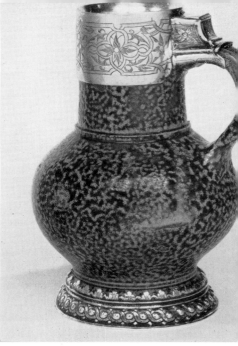

Page 34 (*above left*) Wine cup by Matthew Cobbold, Norwich, c 1595; (*above right*) Tigerware j
decorated in the typical Exeter way, by John Ions, 1570; (*below*) A set of three lighthouse sug
castors, by Andrew Law, Edinburgh, 1693, some years before they were normally made in sets
Scotland

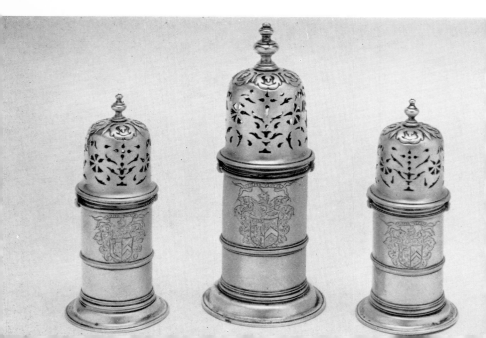

cups abound, for the need was so urgent that many were simply knocked up by the local smith; others are marked but by goldsmiths of varying standards who were frequently the only representative of their craft in their town. Lawrence Stratford, for instance, is the only name known for Dorchester, but some thirty of his cups belong to local churches, including one c 1575. This was sold at Sotheby's in 1967, and is very similar to another of his at Charmouth, Dorset. Richard Orenge, of Sherborne, made many spoons in addition to several cups, including a lovely one for the church of Gillingham, in Dorset. Inside the cover, the boss is inscribed '1574, GYLLYNGAM', nullifying the lack of other marks.

Although this was the great age for communion cups, a few were made later, perhaps as poor parishes grew in wealth and were able to afford finer plate. Many of these were the work of London makers, but

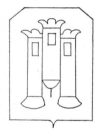

some were made by West Country craftsmen, such as Pentecost Symonds of Plymouth, who made several for Cornish churches in the early eighteenth century. As all the West Country craftsmen registered their mark in Exeter after an assay office had been established there in 1701, these pieces are fully hall-marked and stamped with Exeter's new mark, a triple-towered castle.

Exeter after 1701

But the most interesting cup of later date was a small one made by James Strang in 1729, at St Martin's, Exeter, intended for use when visiting the sick. On the cover, which is not domed, are four studs, rising to the same level as the flattened knop, to give extra support when used as a paten, perhaps balancing on the bed itself. Exeter Museum also has a small paten on a trumpet foot, made by this same craftsman in 1724.

With the exception of communion cups, the change the Reformation brought to church plate was one of loss, the magnificent plate of the Roman Catholic faith having disappeared. But, as we have seen, the restoration of the use of the communion cup to the laity in 1547 necessitated larger pieces generally, so that in addition to melting down and refashioning their own plate, the churches were quite often presented with cups and plates made for domestic purposes. These were usually given in thanks, sometimes personal, although the king's safe

c

return on the Restoration appears to have been of particular benefit to the churches.

Flagons were the one altogether new form of church silver that appeared as a result of this increased need. They were tall, sometimes pot-bellied in various forms but more often straight-sided, like the secular tankards of the period. A very few were pleasingly decorated, but the majority were literally plastered with ornamentation. Almost all were made after 1603, when it was decreed that the wine for communion be brought to the table in 'a clean, sweet standing pot of pewter, if not finer metal'. The majority were made in London, and the few of the West have no particular distinguishing features.

Because of special circumstances, the proportion of church plate made in Elizabethan times was extraordinarily high, but even before the establishment of Exeter's official assay office, all forms of contemporary plate were made in the West Country and enough remains not only to be seen in museums but also to appear occasionally in salerooms and shops. Examples which came up in local salerooms during 1967 included a James I apostle spoon, c 1610, and a James I seal-top spoon, pricked on the seal 'I.I. 1616', probably by John Ivy, of Salisbury, who is remembered for his gallantry during the time of plague in the city. There was also a seal-top spoon believed to have been made by Richard Orenge, of Sherborne, c 1600—enough to show that really early work in the West Country can be collected.

Truro also made quite a lot of silver, of which some fine spoons have survived. Local goldsmiths were most probably employed in the royal Mint, when it was in the town for almost a year during the Civil War. Marks taken to represent Truro are the conjoined 'TR', sometimes in a dotted circle; or an anchor, which demonstrated the town's authority over the river Fal.

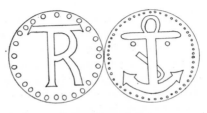

Truro (A and B)

The inconsistency of marks is quite bewildering at times. In Exeter before 1701 the mark varied so considerably that it has been suggested that each worker may have held his own stamp and punched his version of the town mark himself. A look at the early tables will show the 'x' alone; crowned (or uncrowned) within a circle of pellets; crowned in a circle, or in a circle of pellets with an additional pellet on either side of the 'x'; or with a large crown in a shield, following the general outline:

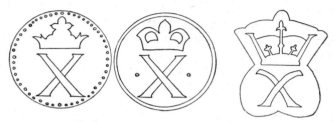

Variations on Exeter mark before 1701

But a second look will show that although several of these were in use at the same time, each was not confined to one craftsman, nor was the work of one man always stamped in the same way. Six separate varieties of the mark on plate made by I. Ions are shown in Sir Charles Jackson's classic work *English Goldsmiths and their Marks*.

It is mildly interesting to wonder about the reasons for this, but the important fact is that the mark invariably contains the Roman 'x', and is always recognisable as early Exeter. In those unofficial days, standards seem to have been well maintained in the region by those who stamped their own work, but there are no records to show how control, if any, was exercised.

During Elizabethan times a fashion raged for mounting various types of pottery jugs in silver; these were occasionally of porcelain, but more usually earthenware, Turkish, Sieburg, Rhodian or Wrotham ware. In most cases the jugs themselves were totally unworthy of the beautiful workmanship put into the mounts, and this is certainly true of the mottled brown Rhenish tigerware in which Exeter specialised. (Illustration, p 34.) Examples can be seen in Exeter Museum, and there is also a jug in the Victoria and Albert Museum, London, with superb silver mounts made by John Eydes, (who marked his work 'I YEDS') in

1580; New York's Metropolitan Museum of Art also has two, one by Eydes, 1580, and the other by Peter Quick of Barnstaple. All these clearly show the startling contrast between the jugs themselves and their magnificent gilded workmanship. Sailors brought these jugs home from Germany, landing at Topsham, just a few miles downstream from Exeter and an important port in those days.

Sailors also patronised the goldsmiths of Barnstaple, where craftsmen had probably been working since the town's first mint was set up under Ethelred, although Hugh Holbrook and his wife Alice, who registered their marks in 1370, are the first known names. After the wool trade moved away, this remained quite an important naval port. Now only small coastal boats sail up the river Taw, but in the late sixteenth and early seventeenth centuries, when sailors returned there from the east, it is possible that they introduced the idea for spoons known variously as Khrishna, Buddha, or Vishnu knopped, which had queer hooded kneeling figures, usually full-faced, as finials. There are many other theories about them, one being that they originated in Germany, where spoons were made with human terminals in many strange forms. But this would not explain their being primarily a Barnstaple speciality, with only a very few from Plymouth, also a port.

Spoons with fig-shaped bowls, hexagonal stems, and a figure on top, had long been in vogue; maidenhead, lion sejant, and apostles were among the most popular, while oddities such as Wodehouse or Moor's Head showed that virtually anything could be expressed in this way. If sailors were responsible for Buddha-knopped spoons, it may have been that they had come under the influence of eastern religions and had commissioned the spoons to remind them of it; or possibly they simply wanted to show off about their travels. We shall never really know the origin of these spoons, or even which deities the spoon heads represent, unless some old letters are found.

There are also a few spoons topped by a half-length nude female figure which were probably made by a Barnstaple maker between 1590 and 1630. Again, the choice of design is unexplained, and was possibly only a personal whim.

Spoons of all sorts were made in the West, prolifically and often well, but because they form the bulk of early collectable items they are the most widely faked. Sometimes only the finial has been copied and added to an old spoon, complete with marks, which has lost its own top. Others, particularly apostle spoons, have been manufactured wholesale; these will not be found for sale in reputable places, but it is as well to be aware of the danger. The method of splicing spoon finials is a good point to look for, as the provincial way of lapping looks more like a cabinet maker's dovetail joint, whereas the London goldsmiths joined theirs with a V-shaped splice. No genuine spoon has finial and stamp cast in one piece.

Forks did not come into general use until after the Restoration, although a few were known earlier. In fact, the oldest fork found in England, two-pronged and probably ninth century, was found at Semington, in Wiltshire, which shows that the messy table manners of the middle ages were not entirely due to ignorance of cleaner ways. This one looks rather like a farmer's pitchfork, although its handle, in several rudely joined sections, would hardly stand up to the job. Useful, date-fixing coins were found with it, as well as a spoon, 8½in long, obviously made as its pair. It has a horseshoe end, joined in the same crude way to a section attached to a central disc, before a similar piece joins the elongated balloon of its bowl, which is only 1in wide. While neither could be considered a thing of beauty, the trouble taken over so complicated a design must have had meaning. Nevertheless, the earliest undoubtedly English fork is hallmarked 1632.

Spoons were very personal possessions in the early days, and each man carried his own, which, if he was sufficiently wealthy, was made of silver. The spread of affluence, not to mention theft and accidental loss, would constantly have created a need for more, and this could be a reason for the number of spoons throughout the West Country which bear unascribed marks. As with the communion cups, some men may have attempted to make their own, though spoon making was really

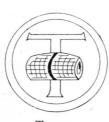

Taunton

a specialist's job requiring a high degree of skill. Local museums throughout the West Country, particularly the Holburne of Menstrie Museum at Bath, have good collections which include spoons made by fine craftsmen whose names have never been traced, while Poole, Bath, Shrewsbury and Taunton are among the towns known to have had men making spoons with varying degrees of proficiency. Taunton, whose mark is the rather obvious 'T' on tun, can, in fact, boast one of the very rare Norman spoons, revealed when excavating the castle there. Possibly of the twelfth century and probably locally made, it may be seen in the Castle Museum.

It was the custom to give apostle spoons as christening presents during Tudor times, the number given and the standard of workmanship depending on the status of the donor. Giving a whole set was rare, and because of this many apostle spoons were made individually for the donor; the four evangelists, perhaps, or in the case of only one spoon, the birthday saint of the child, when applicable. All apostle spoons to be found now are not, therefore, necessarily part of a broken set. Nevertheless, whole sets consisting of the Master spoon, which represented Christ, and the twelve apostles, each bearing his own emblem, were made in Exeter as in other places, and have now been entirely dispersed. In fact, only very few sets made by one maker at one time remain in existence. Loss and damage through the centuries are inevitable, but when people deliberately divide complete sets of anything worthwhile between their heirs they are devaluing to an extent they surely cannot realise.

Most of the great spoon makers did occasionally make other objects, and most true craftsmen also made spoons. Edward Anthony and Richard Osborn are two of Exeter's great spoon makers, but Truro Museum has a seal-top spoon and an apostle spoon, both made in 1576, by Thomas Mathew of Barnstaple, who was chiefly known for his communion cups.

John Lavers also made both apostle and seal-top spoons in the mid-seventeenth century, and Jackson also notes his marks on a chalice. Seal-top spoons were made from the fifteenth century until just after the Restoration, and varied only minutely through the ages. One made by John Lavers in 1634 will serve as an illustration. The gilded knop ends in a flat, round seal on a short baluster section and is pricked with the initials 'M.S.'. The hexagonal stem looks flat, tapering, and thinning towards the knop, although the narrow sides are actually angled to make two tiny edges, six in all. On the back of the stem, near the base, 'I.L.' in a shield is stamped three times. The Roman 'x' with a pellet on either side is surmounted by a large, bold crown, its shield following its own shape; this is struck in the fig-shaped bowl, on the back of which the date '1634' is pricked out, among ornamentation and the initials 'E.H.'.

Spoons according to the fashion of the moment continued to be made in the West, and John Elston, Exeter's greatest goldsmith of the official period, made several, although he was better known for his larger objects: mugs and tankards, chocolate pots and punch bowls. Bridgwater, however, supplied some of the last spoons that were truly different. A few trifid spoons were made in about 1670 and stamped in the bowl with a bridge surmounted by a tower, a mark attributed to this Somerset town. The trifid end of the spoon is somewhat incurved, and on the flat surface, just below it, is stamped a small medallion portrait of Charles II, possibly because a strong royalist sentiment remained in this place where the king had hidden during his wanderings. The first mention of a Bridgwater goldsmith referred to John Brooking, who disobeyed and rebuked the wardens when searched in 1460.

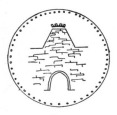

Bridgwater

Plymouth also made spoons, but they do not provide her chief claim to fame. The Eddystone Lighthouse salt, or spice box, if hardly a thing of beauty is still a major piece of outstanding interest. Basically it is a 17in high model of the polygonal lighthouse originally set on the storm-swept Eddystone Rocks, fourteen miles or so out to sea from Plymouth. The salt itself has been so frequently described that detail is unnecessary; if it was ever used at all it would have been as the cere-monial salt, above or below which people sat, so the inconvenience of dismantling it to take salt, sugar, pepper or other spices from the six containers into which it was cunningly divided would not arise. This is now in the City Museum, Plymouth, and is very well worth examining.

Its main interest lies in the history of the lighthouse itself and the consequent dating of the salt, for it bears no date letter or other formal marks. The fate of this extraordinary, galleried lighthouse, which was seriously intended to withstand the worst that weather can do, fixes the date of the salt almost exactly, for the lighthouse was completed only in 1698 and swept away in the storms of 1703. The maker of the salt, Robert Rowe of Plymouth, would have registered his mark at Exeter in 1701, and the piece would have been fully hallmarked had it been made after that date; but as a faithful copy it could not have been made

41

before 1698. This was after the higher standard had come in, and all silver, legally, had to be marked in London. Rowe had made his model of the lighthouse, one of the last upright salts, in silver of the higher standard, 11oz 10dwt, but had foregone the trouble, expense and danger of sending it to London for assay. He therefore showed what he had done by marking it 'Rowe, Plm° Britan', leaving only the date to be deduced.

The fame of this salt, all that now remains to perpetuate a design that failed, can, in a way, be compared with that of Paul Revere's 'Sons of Liberty Bowl', one of the best known pieces of early American silver, but by no means its best. Lack of hallmarks in America leads to loss of identification, so that when a history is known, particularly if it is romantic, interest in the piece is naturally heightened. Rowe's salt was ambitious and sufficiently unusual to become widely known. Plymouth is rightly proud of it, but it would be unfair to the craftsmen who worked there through the centuries to take it as fully representative of their craftsmanship.

Major works, such as steeple cups and standing salts, were not often made in the provinces, but a drum-shaped salt by C. Easton of Exeter was fully up to London standards. Eight and a quarter inches high, its body is heavily embossed with bunches of fruit, flowers and strapwork, with cartouches enclosing boldly stamped lions' heads, all set on three demi-horse feet. This fine body has a projecting cornice above, in which the salt was kept, with a domical cover, embossed with cartouches and garlands of fruit, ending in a vase-shaped finial with four scroll handles on which stands the figure of a man holding a spear and shield. It is a most ambitious piece, really well made. Thomas Mathew of Barnstaple also made a standing salt in 1582 and on the coronation of Charles II the city of Exeter presented one in the shape of a castle, long after such fancy salts had ceased to be made elsewhere.

There seems to have been a strong desire for self-expression among Plymouth goldsmiths, almost as if they felt they had to be different in order to be noticed; yet it is good solid workmanship, sometimes rather unusual, and often marked in a way to arouse curiosity.

A salver in Plymouth Museum is described as 'By R. Rowe, (of Plymouth) 1695–1700', although Rowe is now believed to have continued after that date, marking his silver correctly at the Exeter office. Yet he obviously enjoyed setting puzzles with his illegal marks.

Another example is a tankard with a flat cover, itself within the bounds of convention at that time, marked in different shaped shields: 'Rŏw', with the 'e' above, 'Ply°', and 'new', which suggests that it was made before his salt, (when the new standard had become known by the word 'Britannia') but after 1696, when it came in. Nor does he appear to have made things easy at Exeter, for his name is never mentioned.

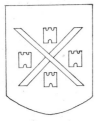

Plymouth

Yet there is no other craftsman known with a name beginning RO, and this mark in bifoil is found as a rosewater dish of 1704, in a private collection; a paten, 1704, at Wembury church, near Plymouth; a 1706 flagon at Whitchurch, and several fine pieces near Yelverton of 1711, all of the same high standard previously shown.

Another oddity of Plymouth marking was the use of the word 'Sterling', stamped with or without the city mark, and no date letter. There were many ways in which this word was used on silver, but pieces so marked in Plymouth are most unlikely to be met outside a museum.

An unidentified but fairly prolific Plymouth craftsman who stamped his work I.M. in conjoined italics, sometimes added the word $^{Brita}_{nnia}$ and within the same period of time (1695–9) $^{Star}_{ling}$. This indicated the standard metal he had used, but on a plain, straight-sided mug with reeded bands made in 1694 he first stamped his mark 'IM', and then the 'S' of Sterling, with 'g' in its proper place. Between these he stamped 'IM' again. Such gimmicks create a certain interest.

Another well-known Plymouth craftsman was Henry Muston who, before the establishment of Exeter, marked his work 'HM'. Jackson shows the marks on a spoon of his pricked 1694. It gives the Plymouth saltire, 'HM' conjoined in a shield, and $^{Ster}_{ling}$ in the same shaped shield. The addition of this word was unnecessary, for the new standard had not yet been thought of and the town mark and his own should have been sufficient warranty of the piece's sterling quality. In the same year Muston made a trifid spoon and marked it in the same way, but after the establishment of the Exeter office and the ill-considered ruling (1701–19) that the first two letters of the maker's surname should be used, his mark changed to 'MU'. His most interesting piece of work is a flat-topped posset pot, sold at Sotheby's in 1935. This was made about

1690, and is in the form of a tankard with plain straight sides and moulded base, and a tapering and curved spout set at right angles to the handle, like an American spout cup. It has a scroll handle and volute thumbpiece, and its cover also has a reeded edge, the overall impression being that of someting squat, plain but really interesting. It is marked with a Plymouth saltire and maker's mark stamped twice on the body, the same reversed on the cover, 'HM' once, and the city arms twice. Tankards, when given to the church for use as communion flagons, sometimes had a spout added later for convenience in pouring, but this is not the same thing at all.

Plymouth had a long history of the craft and it is remarkable how much of her surviving silver was made at the close of the seventeenth century, almost as if her craftsmen, with nothing to lose, had decided to cash in on the situation resulting from the Act of 1697 which abolished all provincial assay offices, as well as raising the standard of silver plate to stop coin from being melted down for other purposes. Some Exeter men seem to have made the best of the port's lax attitude towards the new law, and worked there during the close period; it is even possible that Plymouth's 'IM' was, in fact, John Mortimer of Exeter.

When the 1697 Act was repealed in 1701 and Exeter, for the first time, figured among the provincial cities appointed to assay silver, her goldsmiths lost no time in registering their new marks and electing officers for their guild, so that they were ready to open for business on 29 September 1701. From that day silver in Exeter was marked by the first two letters of the maker's surname; the city arms, a triple-towered, turreted castle, in place of the old Roman 'x'; the lion's head erased; Britannia, which they struck with a bolder punch than elsewhere, and the annual date letter, which followed their own cycle and in no way resembled the date letters then being used in London. These five marks continued unaltered for the nineteen years that are known as the 'Britannia period'.

In theory, the unofficial marking of silver came to an end with this Act, all West Countrymen thereafter sending their work to Exeter for stamping. In practice, a few maintained their independence, including Gabriel Felling who created silver of the very highest quality at Bruton in Somerset, marking it only with his initials in a rectangle. A tankard of his, c 1710, was shown at the 1970 Antique Dealers Fair—a large piece with a slightly domed lid, scroll thumbpiece and skirted moulded base. Though its standard is so high, it was far from his best work and Felling's name, discovered only recently after months of research, should now rank with those of the masters, and not only of the West Country.

After 1720, when craftsmen were allowed to use the old standard once more, the maker's mark, it will be recalled, reverted to the initials of first name and surname. Most craftsmen, however, preferred sterling, and this was marked with their initials, town mark, leopard's head crowned, the lion passant, and date letter. Thus in Exeter, as elsewhere, the leopard's head previously considered the London mark was used by craftsmen in addition to their own town mark, making one more stamp for them than London now used.

The mark of the triple-towered castle could, however, cause some confusion because it was used in slightly different forms in several places, including Newcastle and Edinburgh. Nor were its forms really constant in any place, all changing a little from time to time in much the same way as the Queen's head changes on a postage stamp. Even the variations in the basic castle itself, such as the large door of Barnstaple, (which ceased to be used when Exeter was appointed, and so never appeared on fully hallmarked silver) or the three separate towers of Newcastle or Aberdeen, are of no great significance as no one mark should ever be taken alone in deciphering the information provided by a group. After 1701, when virtually all silver was fully hallmarked at only a few designated places, guessing became a thing of the past, and the expert, then as now, could read the date at least of London work, at a glance. The rest of us look them up in a handy little pocketbook.

Date letters, when taken together with the town and maker's mark, are of major importance as they were changed annually, a new punch coming into use when new wardens were elected. Thus each letter or its type covered part of two years but belonged to no other, ever, because both the type of letter and shape of shield were also changed in twenty-year cycles. These, and their occasional exceptions, are clearly shown by the tables, and no complete sets of marks were ever identical. Therefore, although the date letter cycle that started with a Roman 'A' in a plain, angular shield in Exeter in 1701 looks very much the same as Newcastle in 1740, resemblance goes no further because 1701 was in the Britannia period, while the same 'A' in Newcastle in

1740 was usually accompanied by the lion passant and leopard's head crowned. The Roman 'A' in a very similarly shaped shield to the one Edinburgh used in 1705 could never be mistaken either, because Edinburgh used neither Britannia nor the lion in any shape or form.

In Exeter, the leopard's head was discontinued in 1778, and for six years, until the sovereign's head duty mark, (described in the first chapter) was imposed in 1784, only four marks were used. This head cannot altogether be relied upon as an alternative proof of date, for Exeter was lax about changing the punch; the head of William IV, for instance, did not appear until four years after the death of George IV.

John Elston, Exeter's greatest craftsman of this era, first registered his mark in 1701, and from 1703 onwards the lists include a high proportion of men who might previously have marked their work elsewhere, if at all. They came from all over the West: Dartmouth, Launceston, Totnes, Dunster, Liskeard, Falmouth, Bodmin and Fowey. Truro and Barnstaple gradually drop out, but Plymouth continues to the end, supplying large numbers of craftsmen to the Exeter office.

But as time went on the standard slackened, and although in 1848 it was reported that more plate was being stamped in Exeter than in any other office bar Sheffield, this was largely flat-wear, which makes for a lot of stamping. In fact, work had fallen off from the turn of the nineteenth century, not only because the new railways had speeded up transport, but also because Australian wool is said to have scotched the wealth of the West Country. This, however, can only have been part of the story. The methods used in Birmingham and Sheffield were having a devastating effect on the provincial craftsman, while the great Huguenots in London, such as Paul de Lamerie, David Willaume, Pierre Harache, and Charles Kandler, had raised the standard of the craft to such a height that it was difficult for anyone in the country to compete.

When the Exeter office first opened in 1701, however, all was well. Willaume and Harache had already registered their mark in London, but the overwhelming influence of de Lamerie had not yet arrived, nor the much more difficult medium of rococo.

The reign of Queen Anne (1702–14) was notable for good, solid silver, simple and symmetrical, particularly during the first six years. John Elston excelled at this, and the tankards, coffee pots and mugs he made were of first-class workmanship, and not noticeably lagging in design. Indeed, Pentecost Symonds of Plymouth made two identical teapots in 1712 and 1713, one of which is in Exeter Museum, at a time when very few teapots had been made anywhere. One of the earliest square tea caddies was made there in 1718, and in 1707, Edmund Richards, their first assay officer, made a porringer with crane-head handles, the first appearance of a device that is still used today, not only in silver, but in other metals, as well as in textile design. In fact, West Country silversmiths were often in the forefront of fashion at this time.

Two examples, both by John Elston, prove this point. A tankard he had stamped with the Exeter marks for 1704 is identical with a type given in *The Price Guide to Antique Silver* for 1710–40. This has a serrated front edge to the flange of its slightly domed lid, the same scroll thumbpiece, and a moulded band around the cylindrical body, which has arms engraved on the larger part of its otherwise plain body. A simple scroll-handle, ending in a shield and a moulded base, complete the tankard. Castors given in the same guide for 1715–25 also show that John Elston's 1720 octagonal castor, beautifully pierced and engraved with arms on one section, was fully in keeping with the times and well up to London standards.

This was a period dependent on line for its beauty, the circular, hexagonal or octagonal forms being ornamented only with stepped mouldings or faceted surfaces. From 1720, the tendency in London was increasingly towards complicated elaboration, until, between 1730 and 1740, rococo really took over. The country craftsmen, removed from the stimulus of competitive business, could not keep up, and when the great days came they rather lost heart. No sooner had they mastered one technique than it was outdated, leaving them behind the times, for they lacked that extra something the great masters were able to give in the more difficult mediums. Exeter work was, therefore, inclined to be kept simple. Not that this should really matter except to the expert, provided it is pleasant to look at. Up-to-date fashion is something to live with; a few years out of date two hundred years ago is hardly the same thing. If an Exeter coffee pot, for instance, happens to be octagonal after that style had passed in London, it is still preferable in many eyes to an over-ornate piece.

Brandy warmers were always well made in Exeter, and an example by Peter Elliott, 1738, is typical, for its small shaped bowl has a moulded lip and a straight ivory handle. But some tiny ones were also made in

47

Exeter and nowhere else, roughly between 1720 and 1740, with looped handles instead of the usual straight one, making them look more like a cream jug.

The late Georgian period produced an ever lessening quantity of Exeter-marked silver, other than flatware, but even this has distinct collector's interest. Most of the types of spoons fashionable in their turn throughout Georgian times were made in Exeter, and the variety is so great that it is always possible to find something new. The fiddle pattern, from about 1780, was extremely popular with Exeter gold-smiths, and while the variety is not as great as in the earlier Hanovarian type—with their lace backs, shell backs, flowers, feathers or bird backs —there was more variety in decoration than might be expected. Quite frequently the Exeter town mark is missing on these, but the other marks are set in distinctively square shields, with the duty mark in a circular shield. Nevertheless, teasets, cream jugs and so forth, were made, sometimes very well, in the nineteenth century. The churches of the West contain a considerable amount of communion plate made in Georgian times, sometimes copying the old pieces it was made to replace but more often following the style of the day. The Victorians, however, had a deplorable habit of melting down wonderful old plate and replacing it with the monstrosities they preferred. Unfortunately, this was also true in the West.

Old silver made in the West Country really represents better oppor-tunities for the collector than in any other region. Silver made locally has the added interest of its historical association with the region, and there is much to recommend it as the starting point for a collector.

# Three

# York

It was just 1,900 years ago, in AD 71, that the Romans enclosed with wooden palisades the site that was to become the city of York, the temporary beginnings of something too permanent for any evil force to destroy. Through the centuries, wars, fires, and social changes wrought internal havoc with this northern capital of England, but the city still stands proudly; proud of its ancient place, ecclesiastical and civic, in the history of England and of the many honours it was the first to receive.

Clearly, a city of such importance must have owned magnificent plate from the beginning, and it is equally clear why little remains. An inventory compiled in AD 1500 gives a rich picture of plate belonging to the high altar of the Minster, a tragic glimpse of a priceless heritage lost throughout the country, for nothing now survives. Chalices found in the graves of archbishops give valuable clues to the styles of the times, though, naturally, the finest examples were rarely buried. Two thirteenth-century chalices and patens have been found in the graves of unknown archbishops, and a third, c 1320–40, in the tomb of Archbishop de Melton. The deep conical bowl of this chalice is smaller than in the earlier pair for at that time the chalice was not passed to the laity, but the crucifix engraved on its round foot proves that it was made for the celebration of Mass.

By the time the Goathland chalice was made, in the mid-fifteenth century, the hexagonal foot had been devised in order to prevent the chalice rolling when laid on its side to drain. This particularly fine piece has the sacred monogram 'I h c' engraved on one of the six panels of its foot, a feature known through descriptive inventories to

49

have been less rare than it now appears. Although unmarked, it may well have been made in York, as may the exquisite chalice at Hinderwell, c 1490. This follows the same overall plan, although the bowl is deeper and more conical and the decoration, particularly on the knop, far more ambitious. On one of the six panels of its beautifully moulded foot, a crucifix is engraved showing St Mary and St John standing on either side. The paten of this glorious cup, beautifully and pictorially engraved, is also worth a very long journey to see. Interest in the remaining pre-Reformation chalice, at Beswick, lies in the ornamental toes of its hexagonal foot, a fashion which lasted only a very short time in the last years of the fifteenth century.

So civilised a countryside, of course, also had its domestic plate, and although it is said that almost all in Anglo-Saxon times was of foreign workmanship, there is some evidence of northern independence. For instance, a bowl of the early eighth century was found in Cumberland showing every indication of having been made in north Britain. A marvellous silver bowl of about 1016, containing 379 silver pennies of Canute, was also found near Lancaster, and there have been enough others, of which the Ormside bowl in York Museum is the outstanding example, to indicate that such work was not unusual before the Conquest. Mazer-shaped and possibly dating from about AD 670, the Ormside bowl is raised from a single sheet of thin silver, decorated with repoussé work that shows a high degree of skill, and is lined with a similar sheet of smooth copper, both of them gilded.

Then there is the exceptionally fine Studley bowl, now in the Victoria and Albert Museum, chased all over with a leaf pattern, the stalks bearing letters of the early English alphabet. This was made in about 1380 for domestic purposes, and was kept at Studley Royal, near Ripon. The fact that another silver bowl with the alphabet inscribed on its cover is mentioned in the will of a York man in 1431 encourages wishful thinking regarding its origin.

Wills, in fact, are a major source of information regarding habits in early days. A beaker was mentioned in 1346, and these were most popular at that time, their ancient origin probably deriving from the straight part of an ox horn; silver coconut cups were another reminder of the natural objects man had used for drinking, and one of these was mentioned in a Durham will of 1259.

With the Scrope mazer, c 1400, now in the Chapter House of York

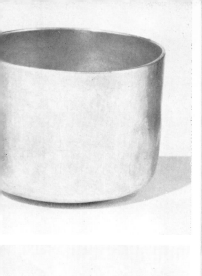

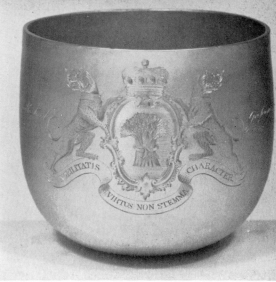

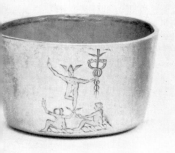

*Page* 51 Tumbler cups showing regional differences: (*above right*) the London normal, 1765; (*above
left*) one of a pair by Elizabeth Hazlewood, Norwich, 1697; (*left* )very rare, and not really a tumbler,
by Abraham Barachim, Hull, c 1685; (*below*) a most
unusual mounted coconut cup by John Plummer,
York, 1667

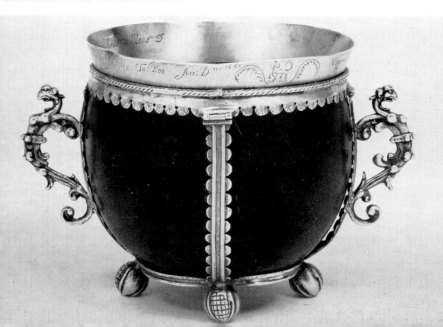

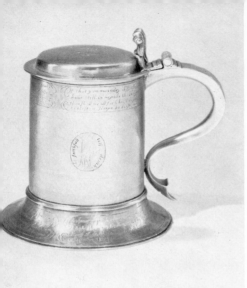
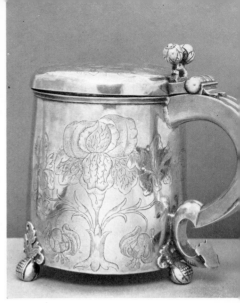

*Page 52* Tankards not only evolved in style, but varied from place to place: (*above left*) Jam Plummer, York, 1649; (*above right*) magnificent peg tankard, John Plummer, 1657; (*below le* William Ramsey, Newcastle, 1670; (*below right*) Ralph Walley, Chester, 1686/90

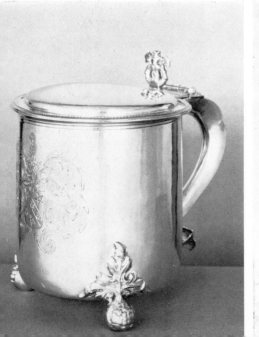
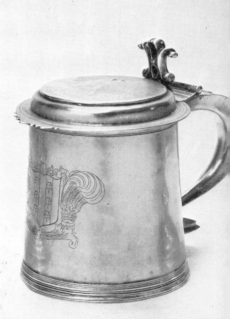

Minster, we come one step nearer to known York work, for mazers were definitely made in the city at that time. This one was presented to the fraternity of Corpus Christi by Agnes Wyman, widow of Henry Wyman, three times lord mayor of York. But the inventory that records this in 1465 does not mention that Wyman was also a York goldsmith, made free in 1386. What would be more natural than that Agnes should have presented her husband's own work?

This maplewood bowl, 12½in in diameter, and 4½in high, has a silver rim ¾in deep, on which is inscribed the name of Archbishop Scrope who held the see of York from 1398 to 1405, and the promise of forty days indulgence to those who drank from it in pure repentance. Old wills mention similar indulgences associated with other mazers of that time.

The Guild of Corpus Christi, established at York in 1408, was dissolved in 1546, and the 'Indulgence Mazer' is next heard of as owned by the Cordwainers' Company in 1622. It was they who had two repairs made to it, both hallmarked and dated by York goldsmiths. Peter Pearson bound two cracks with silver straps and raised the bowl on three beautiful cherub's-head feet attached to a rim around the base. Then, in 1669, the bowl was lined with silver by Philemon Marsh and, below the Cordwainers' arms, filling the centre, a long inscription was engraved telling how Archbishop Scrope had given the bowl to the company in 1398. By such apparently authentic means are facts distorted.

In York, as elsewhere, guilds played a large part in the town's early history, the goldsmiths forming themselves in about 1270, although names of members are not on record before 1313. The Act of 1423, which named York first of the seven towns to be given touches, could

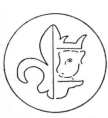
Early York mark

hardly have interested her officers for the guild was always run in a businesslike manner and a document exists, dated 1410, which refers to the town's searchers. York's early laws were very strict, and after 1411 anyone found guilty of selling an article of silver that was not stamped with the maker's and the city marks was fined 6s 8d, surely a monstrous sum when one penny would feed a family. This very early town mark was a half leopard's head and a half fleur-de-lys

D

conjoined in one stamp; the earliest existing example known is stamped in the bowl of a spoon made between 1475 and 1500.

In 1560, when the ordinances were reaffirmed, it seems almost certain that the use of a date letter was also decreed, and a seal-top spoon made by Robert Beckwith in 1561–2 marked with his initials, the letter 'C', and the town mark, is the first fully marked and authentically dated piece known anywhere in the provinces.

A large number of Yorkshire's Elizabethan communion cups are London made, but those made by York craftsmen are of considerable interest. New communion cups to replace the old Massing chalices were ordered in 1562, but York ignored the decree until after the suppression of the Rising of the North in 1569. Then, under pressure from a new and truly zealous archbishop, York found it necessary to toe the line quickly, so that about 80 per cent of the county's Elizabethan communion vessels were made in 1570.

Such urgency was not conducive to the most careful work, and although the communion cup, in contrast to the profusely ornamented domestic plate of the day, was essentially a simple thing, those made in York in 1570 show variations in decoration that suggest haste, though mainly conforming to the basic shape. Throughout the country these cups, with a few local exceptions, had bowls of inverted bell shape or straight tapering sides, and were decorated with an engraved intersecting band of strapwork, filled with woodbine foliage or arabesques, a spray being carried above and below each intersection. Given time, such uniform decoration was not difficult, but a great number of York make were without any engraving at all, while others either substituted bands of dots (not even the hyphenated 'hit and miss') only occasionally interlaced, or had the normal foliage without intersections or sprays. Stems, with their small central knop, and the round, slightly domed feet, mainly conformed, even to the reeded mouldings at the junctions, but the majority appear to be without their covers, designed for use as the paten and virtually obligatory. One must assume them to have been lost.

The main interest in church plate in Yorkshire, however, does not depend on the Elizabethan period, as it does in so many other parts of the country. Communion cups continued to be made profusely by York and London goldsmiths, and the last recorded piece of York silver, made in 1856, was a communion cup. The city's position as royalist headquarters during the Civil War, and consequent losses, might account for the large number made as replacements in the 1660s, but it does nothing to explain the profusion of cups, many more than in Elizabeth's time, that appeared in the 1630s when very little silver was being made in England and most of the country's churches were already fully furnished.

Cups of the Elizabethan type continued to be made coincidentally with the graceful 'wineglass' cups with their slender baluster stems that so typified the reign of James I. Many of these were made originally for domestic purposes, one of the finest being the lovely cup at Dunsforth church, beautifully decorated with repoussé work by Robert Williamson in 1626. This craftsman, made free in 1623, was the second and most important of three bearing the same name registered in York, the first having been made free in 1597 and the last in 1653. At the same time, cups of the Commonwealth type were also being made, their almost square-shaped bowls sitting squatly on a foot like a truncated cone.

Many variations also occur on these styles. At Guisborough church, for instance, there are two steeple cups which, without their covers, could have been copied from later champagne glasses, with shallow, broad bowls on delicate baluster stems. The covers reflect the bowl, so that when combined they give the appearance of a globe on a long stem surmounted by a spire. One was made in London in 1604, and is very beautifully decorated. The other, made by Robert Harrington of York in 1641, would appear to be a copy in outline, but it has been left plain, decorated only by an inscription around the bowl.

Occasionally, too, the styles combined. For instance, a pair of cups at Pocklington church, made by John Plummer in 1655, have the Elizabethan bell-shaped bowls and are engraved only with armorials and set on baluster stems with plain feet. Another of this craftsman's many church cups, made for Thornton Dale in 1660, has the bell-shaped bowl but with a curved lip, set on the usual Elizabethan-style stem with a knop, despite the date. Around the bowl is a belt of leaf ornament, in addition to the long dedication so popular in York; a most attractive wheat-ear pattern is engraved on the foot and cover.

But perhaps John Plummer's greatest work, and the finest of any provincially made ecclesiastical plate, was the altar set he made for Ripon Minster in 1675. The pair of communion cups for this are taller, larger versions of the old Elizabethan style, set on stepped feet;

on one side of each armorials surrounded by scroll-work are engraved, together with an inscription. In London, at this time, the second half of the seventeenth century, engraved decoration, other than for armorials, had given way to applied ornamentation (the Huguenots later revived it), yet the chief feature of these cups are the pictures engraved on the other side, showing Ripon Minster as it was before 1660, complete with three spires. Perhaps this was intended to commemorate a glory that was past, for the central spire had fallen in a gale in 1660, while the other two were removed four years later.

The flagon of this Ripon Minster set, a massive version (13in high) of the straight-sided tankard with widely splayed, torus-moulded base, also shows engravings of the Minster, while on its flat lid, as on the conventional Elizabethan covers of the cups, the Holy Lamb is shown with scroll work and the Jennings crest.

There are also two patens in the set, simple plates in themselves, on round, truncated cone feet, on which the Minster is engraved centrally, with armorials and inscriptions below. What makes for rarity is that each has a cover, known as an 'aire', borrowed from Greek ritual, with a beautifully ornamented dome raised on three claw and ball feet, and surmounted by an orb and cross. The effect is magnificent, and the workmanship fine; sadly, one has evidently been lost and replaced by a rather inferior copy.

In the late seventeenth century, York communion cups were frequently engraved with bell-shaped flowers pointing downwards placed at the intersections of the bands of leaf pattern which were normal. These flowers were a distinctive feature of York work at that time, and are found nowhere else.

The church cannot be left without introducing the craftsmen of Hull, for fine cups in both Yorkshire and Lincolnshire bear the mark of this city's three ducal coronets, one above the other, which they adopted some time in the seventeenth century, when the majority of their known work was being made (see diagram, p 23).

Goldsmiths' names are known from 1427 but, as they had a mint in the reign of Edward I, the probability is that they existed even earlier. Their guild, however, was never officially recognised, and their date lettering system, somewhat spasmodic, does not appear to have begun before the second half of the seventeenth century. Nevertheless, there are several Elizabethan cups by Peter Carlille, mostly in Lincolnshire churches, the earliest being one of 1569 in Wooton church, Lincs. This craftsman usually marked his plate only with his initials, sometimes in conjunction with a large 'H', presumed to be the early Hull mark, and in most cases the exact date is a matter of conjecture. A fine example of his work is in Beverley Minster, a richly decorated communion cup and cover, c 1580, which, with its bell-shaped bowl and knopped stem, otherwise conforms to the Elizabethan style. Carlille's cups are well worth seeking out and there are others belonging to churches at Beeford, Catwick, and Cabourne, Hull.

Hull craftsmen of the seventeenth century largely continued to use the overall Elizabethan pattern in communion cups, but decoration was more varied and often of a high order, showing initiative and imagination. A fine example of this is the cup at Hornsea church, made by Edward Mangy, (free 1660), its interlacing strapwork punctuated by dainty four-petalled roses, with a spray carried down at the intersections consisting of leaves and five-petalled roses. Between the sprays there is an inscription in dainty, cursive writing, a feature of Hull, although the more customary capital lettering is also used. These inscriptions are sometimes quotations from the scriptures instead of the normal dedication.

Edward Mangy always marked his work with his initials in a pointed shield between the Hull mark, stamped twice. All his work was not as finely made as the Hornsea cup, but most of it shows the same rather square bowl on a thick stem with a large knop and moulded foot; a cup at Elloughton church, while utterly plain, is of exactly this shape.

The Mangy family, who were Huguenots, were widespread in Yorkshire, and six of that name registered as goldsmiths in York, starting with Christopher, 1609, who made a tiny cup for St Cuthbert's, York. In Hull, Katherine Mangy, free 1680, also made communion cups, one of which is at Trinity House, Hull, where Edward Mangy has a paten—a circular plate on a hollow, cone-shaped stem. In Leeds, where silver was also made but to a lesser extent than Hull, the only name known to have been recorded is that of Arthur Mangy, who made the civic mace in 1694 and was hanged two years later on the Knavesmire, York, for clipping coin.

Names of more Leeds craftsmen are now coming to light, but their work for the church is so rare that only one communion cup is known to be stamped with the golden fleece, the town mark adopted from the city arms. This piece belongs to Almondbury church, near Huddersfield, and is of exceptional interest. Its shape and style—albeit copied from an earlier London cup at the same church—is most unusual, having a straight-sided, tapering bell bowl on a conical stem, with a thin flange just below the flat base

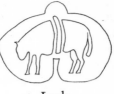

Leeds

of the bowl, slightly damaged, and no knop. Around the centre of the bowl is a most effective thistle leaf pattern, without the strapwork of dedication, although its London-made partner carries one. The golden fleece mark shows plainly between the twice-stamped maker's initials 'TB', a valuable point this, for when a plain tumbler cup weighing only 1½oz was sold for £950 at auction in June 1967, the clarity of its Leeds mark was held responsible for the high price.

The one other communion cup known to be Leeds, although stamped only with the maker's mark 'ST', three times, is at Darrington. The clue to Leeds comes through a pair of patens at Harewood church which bear the same maker's mark on either side of the golden fleece of Leeds. These patens, c 1700, are perfectly round plates with squarely upturned rims standing on trumpet-shaped feet, 3¼in high. Described by Fallow as 'crudely made', they nevertheless strike an important chord for they are attractive as well as exceedingly rare.

'ST' in monogram, the mark of Samuel Todd of Leeds, differs only in the shape of the shield from what is believed to be the mark of Timothy Skottowe of Norwich who, in 1639, made a fine flagon now belonging to Sigglesthorne church. The considerable difference in date, and the golden fleece mark clearly seen beside it on a trifid spoon as well as on the Harewood patens, precludes it from being the work of the same man.

In many ways the main interest of York-made church plate lies in date rather than form, and this applies also in later years when, except for those with the bell-shaped flowers, the majority of York-made communion cups could not be dated on their style alone. Up to a point the same can also be said of flagons, for those of York make generally followed a form long outdated, and no early examples appear to exist, possibly because the Civil War, responsible for so much melting down, also left the churches unable to afford fine silver where pewter would do.

Though the communion cup was restored to the laity in 1547, the making of flagons specially for the church did not really get into its stride until the previously mentioned canon of 1603 stipulated the type of vessel in which wine should be brought to the communion table. Yet, even so, in the whole of Yorkshire we find none of local make before 1781, with the exception of that at Ripon.

The pair of altar candlesticks in the Lady Chapel of York Minster are also interesting for date because, except during the High Church period of Archbishop Laud, such furniture had disappeared from the church in England at the Reformation, only to return in comparatively recent times. Yet these were made in York by William Mascall in 1672.

Possibly the most historically exciting silver belonging to the church in Yorkshire is a pair of recusant chalices at Ugthorpe, near Whitby, used for the illegal celebration of Mass by Father Postgate. Generally, such chalices were made to unscrew into three parts so that they could be hidden more easily in the priest's clothing, but of this pair only the one made in France does so. All such cups were unmarked for obvious reasons, but the second of the pair, probably locally made in about 1630, must have formed a tell-tale bulge as the priest trudged over the moorlands near Whitby, or through the streets of the town where white sheets were hung out to dry on hedges as a signal that Mass was about to be said in a neighbouring house. But the bulk of this cup never gave Father Postgate away. That was left to a traitor who reported him for the reward of £20. At the age of eighty-two, the gallant priest was tried and hanged at York in 1679, while the wretch who betrayed him was found drowned in Ugglebarnby beck, swift justice before he had even collected his reward. Ugthorpe owns a treasure in this fascinating cup, which is also a thing of beauty.

Roman Catholic perseverance, however, did not die with Father Postgate. A set of six recusant candlesticks belongs to the magnificent collection of Irwin Untermyer, in New York. Four of these were London made in 1675, and are described by C. C. Oman as 'the earliest yet identified'. The other two were made in York in 1684, and are very fine indeed.

There are very few surviving York-made ecclesiastical spoons, and most of these have perforated bowls for clearing the wine of foreign bodies. But every sort of spoon in general use was made in York, and their marks well illustrate the history of the city's assay office. The marks of the finest craftsmen are shown on them, and date letters have been proved with their help. Some experts have seen a slight change in the York town mark of 1631, and believe that the half fleur-de-lys in the old mark became a half seeded rose crowned, still in conjunction with the half leopard's head. Needless to say, this is none too clear.

These spoons were well in keeping with the styles of the times, and mention of a York-made apostle spoon in a will of 1494 shows how quickly they took up a new style, for it was then in its infancy; a flat-stemmed spoon, dated York 1661, is also one of the earliest of its type in England. There were few deviations from the normal; a fine apostle spoon by Thomas Pindar, York, 1585, shows St Matthew carrying a carpenter's rule as an emblem, but this is more of a personal fancy than a York speciality.

The great exception to rule is the Death's Head spoons made for the Strickland family of Boynton and Howsham, in the mid-seventeenth century. The spoons themselves are somewhat hybrid, with rather broad flat stems of the Puritan, or Scottish type, egg-shelled bowls with rat tails, and medallion ends on which a skull is engraved. On the stems 'Die to Live' and 'Live to Die' is inscribed. It is possible that these were given away as christening spoons, but more likely they were used as mementos, like American coffin spoons, in place of mourning rings at a funeral. Only seven survive, which might be because they were macabre and so reminiscent of unhappy associations that they were quickly disposed of. John Plummer made one dated 1661, and Thomas Mangy the others, the latest 1682. A similar medallion ending is also seen engraved with the head of Charles I on some Leeds spoons made towards the end of Charles II's reign, possibly for a remembrance service of some kind.

Leeds spoons, roughly between 1637 and 1680, show the golden fleece, sometimes stamped three times on the stem. Some of these show variations in marking that excite interest. A fine trifid spoon, for instance, is clearly marked with the initials of the maker, 'BB' and the golden fleece; in addition there is a monogram which could mean anything. Another trifid, presumably by Arthur Mangy, is stamped 'AM', with the Leeds marks and that most controversial fleur-de-lys.

Commonwealth Puritan spoons were also made in York, where work of this very rare period is well represented, particularly in the church. Chance decreed that many of York's finest goldsmiths were born during the first half of the seventeenth century, but it is very much to their credit that they became apprenticed to such a trade at a time when fine silver was being thrown into the melting-pot by the ton. Leeds, and Hull, where James Birkby was working, also kept their heads above water, but three of York's finest goldsmiths were among many to gain their freedom at this time; John Plummer, free 1648, twenty-five years junior to his brother James (1619); Philemon Marsh, 1652, and Marmaduke Best, 1657. William Plummer, incidentally, was a Georgian Londoner, and had no connection with York. Richard and Michael Plummer both gained their freedom in York in 1659, but are not of comparable importance.

Philemon Marsh made cups, spoons and lined the Scrope mazer; Robert Williamson made an exquisite wine cup with an hexagonal bowl on a trumpet foot, decorated in a manner that makes it look far from austere. And among other fine things, James Plummer made a tankard of typical Commonwealth form in 1649 which, with its splayed foot, simple 'C' scroll handle, and once-stepped flat cover, is chiefly interesting for the inscriptions, in script, that completely cover the foot and upper part of the straight body. The design also includes a medallion, centrally placed, in which the words 'Be faithful unto Death' surround a figure. (Illustration, p 52.)

During the later part of the Commonwealth, when the régime was well established, life was less austere than it had been in the years leading up to it. Foreign craftsmen had departed, but enough customers had profited by the war to be able to afford to give good commissions to the best native craftsmen, of which they could take their pick.

That John Plummer was considered among this élite is obvious by the amount of important work he produced. Nevertheless, a coconut cup at this time seems strange, for there was nothing remotely necessary about them. Mounting these easily polished cups in silver had become almost a status symbol by the middle ages, when the adornment of primitive man's necessity showed a march of progress. In 1653, when silver was scarce and normally fairly functional, John Plummer mounted a coconut cup in an unusual porringer style, setting it on a round base with cast twist scroll handles, on each of which a bearded head stands out. There are also bearded busts chased on the upright straps on the bowl, and the whole work, including the lace collar below the well-marked lip, is of the finest-quality workmanship.

More conventional in shape are two York coconut cups, recently presented to the civic collection; one, by Robert Williamson, 1624, is quite simply mounted on a plain baluster stem, but that of George Gibson, 1682, who was a great asset to York towards the end of the century, has its stem in the shape of the infant Hercules.

Tankards, however, were a more specialised York work, and one of the most frequently illustrated, now in the Victoria and Albert Museum, London, was made by John Plummer in 1657. This is a fine example of a peg tankard, so popular in Scandinavia at the time, and very much a speciality in England of York, Newcastle, and Hull. The squat, tub-shaped body of these tankards is raised on three feet, cast in different ways, such as pomegranates or ball and claw, usually with applied scrolled leaves on the drum at the joining point and a thumbpiece which sometimes reflected the feet. Inside the tankard, in line with the handle, are eight pegs, designed to prevent brawling in communal drinking by ensuring that each man drank no more than his 'peg'.

John Plummer was, perhaps, the chief maker of these tankards, with their flat, round-edged covers that fit flush with the squat bowls. On these he displayed his love of engraved decoration, the 1657 example being covered with beautifully balanced flowers, including a full-blown iris. On the magnificent cover the arms and crest of Sayer are seen surrounded by flowers, charmingly executed. (Illustration, p 52.)

It is interesting to compare this solid but dainty-looking tankard with another made by William Mascall in 1666, for this has the same rounded lid and base set on pomegranate feet with scrolled leaves above them, pomegranate thumbpiece, and 'C' scroll handle. It is even decorated with a flower design, but here similarity ends for this one is heavily embossed in the typical manner of Charles II, and the effect is totally different; although smaller, it is handsome rather than exquisite.

York has a very fine civic collection of silver, housed at the Mansion House along with the insignia and regalia belonging to the city. Unfortunately, only a very small proportion of it is York made, and almost all originating before the Civil War has gone. This was not only due to the war, which broke out nearby, but also to the fact that lord mayors were expected to supply up-to-date silver plate. In consequence, lovely pieces considered old fashioned were either melted down or drastically altered.

Those pieces which are of York make, however, are of a magnificent standard. John Plummer made one of a pair of large tankards in 1673, as fine as anything one could wish to see, in the typical Scandinavian style. These are raised on three lion sejant feet, beautifully and realistically cast, with a fine, bold lion sejant thumbpiece. The lid, rounded as before, has a projecting band of cable twist moulding, repeated near the bottom of the drum, while the base is triple reeded, giving a double line effect. The large, 'C' scroll handle has an applied beaded rat tail on its upper part, a speciality of the northern goldsmiths, while on the front the city arms are engraved, with a shield below and the donor's gift inscription.

The second tankard of this pair, which hold two quarts each and are almost identical, was made by Marmaduke Best in 1673. Could it be that rivalry between these two was so great that the commission had to be divided? Best had already made a glorious gold cup in 1671 in simple goblet form, decorated with tasteful cut-card work and cable twist moulding. On one side an inscription states that it was the gift of Marmaduke Rawdon, a gentleman who always made quite sure that his name would not be forgotten, while on the other side the city arms are engraved within a cartouche. These arms, a Maltese Cross charged with five lions, were to be adopted as the town mark of York in 1700, a very much more clean-cut stamp than the old. Engraved on pieces such as this they are easy to see, but the finest illustration imaginable is provided by the waits' collars, formally worn by the musicians, on which the arms fill a shield 2in × 3in. The butler at York's Mansion House, who takes an obvious pleasure in showing his fine collection of silver, now wears one of these collars on civic occasions.

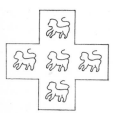

York after 1701

Among others who made important tankards were Thomas Mangy, who has one in the civic collection dated 1679, while George Gibson and William Busfield were also prominent. Peg tankards were also made in Hull, particularly by Thomas Hebden, some with a plain body except for the leaf ornament above the feet and on the thumbpiece.

Marmaduke Best's gold cup, from which the lord mayor drinks the loyal toast at civic functions, was enough to turn any rival craftsman green with envy, but Rawdon had already commissioned the same goldsmith to make the city's famous silver chamber pot in 1670.

Weighing 50 oz, eight less than the larger lion tankard, this magnificent piece is extremely rare and very much finer than the plain example, weighing 31 oz and engraved only with a coronet and cypher, made by Isaac Liger in London in 1725, which appeared for sale late in 1969. One other example—six are said to exist—is by Simon Pantin, 1716, London, which is a trifle smaller and also engraved with a coat of arms. When Best made his pot, the idea of an indoor 'convenience' was as remote as a trip to the moon, and as such objects were made for dining-room use, there was good reason to invest them with due pomp. On one side, the arms of the city of York are engraved; on the other those of Marmaduke Rawdon. There is also an inscription telling about himself and recording his gift. Perhaps as self-advertisement this falls short of the efforts of Sir Martin Bowes, a Londoner, who had given a sword to the city of York in 1549 and decreed that a prayer should be said at civic dinners . . . 'God have mercy on the sowle of Sir Martin Bowes, knight and sometime mayour of the citie of London, and all Christian sowles'. Rowdon merely decreed that his pot should continue to be used in civic service, or that, if converted to other use, the ten pounds he had paid for it should be returned to him or his heirs.

The pot is now a much-prized item in the Mansion House collection and worth several noughts more than its original ten pounds. But in 1909, when a booklet was written describing the collection, it bowed its head in shame. Photographed with its tell-tale handle turned away, it was described simply as 'a pot'. This handle, incidentally, has a whistle, similar to those found in the handles of certain tankards later on and reputed to have been used to summon a servant when replenishments were needed; in fact, they are simply air vents. A domed 'whistle' tankard by Isaac Cookson of Newcastle, 1738, is also in this collection.

Any visitor to York will want to visit the Castle Museum, if only to see the Fishmongers' tankard, but time should also be allowed to walk around the museum's re-creation of old Yorkshire life, which is so realistically laid out. The Fishmongers' tankard, again by Marmaduke Best, 1672, is drum shaped, with the typical thumbpiece, but no feet or rounding of the lid's edge. This was the first piece of silver presented to the Fishmongers' Company, and their coat of arms and an inscription fill the whole front of the bowl, while another long inscription covers the flat lid, below which is a projecting flange.

The silver collection of this museum is not large but includes several interesting spoons, one by Christopher Harrington dated 1599, a 1682 porringer, and a tumbler cup by William Busfield, 1687. This craftsman made several of the many York tumbler cups of the late seventeenth century which are recognisable as being shorter, and also wider in comparison to their height, than those of London. This is very easy to see when any two are placed beside each other. Mark Gill, who was to be lord mayor in 1697, made several that were noticeably larger than average, in the 1680s. Chasing on them was also more common in York than elsewhere, but many York-made tumbler cups are absolutely plain, or simply carry a crest; one such cup, by William Busfield, 1685, has finely engraved initials, and this was also fairly usual. From Jackson's list of marks, it would appear that Busfield carried on working and marking his plate, mostly communion cups and plain tumbler cups, with the old York stamp throughout the period when all provincial assay offices had officially closed their doors. He was also among the few who registered his new mark after the reopening, using the higher standard to continue his work.

The tiny Leeds cup has already been mentioned, and another, very small and plain, was recently for sale. But large pieces were also made in Leeds. A flat-topped tankard, stamped with the maker's mark once and the golden fleece twice, was made by Robert Williamson of York, who evidently had interests in both cities. He also made a very fine chocolate pot in 1685 and stamped it with the rare Leeds mark. This is of plain baluster vase shape, with a cylindrical, reeded neck, and a slender, tapering curved spout reaching upwards from near the base. The lid is attached to the silver base of the handle by a well-made chain secured to the flange below the dome, which is nicely decorated with cut card work, the only ornament on a piece well able to rely on line for its beauty. (Illustration, p 155.)

With the exception of the Harewood patens, 1702, no silver is known to bear the Leeds mark after 1697, when work in the provinces officially came to a standstill. But Hull, the most inaccessible of places, apparently kept up business as usual at that trying time. Their unofficial status made this simple enough, for since their 'Company of Goldsmiths and Braziers' was not officially recognised, they could not be beholden to any laws but their own. So far as the standard of silver they produced was concerned, there seem to have been no complaints, and their goldsmiths' names, many of whom have had no mention here, are well respected. But if they knew what they were doing regarding date letters, they have not passed on the secret. The cursive capital '*A*' found on a porringer by Edward Mangy and believed to be for 1670, gives a rarity value to an otherwise ordinary piece, but there must have been at least one other letter cycle before this.

Only one name registered during the Britannia period, that of Abraham Barachim, a Huguenot, is worthy of mention. Jackson records him as free in 1706, but it seems certain that he was working in the '90s. His mark, a very grand affair with the 'AB' crowned upon a rose, is shown for 1706 on a communion cup, near Hull, and a most unusual bleeding bowl, sold in London in 1969, was attributed to him. This round bowl with straight sides 1½in high, is almost like a tumbler cup on a flat base, and is described in the catalogue as 'naïvely' engraved. The word is apt, but the ambitious picture serves only to add interest to a most unusual piece. Names in Hull continued to be registered up to 1774, when the goldsmith's art in Hull, as in so many of the unofficial places, just fizzled out.

This was very far from being the case in York, however, where a major row was brewing. Relations in the assay office would appear always to have been strained, and whether the tight discipline exerted there was the cause or the effect of the many irregularities, is difficult to say. York always had more laws than average and it could be that while the best goldsmiths there were turning out consistently fine work, lesser men, offended perhaps by tactless treatment, avoided the office and resorted to queer markings of their own.

The effect is more important than the cause to us and, in a nutshell, it has meant the almost total absence of York-made silver of the finest collector's period. When York reopened her office in 1700, after the enforced closure of all regional offices, very few craftsmen registered their marks and no York plate has been found bearing date letters between 1713 and 1779. Of those who carried on, John Langwith was the most important user of the five stamps of the higher standard, which were: the Maltese Cross with its five lions passant indicating the city of York; 'LA' in a shield, the first two letters of his surname, as maker's mark; the figure of Britannia and the lion's head erased, for the higher standard of silver; and the variable date letter.

Marks of the higher standard period were rare in York, but examples can be found by diligent collectors. Three flagons, for instance, were recently sold in a London saleroom at remarkably reasonable prices; two were plain cylindrical, with domed lids, while one was acorn-shaped, with an acorn finial. The markings on these do not give a clear picture and appear to be an example of what caused York to close her assay office in 1716, so missing the great inquiry of 1773 which might have revealed the cause of trouble. John Langwith and Joseph Buckle, free 1715, carried on alone, sending their work to Newcastle for marking, by special arrangement. Jackson has listed other York craftsmen in the Newcastle list, but there is no evidence that any but these two had work marked there.

By the time the office reopened, many changes had come about, particularly in the manner of producing silver. Machines were now able to roll the metal to a thinness never before possible or required, while others could take care of all repetitive decoration. Costs of production had tumbled and the ownership of domestic silver had ceased to be the monopoly of the rich. Nevertheless, the change was not complete. The best workmen continued to make silver to order in the old traditional way, and the difference is not difficult to see. A bullet teapot, delightfully plain and beautifully shaped, now in the Victoria and Albert Museum, makes an excellent example. Produced by the firm of J. Hampston & J. Prince, for whom the assay office was largely reopened, it bears the York mark for 1784. Partnerships of this sort were another change that had come about during York's absence from the scene, and though this tended to shroud work bearing a firm's mark in anonymity—no doubt an advantage where machine-made work was concerned—it does not follow that pieces such as this teapot were not hand made. Old prints will show that, from the earliest times, the making of silver plate had always been something of a team enterprise.

Style, of course, went through many changes, and when the York office reopened the neo-classic vogue was in full swing. Robert Adam, having been to Italy and seen the wonders of Herculaneum and Pompeii, was already reflecting his impressions of them in his architecture. Furniture styles were then made to fit in with his elegant interior decoration, and silver plate naturally fell into line. Among the lesser goldsmiths, particularly in the provinces, a book of 'howlers' could be compiled from the mistakes made by those without classical education who did not understand the medium, but in York, Hampston

& Prince avoided the pitfalls of over-ambition and produced good and usually dainty work. A tea caddy of theirs in the Victoria and Albert Museum is a fine example, for it combines the straight lines and symmetrical curves which were then so much in vogue. This was made in 1784, the year the number of marks used in the city rose to six with the addition of the sovereign's head to show that duty had been paid. This oval, straight-sided caddy, with horizontal lines of decoration surrounding it at top and bottom, has a plain, smooth surface in between, relieved by bright cut engraving, employing the garlands and bows and ribbons of symmetrical curves so frequently seen in Adam interior decoration. An exquisite piece, it is typical of an age when York was still producing more of quality than quantity.

The drinking of tea was, by this time, very much a part of the elegant way of life, enjoyed by the rich and the new middle classes alike, both of whom were anxious to furnish their homes with every item necessary to the ritual of the tea table. This was essentially a dignified occasion, with ladies sitting in elegant posture, holding conversation which, if not deep, was at least formal. And so was the silver to go with it, for the vulgar age of massive plate had not yet arrived. Hampston & Prince made tea-table pieces in many forms, but all of them were dignified. They also made a quantity of church plate, for the vogue for replacing Elizabethan communion cups with something more up-to-date was just beginning a new and horrible lease of life which was to reach a crescendo during Victoria's reign.

York continued to make silver up to 1858, alas without diminution of the irregularities and discord that had dogged her steps from the beginning. The names of Barber, coupled at first with William Whitwell and later with George Cattle and William North, were the only ones of note which appear to remain and these, in one form or another, continued until the end. A lot of silver was made by them between 1800, a time when H. Prince & Co were still trying to uphold the old names, and 1830, but although this work was good enough, it followed the ugly styles of the times. The work became increasingly unimportant, and no further pieces marked in an assay office that had handled so much magnificent work is worth particular mention.

# Four

# Newcastle

Although the assay office in Newcastle closed down in 1885, it could be said that the wheel has now turned full circle. Not far away, in the village of Allendale, the old silver-bearing lead mines were recently reopened, the high price of silver having made it appear economical to extract even small amounts from them once more.

Newcastle's original name, Pons Aelius, means 'on the Roman Wall' and the Romans were known to mine for lead extensively. As silver was most easily obtainable from the upper layers of a lead mine, it is safe to assume that they also extracted silver from them. Various silver objects have been found in Northumberland, and while it cannot be proved that the Romans used locally mined silver to make them, it is at least a logical assumption. An amusing example of these local finds is a silver earpick and nail cleanser, such as were made from Roman times down to the middle ages, with a little spoon-like scoop at one end and a pick-like point for the nails at the other, flattened, end. Three and a half inches long, the stem between the effective parts is twisted, and the whole thing is gilded. Spoons, however, are more usual discoveries, and one found at Benwall has a bowl similar to those we know today, and a long, pointed stem, roughly joined but showing considerable workmanship.

Later, after St Aiden had founded the great monastery at Lindisfarne on Holy Island in AD 635, which was 'greatly enriched by gifts', his Irish monks spread over Northumbria, which went through a period of high Anglo-Irish civilisation. If the Romans did use local silver, at least for coin, these monks would certainly have employed it for the creation of art. They were magnificent craftsmen in silver at that time,

E

and the illumination of the Lindisfarne Gospel Book, second only to the Book of Kells in surviving manuscripts, is evidence of the high standard of their culture. The colours of its Celtic designs are still marvellously rich, and the book itself was originally bound in silver gilt, magnificently bejewelled. Lindisfarne was sacked by the Vikings in 793, and that would appear to have been the end of an era, with little more than conjecture to show for it.

The turbulent history of the north of England is such that surviving treasures are mostly of much later date than elsewhere, yet we have every right to believe that they were of the highest order. There was no lack of fine monasteries, and in describing the Tassilo communion cup, dating from about 770, the Rev James Gilchrist says that, if not of Northumbrian make as suggested by C. H. Elburn in the catalogue of the Charlemagne Exhibition in Aachen in 1965, 'it certainly reflects the influence of northern English artists who travelled abroad'. Little enough to go on perhaps, but this cup, made of copper and decorated overall with silver niello, is a magnificent example of work which may have been typical of the treasures in those monasteries. Seven inches and four-fifths high and holding three pints, the bowl rests upon a ring of pearls, supported on a knop with spreading foot. On the foot of the cup are oval pictures of Theodore, Martyr; John the Baptist; Our Lady and Saint Theodolinde, whilst the bowl itself is decorated with five oval pictures depicting Christ in Glory and the symbols of the four Evangelists. The spaces between the pictures are engraved with patterns of gilt; 'the whole', says the Rev Gilchrist, 'is brilliant and overpowering in its beauty'.

He also mentions a portable altar and a pectoral cross, possibly fifth century, found in a coffin believed to be that of St Cuthbert (686) at Durham, but this magnificent cup must stand alone as an illustration of a northern glory that is past. But what a picture it affords.

Because communities grew up around the lead mines and places of worship were built to accommodate them, many of the churches of Northumbria stand on really ancient sites. In fact, almost all built before 1800 owe their origins to pre-Norman or Norman times, although some were rebuilt during the intervening centuries.

The first mention of goldsmiths in Newcastle refers to the election of assay officers for the mint there in 1248, but although it was one of the seven towns given its 'touch' in 1423, nothing is known of goldsmiths who may have worked there until 1536 when 'The Company' was established. No silver survives from this period, but some of the most fascinating reflections on history emerge from it.

In broad concept the Company was a trades union, incorporating freemen of the goldsmiths', plumbers', painters', pewterers' and glaziers' companies. This charter still exists among the archives of the Plumbers' Company and fine reading it makes, redolent of border strife. The Company was to be governed by four wardens, including a goldsmith, and its laws incorporated most of the usual clauses we know so well. No brother, for instance, was to put his hands to another man's job on pain of a 3s 9d fine, and if any should take as an apprentice 'A Scotsman borne in Scotland', the fine rose to 40s. On the other hand, 'If any member should lie or brawl at a meeting, use malicious or slanderous words, or draw a knife or dagger or any other weapon in malice . . .' he was to be fined a mere 3s 4d. But any member who so far forgot himself as to call a brother 'A Scot, a murderer, or a thief', was to be expelled from the Company and not readmitted until 'such tyme that he be clerely and duely purged and acquited by dew order of the law.' One shudders to think what that may have entailed.

Five goldsmiths were enrolled among the original members of the Company, Thomas Cramer representing the craft amongst the wardens, but the art could not have played a prominent part in the city life for the names of only thirteen goldsmiths appear on the Company records before 1656, and none at all from about 1609 to 1656. Jackson's assumption that trade must have flourished in the sixteenth century would therefore appear ill-founded, even though he has listed the names of twenty-six goldsmiths active during that period. Some of these may have been concerned solely with coin, but as no names appear in his 'made free' column and we now know that thirteen of them were freemen, the list seems somewhat unreliable. Nevertheless, with virtually no silver surviving to prove the point, assessment of their output or the quality of their work is somewhat academic.

All we have to go on, and that without indication of the place of manufacture, are continual references in church inventories compiled during the reign of Edward VI, to 'Challice with patten . . . parcel gilt', sometimes with the addition of something like 'weying xiiij unces', an entry which appears at Wolsingham. Wills also mention secular silver, and one dated 1448 refers to a silver cup inscribed 'En bon Estreyn'. It is unfortunate they are not more descriptive.

It would appear, therefore, that the total lack of locally made Elizabethan communion plate, which figures so largely in all the other early provincial records, is due to the fact that next to none was made. Only seven Elizabethan cups have survived in Northumberland, fewer than in any other county of England, and all of these were made in London between 1570 and 1571, which at least pinpoints the time when the bishop decreed that his parishes must conform by changing their old Massing chalices. In Durham, the situation is not much better, seventeen London-made cups having survived, and there are also two pre-Reformation patens in that county.

This would seem an appropriate point at which to mention the possibility of silver having been made in Carlisle, for the history of its guild, of which little is known, appears to end with the Siege of Carlisle in 1644–5.

We know that a guild existed there during the sixteenth century and incorporated blacksmiths, whitesmiths, goldsmiths and silversmiths, and that it continued as such until 1728. Nevertheless, records from 1660 show that city maces were sent to Newcastle for repair, and from then on no further evidence appears of work undertaken in Carlisle. Newcastle became the silver centre for Carlisle, and connection between the two cities remained strong, as later references to Newcastle silver in Carlisle will show. There are, however, ten communion cups in existence, made roughly between 1565 and 1571, which were probably made by a Carlisle man called Edward Dalton and, in this case, 'roughly' could be taken to have a double meaning. These cups struggled to copy the Elizabethan pattern of the times, and if no things of beauty they are undoubtedly of interest. Old records mention a silversmith named Dalton at various intervals up until 1644, which would indicate a family business spanning several generations.

The original cups were marked, if at all, with the initials 'ED' linked, followed by a four-petalled rose in a circle stamped twice. The hammer-men of Carlisle had had their pewter marked with such a rose, and a hammer appears to have been the chief tool used in the making of these cups. Incidentally, this same rose was stamped, again

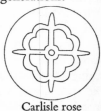

Carlisle rose

72

somewhat crudely, on the coins minted in Carlisle during the Siege—but then, they were rather crude coins. Carlisle, after all, was not a mint town. The city had been under siege since October 1644, and when, on 13 May 1645, they decided to make coin for themselves, resources were pretty nearly exhausted. The good royalist citizens cheerfully brought in their plate for melting, and between them they raised 1,162oz of what would now be priceless antique silver. At the time, it produced £323 os 3d worth of coin.

All the old corporation plate went into this melting-pot, consisting of '2 flaggons, 2 gilt bowles, 1 gilt salt and 2 beare bowles', 233oz in all. In an earlier inventory, the two gilt bowls had each been described as 'standing bowle gilt, with a cover', and the salt as '1 double salt, gilt'. Of the private citizens, we learn that 'Widow Orpheur gave 4 spoons; Sir Thomas Glenham, 2 candlesticks; Sir William Dalston, 1 great salt, 1 lesser salt, 1 bowl and 8 spoons'. Each according to his worth, including tankards, tumblers, and dozens of plates. A pity that no one thought to describe them.

The romantic history behind this mark of the Carlisle rose gives it a special interest, and a seal-top spoon, c 1620, struck with this rose once on the bowl and twice on the stem, appeared in a Sotheby's sale in 1964. In the Ellis catalogue of provincial spoons, for which the late Commander G. E. P. How, RN, wrote a foreword in 1935, several more maker's marks had been found bearing the stamp of this rose of Carlisle.

Although in these border counties there is less Elizabethan communion plate than in any other part of the country, there is an unusual amount of later date, and from the mid-seventeenth century onwards very much the greater proportion of this is of Newcastle make, particularly in Northumberland. Church silver, in fact, was made throughout the remaining centuries that the city was concerned with the craft, in all the varying styles of changing times. In County Durham some of the earliest church plate, including one Elizabethan cup, was York made, but later, as Newcastle rose to surpass York in wealth and importance, the position is reversed, and a high proportion of Newcastle-made plate, mostly communion cups and flagons, appears in Yorkshire churches from about 1705 onwards. Many of these are by Isaac Cookson, but John Langwith, who was actually a York man using the Newcastle mark while his own assay office was closed (1716– 76), is also well represented.

The golden age of Newcastle-made silver began about the time that William Ramsey joined the Company in 1656, and from then on the great names follow one another regularly. Wilfred J. Cripps mentions the tall cup, 8¼in high, by John Wilkinson at Ryton church, in Co Durham, as the oldest of Newcastle make, an appropriate possession for Ryton where records show that 'a new church was built in the thirteenth century'. The bell-shaped bowl of this cup sits on a wide straight stem, with a moulded central knop and a domed foot. Its paten is pricked out '1664'. Jackson, however, has attributed the date 1658 to

a cup at Trimdon, also marked with Wilkinson's 🛡️ over a mullet;

he had found Wilkinson's name mentioned in 1650, which makes the attribution possible, and no doubt had a reason for it, although search has not revealed it to me. Nevertheless, Jackson was by no means infallible, and no silver made in Newcastle bore a date letter before 1702. Their marking system, to say the least, was odd, the town mark and lion passant often being omitted altogether. In fact, there is no evidence that any authority controlled marking before 1702.

In the Laing Art Gallery and Museum in Newcastle there are some very beautiful and simple pieces of Charles I communion plate described as 'probably Newcastle'. One is an Elizabethan type of cup, with '1628' engraved on its paten cover, and a pair of standing bowl patens, very lightly and beautifully engraved, are described as 'circa 1628'. They are lovely, uncluttered work, typical of Newcastle throughout its history, for to the craftsmen there the concept of good workmanship and line, with simple decoration, appears ever to have been their guiding principle. But if there were goldsmiths in the city at the time, and Jackson names two possibles, why did they not join the Company? An unwritten history of jealousy and internal strife could be the answer.

From the time of John Wilkinson's first known plate to 1672, Newcastle work was marked with a single castle and the maker's mark. During that same period, and again sometimes between 1721 and 1727, work was also stamped with the lion passant 'to sinister', which means that the lion is walking towards the right when normally it would face

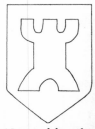

Newcastle's early single castle mark

74

to the left ('to dexter')—mirror writing being the best explanation of these 'back-to-front' heraldic terms. In addition to its independent sense of direction, the Newcastle lion looks straight ahead with a most jaunty expression, whereas the normal lion glares at one full face.

Use of this lion varied in the earliest examples. In John Wilkinson's two communion cups already mentioned it was used twice in different combinations with the maker's own symbol and the single castle, each used once. But on a tankard he made in 1668, he uses the lion and his 'w' only once, with the single castle mark twice.

John Dowthwaite, whose mark also had a rather peculiar cross over the first of his two initials 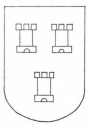 (which were in a shield over a mullet) was another to mark his plate with the single castle and lion to sinister; Jackson records two tall, straight-sided flagons, marked with this single castle, belonging to St Mary's church, Gateshead, dated 1672, the year when the three castle mark is first recorded.

This, the mark for which Newcastle work is really known, was stamped on a variety of shields, the three castles also showing distinct differences before 1702. The important point to the amateur is that the three castles always stood separately, two above one. Similar castles at Aberdeen were mostly in conjunction with Scottish marks.

John Dowthwaite's cups appear in churches throughout the northern counties, and generally have flaring rims and bases, whether the bowl be bell-shaped or straight-sided. He also made a straight-sided, flat-bottomed porringer, again with a flaring rim, with repoussé tulips and leaves on the body. This was an unusual form of decoration in Newcastle, though it was common in York.

Newcastle town mark of three castles

We are inclined to blame the paucity of early Newcastle work on successive wars and border troubles, but an old communion cup of John Dowthwaite's, blackened and unloved, illustrates another cause of loss. Lack of taste in Victorian times caused the melting down, for 'refashioning', of an immense amount of our oldest silver, of every type. In 1917, an old cup, only 4¾in high and hardly recognisable as silver through neglect, was sold for scrap and bought by a man in Carlisle who proceeded to clean it up. When the marks appeared, the single castle of Newcastle was revealed, with Dowthwaite's mark, between the lion to sinister on either side. It must have been thrilling to find them, and then to bring out the pleasing band of decoration with scrolled leaves and flowers at the top of the flat-based bowl of this little cup, which weighs only 3oz 16dwt.

But Dowthwaite did not only make for the church, and a peg tankard of his, c 1670, is in the Laing Art Gallery. These drinking-vessels were very much a feature of the north, where Scandinavian influences were strong, and may have three claw and ball, or pomegranate feet, with applied scroll leaves above them on their rather squat bodies. The lid, usually with a protruding flange, has a flat top, stepped only once, and the thumbpiece often matches the feet.

In this peg tankard of Dowthwaite's, which has the Thorp arms engraved on the front, the pegs can be seen protruding at regular intervals down the inside, which is gilt. It could never be said that anything bearing the Newcastle mark before 1702 is common, for 'rare' is a better word up until 1750; nevertheless, of surviving silver, such tankards, with or without the pegs, are amongst the most frequently found and are easily recognisable as northern work. Another peg tankard, by William Ramsey, has broad simple 'S' handles ending in a plain shield, where quite often initials are engraved. This tankard, c 1670, is stamped with the maker's mark twice, and the single castle of Newcastle twice. (Illustration, p 52.)

The marks attributed to Ramsey show an immense amount of variety, appearing as initials over a little bird, below a crown, in many different shields, or without a shield at all. It is possible that the initials 'WR' conjoined within a dotted circle may have marked the work of William Robinson senior, who was described as a 'goulsmith, late of Newcastle, deceased' on his son's apprenticeship forms in 1657. The only other mention of him refers to an 'imbroderer', a man who would have been chiefly concerned with the making of gold and silver lace to embellish the rich costumes of the day. If he also made silver plate, there could not have been much of it, but a seal-top spoon exists marked in the bowl with this particular 'WR'. The top is pricked out with the date '1642', a time when these initials were otherwise unknown throughout the country. If William Robinson was the maker, then this spoon is the oldest surviving piece of marked Newcastle silver.

But this is not the only complication. William Robinson junior obtained his freedom in 1666, and both he and Ramsey died in 1698. Until exhaustive research is undertaken, the apportioning of these initials must be taken with reserve. Jackson, who did the donkey work on the whole country's marks, is now being proved wrong in many of them. Nevertheless, he has given the 'WR' conjoined in a heart-shaped shield with scrolls above and below as Robinson's last mark. J. W. Clark, the local expert, however, described these marks on a chocolate pot, c 1695, shown in the Bowes Museum exhibition at Barnard Castle in 1961, and attributed them as 'probably by William Ramsey'. 'WR' appears in two forms on this inverted pear-shaped pot, which has a flattened domed lid, the usual detachable domed cap through which the chocolate was stirred, and an unusual amount of decoration for Newcastle work. One mark is the somewhat untidy heart already described; the second a quatrefoil with a star between the initials and a crescent above and below the star. With two craftsmen working at the same time and bearing the same initials, it does not seem safe to assume, without proof, that the majority of these marks were stamped on the work of William Ramsey.

Surviving examples of these marks are prolific, and are to be found on a wide variety of silver. For over forty years pear- and bell-shaped communion cups, flagons, spoons, two-handled cups, at least one pair of standing salvers, (1686), and tankards, some using cut card work on the handle, appear with 'WR' in one form or another. One of the tankards, drum-shaped on three pomegranate feet, has a rather entrancing mermaid holding a tail in either hand, as a thumbpiece. On this a rose in a shield is marked twice, and the initials appear above a bird, together with the three castles of Newcastle. This rose appears on much ascribed to Ramsey, and it has been suggested it may indicate that he came from Montrose, in Scotland. In view of the laws of the 'Company' and its strong feelings about the Scots, Carlisle, to me, appears much more likely.

The Sawley flagon also has the three castles, the five-petalled rose in a square shield twice, and the maker's mark. If this great piece, now in Newcastle's Laing Art Gallery, is really Ramsey's work, as assumed, it would place those versions of 'WR' found in conjunction with the rose with much greater certainty. With it the lion passant was never used, and the rose must have taken its place as standard mark.

This flagon, about 11in high, is typical of the straight-sided, tankard-type flagon of the day, with its flat-domed lid, wide splayed foot, and broad 'S'-shaped handle, with an ordinary double-lobed thumbpiece. On one side the arms and achievements of the city of Newcastle are engraved, while inscriptions tell us that it was given to the mayor of Newcastle in 1670; the other side describes how it was presented to Sawley church in 1756. One of the four donors named on it, William Kay, had been churchwarden at Sawley where his brother was vicar and, when sent to help General Wade keep order in Newcastle during the troubles of the '45, he somehow managed to hide the flagon and so keep it from the general melting-pot; no mean achievement at that time.

Two other flagons in the same museum belonging to All Saints church, Newcastle, were made by Thomas Hewitson, free in 1697, during the period when local marking was illegal. Both were of the straight-sided tankard type, but bigger and with a less widely splayed base than the Sawley example. Several technical differences, mainly of proportion, could be shown, but in comparing these two fine pieces with any other flagon it is the magnificent thumbpiece that seems important. Dated 1697 and 1698 respectively, they are about 18in high and have wide 'S' handles terminating in the most lovely cherub, full face in the centre, with wide wings outstretched. The handle of each is flat and really broad at the top, where applied ornament breaks the surface in geometric design. This is at its finest in the 1698 flagon, on which the ornament is repeated on the body at the junctions of the handle. There is a small finial on the lid.

Thomas Hewitson also made a porringer, or two-handled cup, in 1697, with vertical convex and concave flutes. This has large, broad, hollow handles and, while the shields in which they ended were common enough in the tankards of the day, they were most unusual in such a cup.

A porringer made by 'WR' in about 1690 is unusual for its overall chinoiserie engraving, but is otherwise typical, its bowl, of the usual shape, sitting daintily on a simple, moulded base. A fine acanthus leaf finial stands boldly above its almost flat lid, while light, 'S'-shaped handles recurve pleasantly. This cup is marked with the initials 'WR' conjoined below a coronet twice, and the three castles mark once.

Chinoiserie engraving was rare in the provinces because it was a specialist's job. In fact, one expert believes that all the fine work of this kind was done by just two men in London, who engraved sophisticated scenes in the Chinese manner. One man, possibly from Barnstaple, and another from Edinburgh, tried to copy this style, but only Dublin, outside London, really succeeded. Yet Newcastle appears to have had its own engraver, for the flat chasing on some of its wares could not have been executed by those London masters. The work is cruder in form and less sophisticated, attempting only flowers, foliage and occasional birds rather than the full Chinese scene. They are distinct, however—Newcastle work rather than London copies.

It is possible that this Newcastle engraver was Eli Bilton, a contemporary, prolific goldsmith, free 1682. He had an early mark which varied considerably, showing a plain 'EB', or 'EB' over a star in a shield, or sometimes with a crown above. Secular plate of his survives, including a 1694 chocolate pot, while his communion cups appear in Cumberland, Northumberland, and Co Durham churches, the majority stamped twice with one form or another of his mark, twice with the three castle mark, and in a variety of forms with no lion passant. Carlisle Museum has a fluted, two-handled porringer made by him in 1700 belonging to the Taylors' Guild of the city. It bears his mark as illustrated, although this had ceased to be legal, and the three castle mark, each repeated.

Of greater interest, however, are a spoon, 8¾in long, on which he marked the London date letter for 1699, and a mug he made in 1700, for on both of those he showed that he had used the higher standard silver by stamping it with Britannia, the lion's head erased, and the single castle of Newcastle in a plain shield, although three castles would have been correct were it not for the fact that only London marks were legal at that time. His own mark in the new manner, 'Bi' in a shield, with a star above and below, followed. Markings on provincial silver generally during this period were varied and strange, but the open defiance of including the old Newcastle mark was rare. Francis Batty, admitted in 1674, sometimes used the new form of maker's mark, 'Ba', stamped four times during this period, as did several others, either three or four times. All over the country, provincial craftsmen found their own ways of getting around the ban on local marking.

A large amount of silver was made in Newcastle from 1670 onwards, but spoons were always comparatively rare. The Ellis catalogue (Sotheby's, 1935), however, listed a spoon by Eli Bilton, c 1694, with an unusually deeply indented trifid top, a finely decorated rat tail, and the town and maker's mark struck twice on the stem.

So little silver survives from 'The Company' days, (from which the goldsmiths broke away in 1716) that the appearance of any for sale, let alone so rare an object as the Bilton spoon, was really an event. Yet, among the few, Eli Bilton is well represented. At Christie's in 1964 a two-handled cup and cover of his, c 1695, was sold. This was a very early example of a style of porringer made generally between 1695 and 1715, but rarely with a cover. Set on a low, circular reeded foot, the lower part is chased with spiral flutings, with a fluted rib above; the cover, too, has a fluted border and a tall baluster finial on a rosette of spiral flutings. It has plain 'S' scroll handles, and a rather bold coat of arms has been engraved centrally in a circular medallion at a later date.

At the Antique Dealers' Fair of 1967 a tumbler cup made by Eli Bilton in 1703 was sold, again decorated on its lower half with spiral flutings, quite unusual in tumblers. But at the same fair, a Newcastle tankard, c 1690, was of even greater interest. (Illustration, p 85.) This 29 oz tankard, 7in high, is of another typically northern type, round-bodied, somewhat squat, with an almost flat top, but no feet. The cut card decoration applied to its broad handle is a style rarely used in the south, and generally indicative of Newcastle in the north. It derived from the Scandinavians who had used engraving on handles, but in Newcastle this was rare, engraving there, with the occasional exception of initials, being confined to arms on the front of the body and the chinoiserie already mentioned.

The long rat tail running down this tankard's spine, under the handle, was another feature indicating Newcastle, for it is a speciality of the city's work. Two other clues to its origin show the fascination that a little detective work can give to such silver, for in searching to identify the arms engraved upon it, the expert discovered that these belonged to the Forsters of Edderston, who had been hereditary wardens of Bamburgh Castle, in Northumberland, until 1715.

The tankard was marked only with the initials 'AF', with a mullet below, four times, a mark that also appeared on a communion cup at Medolmsley, twelve miles from Newcastle, a further clue to local manufacture. The record of the Christening of Augustine Float's daughter in St Nicholas Cathedral, Newcastle, in 1681, describes her father as a 'silversmith', the only mention of him in the city, yet no

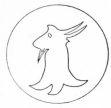

Gateshead

other craftsman with those initials is recorded there at that time. Nevertheless, just across the river, in Gateshead, some silver was being made and marked in an oval shield, with a pellet between, and a goat's head erased; this, described as the 'Gateshead' mark, causes excitement through its rarity, and the maker who used it has always been presumed to be Augustine Float. One wonders why he marked the tankard differently.

Ellis records a rather worn trifid spoon, c 1680, but of far more interest are the magnificent examples belonging to the Laing Art Gallery, stamped with this same goat's head mark from which the town's name is said to derive, and the (A.F) of Augustine Float.

A very fine Charles II tankard, c 1680, is of the same style as the previous example, and its measurements show proportions which can be described as both 'large' and 'squat', for, weighing 32oz it is only 7in high yet has a diameter of 5in. This also has the rat tail rib below the hinge, a flat cover with a moulded rim, corkscrew thumbpiece, and strapwork scrolls applied to the top of its plain 'S'-shaped handle. The bowl and lid are well marked with Float's oval mark and the goat repeated, those on the lid being in pristine condition. Then, all by itself in the centre of the handle well below the decoration, 'AF' appears again as simple initials.

A half-pint-size mug with a very slightly everted rim also bears these rare marks. This is decorated very lightly below the rim with a tiny band of repoussé leaf decoration, which is repeated below the alternate concave and convex spiral fluting on the bulbous lower half of the mug. There is a flat reeded handle, and the whole piece is only 3⅜in high, weighs 4oz, and has very clear marks.

The law-abiding silversmiths of Newcastle suffered more than most during the years 1697–1701, when the silver standard was raised and London alone could mark it, for obviously it was virtually impossible to send silver all the way to the capital. To make matters worse, when other provincial offices were re-established in 1701, Newcastle was left out. Though they could now send work to York and get it back within two weeks, they resented having been passed over and Francis Batty, by then a senior craftsman with much fine work to his credit, headed a deputation to Parliament. Their petition stated that 'whereas in the town of Newcastle-Upon-Tyne there is, and time out of mind hath been, an ancient company of goldsmiths . . .' and eventually resulted in their re-establishment in 1702, one year later than other provincial offices.

This, then, was to be known as the 'Company of Goldsmiths of Newcastle-Upon-Tyne', and the marks were to be as elsewhere: the maker's mark being the first two letters of a surname, such as Francis Batty's 'Ba'; the lion's head erased; Britannia; the arms of the city, the three castles now taking on a more regular image; and a variable date letter which, until 1721, was not stamped in consecutive order.

But although given their own status, the goldsmiths did not yet break entirely with 'The Company'. They held separate meetings and kept their own minute books, gradually becoming more aloof from the Plumbers, though separation was difficult because of investments involved. For one thing, when the Company meeting hall was rebuilt during the 'closed' years, the goldsmiths had been amongst those who had subscribed. The balance was raised by loan, soon repaid out of the fines 'constantly imposed'. These were not only concerned with 'Scots', but with crimes such as the taking of a new apprentice before the last one had served three years. Both Batty and Eli Bilton were fined £5 for this, while Richard Hobbs was mulcted of 1s for going to a Christening, thereby missing a meeting. Traditionally, from the beginning, half the fines went to the Company and the other half to upholding the works of Tyne Bridge.

One of the Newcastle goldsmiths' most precious possessions is a circular copper plate on which, from 1702 till the assay office closed in 1885, every freeman punched his mark, starting with Francis Batty in the centre and continuing in spiral form. Two hundred and eighty-seven marks are recorded upon it, an invaluable and unique guide to makers' marks from that time forward.

Many guilds then flourishing in the north are now defunct, their plate on permanent loan to local museums, while that belonging to the wardens of six of Durham's companies is to be seen by appointment in the town hall. Of these, twelve pieces are of Newcastle make, including six of the fifteen tankards which, like the bowls, goblets and loving cups dating from 1600 to the end of the eighteenth century, are particularly interesting for their inscriptions, which often give clues to local history.

The guilds of Newcastle also had their plate, but only that of the Taylors' Company is still to be seen, by appointment. This includes several fine tankards, and a little straight-sided, flat-bottomed bowl, 2⅛in high, with a flaring lip, c 1676, by an unidentified maker.

Although the silver in the Tuillie House Museum, Carlisle, includes less of Newcastle make, it is of particular interest. Beside the two pieces by Eli Bilton already mentioned, the Skinners' and Glovers' Guild of Carlisle have a 'tankard' he made in 1701, only 3¾in high and without a lid. This really should be described as a small mug. Then there is a tiny tumbler cup by John Younghusband, free 1706, made for the Tailors' Guild of Carlisle in 1707. This is only 1⅞in high and demonstrates that northern tumbler cups are noticeably lower, in proportion to width, than those of London. Although 2¼in high, a tumbler cup there belonging to the Shoemakers' Guild of Carlisle, made by Richard Richardson of Chester in 1721, also shows this same tendency. Apart from these, a tankard by Isaac Cookson, 1744, one of the great Newcastle names; a two-handled cup and cover by Thomas Partis, 1727, and a lidded tankard by James Kirkup, 1722, both belonging to the corporation of Carlisle, are the only other examples still in its keeping.

Yet the gems of this museum must be of interest to Newcastle people, who have always been concerned with racing. The museum's two Elizabethan globular racing bells, one inscribed 1599 and only 1¾in high, are a part of the early history of the sport when bells were traditionally the prizes for horse racing. One of these, of silver gilt, 2³⁄₁₆in high, is inscribed, 'The sweftes horse thes bel to tak for mi lade dakar sake'. Local historians could have fun discovering who Lady Daker was.

Yet these were made many centuries later than Lanark's silver bell, which has been a prize run for since the days of William the Lion of Scotland, (1165–1214), and is still presented by the town's newest bride. And if, in those days, no self-respecting Newcastle horse would have considered competing for a Scottish prize, how different the case now, when the Newcastle and Scottish breweries combine to give one of the north's richest prizes, for which a beautiful mounted cavalier, designed and made by the Northern Goldsmiths' Company in 1960, is the trophy. This is a fine piece of modern silver.

The earliest civic record of racing in Newcastle was in 1632, when two silver 'potts' were given for races on Killingworth moor. Racing, among other pleasures, was stopped during the Commonwealth period, but no time was lost in coming to the start in the more cheerful days that followed, the races and their silver trophies growing in value and interest. These trophies took various forms in different parts of the country. Thomas Partis of Newcastle made a coffee pot, for instance, which was presented for the Ladies' Plate at Carlisle in 1726, while the gold teapot by James Ker of Edinburgh, now in the United States which was sold for £40,000 at Christie's in 1967, was made in 1736 and presented that year for a Scottish race valued at £100.

Gold, which in Newcastle was marked in the same manner as silver until 1798, also featured in the many fine prizes given for racing, and James Kirkup made a two-handled gold cup for this purpose in 1728. Collecting racing trophies gives added interest to those concerned with the sport, for it is usually possible to trace the history, not only of the cups themselves but also of the horses that ran for them, often in circumstances that are unusual and amusing to us now; this applies equally to unimportant trophies which can be bought comparatively cheaply.

In 1740 an Act of Parliament suppressed 'petty' races, held in almost every village in the country, and so put an end to thirty-two meetings in Northumberland and Co Durham alone, including Killingworth. Nevertheless, racing interest in the north was always strong, and there can be few better areas for seeking out old trophies.

During the years between the reopening of Newcastle's assay office in 1702 and its cession from the 'Company' in 1716, the majority of its big names were already well known, conforming to the higher standard required, and (largely) marking accordingly. Communion plate continued to be made, and Eli Bilton, to take one example, made a pair of cups for Stanhope church in 1703 with a straight-sided bowl of the Elizabethan type, with a raised, narrow rib where the old engraved band would have been and a truncated stem divided by a plain knop with a central raised rib, set on a stepped foot.

But new names were also appearing. William Ramsey junior had been made free in 1691; Eli Bilton, son of Josuah, a blockmaker, was apprenticed to his famous uncle in 1704, and the much more industrious Francis Batty junior, in 1706. Jonathan French, free 1703, and John Younghusband, 1706, were the most important of the newcomers.

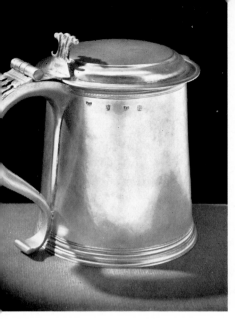
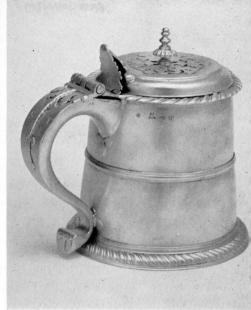

85 Tankards 1690–1864: (*above left*) a typically northern form, marked with the 'AF' of gustine Float, who usually worked in Gateshead. Note the long rat tail beneath the handle; *ve right*) James Sympsone, Edinburgh, 1702; (*below left*) Philip Elston, Exeter, 1738; (*below right*) Victorian at its best, by Elkington & Co, Birmingham, 1864

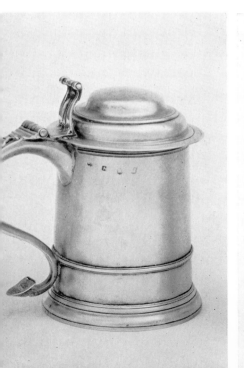
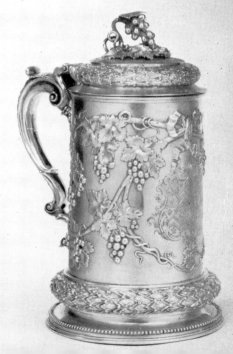

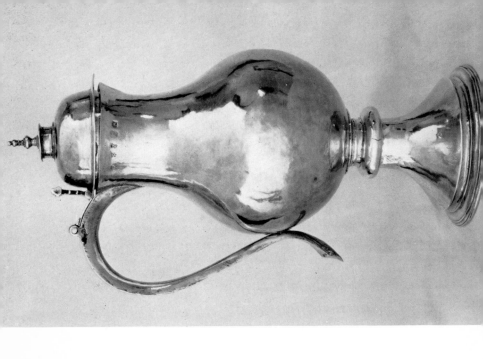

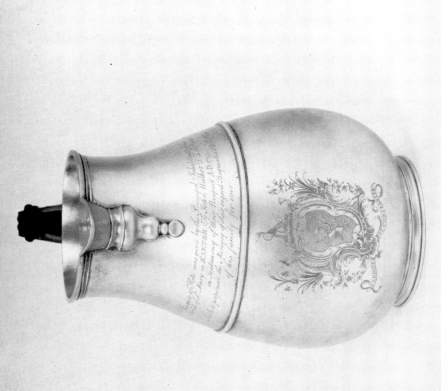

In 1716, when the York office closed for fifty years, two leading silversmiths at the time, John Langwith, their assay master, and Joseph Buckle, registered their marks in Newcastle. Stephen Buckle, who made plate mainly for Yorkshire churches, was also registered in 1740 as 'of York', although he had been trained in Newcastle by one of its greatest craftsmen, Isaac Cookson (1728–54). Jackson also records a tumbler cup, fully marked with Newcastle's higher standard marks, for the year 1708, as made by John Buckle of York, although this name appears in neither his York nor Newcastle lists.

The closure of the York office must have increased the volume of work commissioned in Newcastle, but could not have affected the high regard in which Newcastle-made silver of this period is still held. In most cases they followed the fashions set in London fairly closely, with virtually no time lag; the punch bowl by John French, 1728, sold in 1954, is typical of this, being exactly of the plain, round shape on a circular domed base that was normal at the time, adorned only with engraved arms and inscription.

But in some ways Newcastle was still individual in its work. From about 1730 onwards, when hollow-ware generally had become more bulbous in the body, Newcastle was producing an unusually tall tankard of cylindrical form, with a flat-topped domed lid and gadrooned base, without feet, the gadrooning also appearing around the base of the lid. The Danes had made tankards of this identical shape a hundred or more years earlier, but they had chased the base and lid, and had also been more ornamental about the thumbpiece. Earlier northern forms of tankard had been shared with York and Hull. This form belonged to Newcastle alone.

It is difficult to say whether an arval flagon was more particularly a Yorkshire or a Newcastle speciality, for any tankard could have been used for the comfort of mourners at a funeral, and the idea was, simply, to keep one cup separate from those used on happier occasions. Nevertheless, Bolton-by-Bolland, in the West Riding of Yorkshire, is one church that possessed a flagon, by Isaac Cookson of Newcastle, 1731, especially made for the purpose of serving wine, or warm ale, to the bereaved after the burial service was over. This is a quart tankard with a domed lid, and initials cut on the handle indicate the possibility of a memorial gift.

That Isaac Cookson's work appears all over Yorkshire, particularly

F                                    87

in its churches, must be a direct result of York's closure, but it seems doubtful whether this hard-working craftsman would have achieved less with a more restricted market. In John Langlands he trained an apprentice with the ability to be a real help to him; nevertheless, with every mention of the quantity of his work, the word 'quality' must be added. During York's closure, he provided any civic plate still required by that well-furnished Mansion House, including a domed tankard, typical of the period, 1738, and a very fine set of castors, engraved with the York city arms, in 1735.

He made so much silver for the churches of Northumberland and Co Durham that to have it brought together under one roof would be a great achievement. One fine example is a paten in the form of a waiter, with three claw feet, in Harburn church, Northumberland.

Perhaps because of his industrious habits, more Isaac Cookson silver appears for sale than that of any other Newcastle craftsman, bar John Langlands and his relations. At an exhibition of Newcastle silver staged by the Newcastle Society of Antiquaries at their Black Gate Museum in 1897, examples of his work included: cream pots, a pepper pot, candlesticks, a punch ladle, porringer, a salver and sauce boat, as well as tankards and mugs. The latter appear most frequently, and generally follow the baluster fashion of the times, with the moulded midrib and domed cover, occasionally with a spread base instead of the more usual rim, or stepped base. On many of these he used a heart-shaped, or shell shield to complete a scrolled or double-scrolled handle. The thumb-piece may have had the simple or bifurcated loop, the corkscrew, or the scroll thumbpiece. Very often initials were engraved on the handle, as was usual in Newcastle.

Despite the number of tankards and other work, he was mostly known for his tea and coffee pots, and a beautiful little bowl he made in 1747, with three-lion mask and paw feet, may have been intended for sugar to go with these, in the days before such things were made in sets. This has an everted rim, chased on top, and arms engraved on one side. His coffee pots were of a high standard, again following the variations of shape shown in his tankards, mostly baluster, although the earlier examples were cylindrical. These were mostly quite plain, with leaf decoration applied around the curved spout, which sometimes had a swan neck.

Of his teapots, which are again known more for their workmanship and quality of engraving, generally on their lids, than for any extraordinary style, there is one in the Laing Art Gallery which did differ from the normal. This is a small bullet teapot, made in 1732, with a most unusual spout that comes out horizontally from near the top, and then turns up at a sharp angle, almost vertically. The engraving over the lid and shoulders of the teapot is of Cookson's usual, light, but well-executed standard, and the finial is high.

A large tea kettle complete with stand and lamp, made by Isaac Cookson in 1732, a man who assayed about 150,000 oz of silver and worked until his death in 1754, was a glorious example of Newcastle's uncluttered work, the kettle being of the skittle-ball type, with fine flat chasing around the lid and a well-engraved coat of arms as the only other ornament. For a craftsman of his quality in the mid-eighteenth century, it is to his credit that he resisted any attempt to imitate the Huguenots of London, who had brought rococo to its height in England.

But simplicity was always the byword of Newcastle, and when rococo was at its height William Partis made a beautiful little sugar basin with a swing handle, now in the Laing Art Gallery, that is decorated only with one row of pierced decoration, below the rim. William (died 1759) was the son of Thomas Partis (1720-34), who founded a family of goldsmiths from Sunderland, whose work is in many of the churches of Co Durham and who also made silver of a secular nature for gentry in their county.

Yet, somehow, we have left the new Company of 1716, marking its silver with the three castle mark that is so easy to distinguish from Exeter or Edinburgh because each castle is separate. During the years from 1721 when the sterling standard was restored, until 1728, most

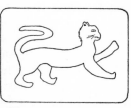

Lion passant to sinister

craftsmen also asserted their individuality by stamping the lion passant to sinister. This happened nowhere but in Newcastle. Francis Batty junior and John Ramsey junior were among those who marked this lion to sinister, as were Jonathan French, Thomas Partis, John Carnaby, and Isaac Cookson's first recorded piece, a small mug, with the date letter for 1727-8. The only exceptions that Jackson records were Robert Makepeace on a coffee pot, and James Kirkup on a tankard, who, between 1722 and 1723, placed their lion to dexter in the proper way. They were probably not alone. This became normal practice in 1728, when the lion conformed by walking in the right direction, that is to the left, with his head turned four-square to glare at the assay master. But in 1846, when the Newcastle leopard's head lost its crown (having clung to it longer than most), the lion passant regained his jaunty expression, looking straight before him as if he owned the world. The leopard of Newcastle had obviously been a moody creature with an ever-changing expression, no doubt due to the stamp being re-designed for the assay office every few years. He also declared his independence by wearing a five-pointed crown until 1779, when he decided to conform with the uniform crown. Jackson remarks that when the sovereign's head duty mark was introduced in 1784, the date letter 'S' is seen both with and without this mark in Newcastle. This, of course, happened everywhere, because the duty mark actually came into force on 1 January 1785, half-way through the date cycle.

Throughout this period Newcastle was at the height of its fame, with fine craftsmen producing good work prolifically. Because most of them largely made the more important type of silver, such as tankards, coffee pots, cream jugs, and plate of all sorts for the church, it is difficult to pick out examples without being repetitive. Throughout the eighteenth century their work retained the simplicity and standard for which the three castle mark is known. To pick out some names, such as Robert Makepeace, is to omit others equally deserving. Yet a prophet is without honour in his own country. After their highly successful exhibition of locally made silver in 1897, the Newcastle Society of Antiquaries proposed a second exhibition of English, Irish and Scottish plate, from which Newcastle work should be excluded, for 'however interesting it might be, it would hardly compare in artistic merit with the silver of London or Irish make'. In that era, of course (1898), plain work was not in vogue.

Newcastle, at this time, was also famous for its glass, but it is interesting to note that William Bielby, a Durham man best known for his fine enamelling of glass, was first mentioned as a silversmith in Newcastle in 1733. No great amount of silver appears with his mark, and it is probable that the greater part of his time was spent in enamelling other people's work, for his last mention as a Newcastle silversmith was in 1765. Well before then, however, he had made his name for the fine enamelling of flint glass, signing his best work with his name and a most lifelike butterfly. Some of these glasses bore commemorative scenes or armorial designs, others were purely decorative. It is an interesting point that Newcastle-made glass, mostly of a lighter form, was all engraved by Dutchmen, but that another of Newcastle's greatest engravers of glass, Thomas Bewick, had first been apprenticed to William and Mary Beilby.

James and David Crawford were both apprenticed in 1763, but never seem to have worked in partnership. A fair amount of silver by both brothers appears from time to time, but a tankard that James Crawford made in 1790, now in the Laing Art Gallery, particularly appeals. This is a tall, plain, pear-shaped tankard, with spiral fluting around its base and the stepped part of its flat top.

John Langlands, however, was the greatest name in Newcastle at this period, and in his time he assayed about 400,000 oz of silver, either alone or with his partners, so it is not surprising that his name is a by-word for Newcastle. Although apprenticed in 1731, he was not admitted before 1754, when he entered into partnership with John Goodriche, who died in 1757, the same year as his master, Isaac Cookson. Without having researched the point, it looks as if he shunned the limelight, and may actually have been responsible for much of Cookson's later work. Having made the break, he remained on his own until joining forces with John Robertson in 1778. This may have been a purely business partnership, as Jackson never records Robertson separately. Nevertheless, Sotheby's, whose catalogue compilers are more up-to-date, sold an oval sauceboat in 1967, with rubbed marks, which they describe as 'apparently Langlands and Robertson, 1757'. This has a waved rim, a flying scroll handle capped with leafage, three hoof feet, and is engraved with a mitre crest.

But the mark of John Langlands alone also appeared in the major salerooms many times during those intervening years, the pieces including a cylindrical teapot, 1773; a plain mug on a spreading foot, 1774, and a tankard of that same year with the heart-shaped terminal to its double-scroll handle of which Cookson had been so fond. These are among a great number of examples that show his standard, but his work, like that of his fellow Newcastle craftsmen, was an open invitation to the 'spoilers' of later days, who loved to add to any plain work.

For example, a baluster tankard bearing John Langlands's mark, 1757, is described in a sale catalogue as having been 'later inscribed and embossed with scrolls and flowers . . . the handle by a different maker, and the cover missing'.

His partnership with Robertson continued until his death in 1793, when his son John carried on the business until his own death in 1804; John junior's widow, Dorothy, then kept up the family name until 1845. It is interesting to note that neither son nor widow was ever mentioned while another Langlands held the mark, and although a great deal of silver was assayed in Dorothy's name, she was obviously merely the figurehead of a family firm that had always been run as such. A set of four alms dishes in the Laing Art Gallery bear the mark of Langlands and Robertson, 1784. These are almost round, very slightly sexfoil, with beaded rims, and are really lovely. A tankard of theirs can also be seen in the same museum, dated 1780, with spiral fluting at the base and on the flat lid.

The Robertson family name also continued, John registering his mark on his father's death in 1795, and Anne, presumably his widow, in 1801, the year he died. John was at one time in partnership with John Walton, another who continued on his own, making teapots in particular, during the early nineteenth century. While some of these were more ornate than the Langlands work of the period, they were still restrained for the times, set on feet of various types, sometimes with the addition of a gadrooned collar with perhaps a little foliage on the handle or spout. A melon-shaped coffee pot made in 1830 was engraved with a crest, but otherwise adorned only with a ribbed spout, capped with a leaf motive, and a melon-shaped finial on the lid.

Thomas Watson, who is also well represented in this museum, worked between 1793 and 1845, and broke away to a considerable extent from the Newcastle normal, his work being much more ornate and, in keeping with the times, sometimes displaying quite heavy ornamentation. But to continue with names is to write a list, and as time and the influence of Birmingham and Sheffield methods took their toll, work for the Newcastle assay office fell away, declining dramatically during the last forty years until closure in 1883. At that time Messrs Reid & Sons, a firm which had been founded when Christian Ker Reid registered his mark in 1778, were the largest assayers of Newcastle silver; when they established a factory in London, little was left for the Newcastle office that had upheld the finest traditions through the years and earned commendation in the great enquiry of 1773.

# Five

# Norwich

Buried treasure found at Caistor-on-Sea, just north of Great Yarmouth, takes proof of civilisation in Norfolk back to the seventh century BC. It does no more, however, for it would be idle to pretend that the gold bracelets, dress fasteners and other trinkets so fashionable in the Bronze Age had been locally made, as no precious metals were mined in East Anglia to give the incentive. This gold hoard, in fact, consists of the type of objects made in Ireland at the time, and other finds in East Anglia show that considerable traffic moved along its shores. A fine torc and fragments of other such collars were found in 1950 at Snettisham, near King's Lynn; the torc is made of an alloy of gold, copper and silver, and although its workmanship and decoration are magnificent, its chief interest is the coin inset in one of its ring terminals belonging to the second quarter of the first century BC. This has helped to date similar torcs found quite recently near Ipswich, one of which had been used to fasten a farm gate. When the crust of time had been removed, the workmanship of its high relief ornament showed a considerable degree of skill.

One could go on, describing the Mildenhall treasure from Suffolk, or the finds on Lord Elvedon's Norfolk estate, both of the fourth century AD, but history has more positive indications of East Anglian culture to show, such as the first monastery at Bury St Edmunds, built in 637. Dates of this sort can read like a list in the area, and where monasteries or cathedrals existed one can be fairly sure that silver adorned them. The story comes nearer home, perhaps, when the see of the bishop of 'the North Folk' was first set up at Elmham, in or a little before 800 AD. This was moved to Thetford in 1075 and finally settled in Norwich in 1094, when the great cathedral was begun. By that time, of course, the early Saxon settlement, a mint town in Athelstane's time, had grown to be one of the three largest boroughs in England.

The cathedral, still retaining many of its Norman features, has been less lucky over its silver which must, originally, have been magnificent. Norman plate, of course, has not survived in England, and 'history' in a broad sense is left to explain the reason why. The sort of thing that happened through the years is illustrated by the edict demanding that Norwich churches, already in the plural, were to give up their chalices in 1193 to help pay a ransom for the release of Richard I, captured on his way home from the Crusades in late December 1192. Although it is rarely mentioned, this was probably a major cause of the loss of Norman silver all over England.

Another very early influence in the area came from the prosperous abbey of St Benet, at Holme, which had been scattered by the Vikings in 870 but grew again to greatness under King Canute. Although none of its treasures remain to be seen, somehow this abbey, the only one in England that was not dissolved by Henry VIII, finds its way into most early East Anglian history, and from it we learn the name of the first goldsmith mentioned. The abbot of St Benet granted a lease of tene-ment in St Peter Mancroft, a ward of central Norwich, to Salamon, goldsmith, in 1142. Jackson tells us that a great number of goldsmiths were working in the city between 1285 and 1305, and then from 1350 to the end of the seventeenth century. It seems more than likely that there was no break, and that having missed Salamon, he simply failed to find the names of craftsmen in those years. Records through the centuries before Norwich started stamping her own silver show that vast quantities were owned, both by the church and homes, and nothing could illustrate this better than the inventory taken at Caistor Castle in 1459, which included 15,000 oz of silver. As the craft had flourished for centuries, one must assume much of it to have been local work.

The city was really wealthy, and by the time of the Reformation every one of its thirty-three churches owned magnificent silver. The tragedy is that now, with Norwich still flourishing, twenty-four of these churches are no longer needed for worship. They are spread over a city that had two main centres: the district around the cathedral, called Tombland from the Saxon market once held there, ('toom' meaning 'open land'), and the Norman market-place near the castle, built in 1130 on a prehistoric mound. This castle, which stands high above its surroundings, was the county prison for five hundred years and now, as a museum, houses a great collection of Norwich-made silver.

Carrow Priory, built as a Benedictine nunnery around 1146, surprisingly leads us to an important feature concerning marks on this silver, for the lovely house, built for its prioress, Isabella Wygun, just before the Dissolution, shows her rebus above the doorway, a 'Y' with a gun. Ever since marks were first read, early Norwich craftsmen have been largely nameless, known only by the device they used. Now, mostly through the researches of Mr G. J. Levine, records have married up many names and marks and, when looked at closely, the marks have obviously been a rebus on the name, giving a clue to the probability of others. Thus we find the orb in Cobbold, which in Norfolk would always be pronounced Corbold; the sun in spendour for Peter Peterson; the flat fish in an oval for Thomas Buttell—butt being a flat fish; 'IV' over a heart for Valentine Isbourne, and the ship for Richard Shipden. This still leaves some unsolved, but time will probably reveal more. The only exception to the use of a device in the sixteenth century was the 'CT' in monogram for Christopher Tannor.

With so much silver made in early Norwich, it is tragic that no stamps at all were used before the full hallmarking system came into being in 1565. The city was one of the seven towns granted its 'touch' in 1423, and had they taken any notice of it and placed even one mark on their work, perhaps a few pieces would turn up that could be ascribed to the city. As it is, there are more pre-Reformation patens in Norfolk than anywhere else in the country, and those that are unmarked are presumed to have been made locally. Nothing is known, and no chalice is even considered a 'possible'.

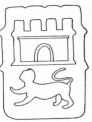

Norwich castle
over lion

There are only about seven hundred marked pieces of Norwich plate known to exist today, and these have provided more talking points than those of any other region. Yet the first marks, in themselves, are simple; the date letter, starting with 'A' in a square in 1565; the maker's mark, and the Norwich town mark, a castle over a lion. So far, so good, with only the maker to decipher; but in 1624

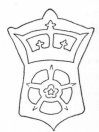

Norwich crowned
rose

a crowned rose was added as a fourth mark, and Jackson has done much to cloud the issue over this, and other marks, which will be more easily discussed in context, when we come to them.

What really had Jackson bemused was the Dutch influence on the city where, in the first half of the seventeenth century, as much Dutch and French was spoken as English. Trade between the Netherlands and Norwich had been brisk for many centuries when, after the Reformation, Protestants from West Flanders first took refuge there from Spanish persecution in their own country. Edward VI encouraged them to go to Norwich by putting churches there at their disposal, but during Mary's reign they presumably moved to Zurich, in whose public library three beaker-shaped silver cups can be seen, one each having been given to the Swiss city by Protestants from Norwich, Winchester, and Salisbury as thank offerings for hospitality received. With Elizabeth's accession they trickled back to Norwich, but flooded in when the city was granted a licence to receive them in 1565. Eventually, of course, they became integrated in the life and worship of the city but, naturally enough, imparted many of their own traditions on the way.

Jackson, by attributing the orb and cross mark to the 'Great' Peter Peterson, also referred to as 'The Dutchman', exaggerated their influence, for this, by far the most prolific device, is marked on all that is finest in the Norwich plate. For many years no doubts were cast upon its ascription to Peterson and the consequent superiority of Dutch craftsmen in the city, until Mr G. J. Levine, delving ceaselessly into old records with the zeal of a master detective, proved not only that Peterson's mark was the sun in splendour, but that the orb and cross was the stamp of William Cobbold, free 1552 and master in 1564. This mark appears in five versions, and he has dated four to different periods of Cobbold's life—or to that of his son, Matthew, after his death. The fifth version, dated 1627, appears only once, on the Attleborough cup, and is ascribed to a member of another generation of the family, Richard.

Jackson recorded the freedom of William and Matthew (1593), but the name Cobbold is not mentioned once in his text, or in his table of drawn marks. Richard, apprenticed to Timothy Skottowe in 1622, is not even listed. Present-day experts writing on Norwich all credit William Cobbold with any work bearing this mark before his death in

1586, but to those who had previously looked only to general reference, the greatest name in Norwich assay history is unlikely to have been heard mentioned before, while that of Peter Peterson is now very much reduced in size. His mark, in fact, appears on only forty-six known pieces, including thirty communion cups, while the orb and cross are found on eighty such cups of an altogether different quality.

Records also prove conclusively that Peterson did not make the font-shaped 'Peterson Cup', sometimes called the 'Ransom Cup', one of the treasures of the civic collection, c 1575–80. This bears an inscription around the bowl pronouncing it to be the gift of Peter Peterson. It is also stamped with the orb and cross in a shaped shield, which Jackson took as conclusive evidence that the mark was that of the Great Dutchman. Mr Charles Oman, nevertheless, while compiling his book *English Church Plate*, found that it was the exception rather than the rule for goldsmiths to make presentations of their own work, and he backs it up with many examples. Generalities, of course, are not proof, but the churchwarden's accounts for 1567, found by Mr Levine at St John Maddermarket, are, for they record a payment to William Cobbold for a piece that still exists and is marked with the orb and cross.

Marks in Norwich read like a detective story, and research in civic records has disposed of another popular myth concerning the 'Ransom Cup'. It had always been supposed that this cup had been made by Peterson as 'ransome' for being excused office as sheriff. He was, in fact, excused all civic duties bar that of chamberlayne—or treasurer—on payment of a fine of £40 and the gift of a standing cup weighing 15 oz. It was a romantic notion that this was the cup made for the purpose, but it is not true. Records show that he paid the fine in full, £40 in two instalments and 'a boll all gylte conteyning XVI ozs.' in 1574. This cup weighs over 30 oz.

To find the probable answer to this puzzle we must look to two other very fine, font-shaped silver gilt cups made in London in 1561 and now in the civic collection, which are almost identical to the 'Peterson' cup. They are beautiful objects on short baluster stems, finely decorated in the Elizabethan manner and engraved on the inside with the arms of John Blenerhasset, their donor, whereas the Peterson cup bears the arms of Norwich. These 'Blenerhasset' cups were used for the city's two sheriffs, and it is a fair supposition that a similar cup, of at least equal size, was needed for the mayor. The suggestion is, therefore, that Peterson's cup was melted down soon after its presentation, and William Cobbold given the job of re-making it to match the other two, keeping only the inscription that proclaimed the Dutchman's gift. If Peterson had been the great craftsman previously imagined, surely he would have been commissioned to do this job himself? Obviously he was not in the same class as Cobbold.

The regalia room in the Norwich City Hall, where these three cups can be seen, is beautifully set out with a dazzling display of civic plate. Pride of place goes to the Reade Salt, the finest piece of provincial silver in the country, made in Norwich in 1568, 'to serve the Mayor and his successors for ever'. Like all the collection, it is still used at civic dinners and is marked with the orb and cross in a lozenge that Cobbold first used, between 1565 and 1569. This great drum-shaped salt, set on a low domed foot, also has a domed cover with an urn finial surmounted by a Roman warrior, a lost-looking fellow obviously out of place in the army holding the butt of a spear and a shield. The workmanship is superb and the repoussé decoration of vases of flowers and garlands of fruit, suspended from tasselled ribbons, is magnificently executed. The arms of Reade, Blenerhasset, and Reade impaling Blenerhasset take up a large part of the body but do not dominate this great salt, which is 15¼in high. (See frontispiece.)

Norwich owns the finest collection of civic plate outside London but, like that of other cities, it does not necessarily represent the survival of all that was best among the pieces committed to its keeping through the centuries. Civic dignitaries frequently lacked appreciation of art, though the majority liked to be associated with it. They cared more that their name should be on record as having given a piece—preferably inscribed to that effect—than that the treasures of another's past should survive. Re-fashioning and melting down, both of regalia and plate, were, therefore, rampant. Among the casualties of the years was a particularly fine ewer and basin given to the city in 1572 by the Archbishop of Canterbury, Matthew Parker, who was a Norwich man; considering the standard of Norwich craftsmen, it would seem likely to have been locally made.

Yet too much must not be assumed. The insignia, which include some incredibly lovely maces, are all either unmarked or London made. There is only one exception: old records have been found proving that the waits' collars were made in the city before Norwich stamped her own wares. These robust chains consist of alternating castles and lions, linked together in a succession as constant as the years since they were first used in the city. The third collar has no past, but symbolises a future for the goldsmith's craft. It is a very much lighter version of the same theme, made by Howard Brown of Norwich in 1951 for the city's first lady mayoress. In this dainty necklace even the lion, slim and jaunty, is altogether feminine, and considerably more chain has been used between the badges. Unfortunately, its maker died in 1956, but a lovely silver ciborium of his, 1952, can be seen in St Peter Hungate Museum; more important, his apprentice, Jack Neild, carries on the good work.

A great deal in the collection was stamped at Goldsmiths' Hall, and the Howard ewer and basin, for instance, are among the most out-standing pieces of English Jacobean craftsmanship, made and gilded in London in 1617. It is really a crime to pick on so marvellous a piece to illustrate a donor's desire for posterity, but the placing of the inscription on this shows how self-importance could cloud all other considerations. The words which begin 'The gift of the Right Honble Henry Howard . . .' are pricked out just below a plaque showing Christ washing the feet of His disciples. Yet to be fair to the future sixth Duke of Norfolk who presented this wonderful gift in 1663, he also gave the city a magnificent mace when Charles II visited Norwich in 1671, on which no more than the Howard crest was placed on the butt.

The 'Spendlove Cups,' another interesting Norwich-made feature of the collection, are by Arthur Haselwood II, a fine craftsman, who did rather more than uphold the good name of his father. The three cups, delightful examples of the simple line, are bucket-shaped with slightly everted rims, each set on a baluster stem and conical foot. All are engraved only with the city arms on the bowl, and the inevitable inscription around the foot recording 'The guyft of Mr Tho Spendlove, sometyme one of ye Alderman of this citty. Ye 3 bowles way 43 oz. 3 qz'. But Mr Spendlove made his gift in 1633, and these were made in about 1670. More, records show that 'Mr. Skottow, goldsmith' was paid £19 15s 6d for making 3 beer cups and 3 wine cups, and for 'graving ye feet wth Aldn Spendlove's name, wch was his gift'. There is no trace of any such cups made by Timothy Skottowe, who died in 1645, and it appears likely that the beer cups, of almost the same weight, were later refashioned. This particular gift was the price Spendlove had to pay for being excused the office of alderman—Norwich seems to have been clever in choosing dignitaries who did not wish to serve.

There is also a similar cup, very slightly larger, marked with a three-quarters profile bust, a device not yet deciphered. This again was created in about 1670 from the refashioning of part of a gift to the city by Mr Justice Windham in 1596. The story of the various changes these objects went through becomes somewhat repetitive, but that very fact serves to illustrate how lucky any silver is to have survived to the present day in its original form. The Dehem flagon, marked with the 'WD' conjoined over an arrowhead of an unknown maker, c 1630, has not quite achieved it, because its lid is missing. Yet it is an imposing pot, 12¼in high, that would have been amongst the proudest treasures in its complete state, with the lid in keeping.

At the time that the goldsmiths' guild of Norwich petitioned the council to allow them to mark their silver with the arms of the city, William Cobbold and William Rogers were wardens of the company. From this fact, two points of pure conjecture come to mind: William Rogers, whose work is not known, was obviously a man of importance for he was warden in three of the next four years. He could have been responsible for the petition regarding marks, and he may well have been the maker of some of the magnificent work known today only by its device. Sixty-seven pieces, for instance, are marked with the trefoil slipped, sixty-five with the maidenhead, and the owners of both punches were working at that time; a name has been found for neither.

On the other hand, William Cobbold had most to gain by a proper system of marks as used in other cities, for anonymity never made an artist's name. The petition declared that great abuses were, and would continue to be, practised because of lack of a mark, which law required them to stamp; that the standard of Norwich craftsmen should be known by its marks to be as high as that of London, and that goldsmiths should be regularly searched to see that all was in order. It is a fact that Cobbold, having served the required seven years' apprenticeship, had already been a freeman for twelve years, yet none of his silver is known to survive prior to 1565—or that of the other master craftsmen who suffered this lack of recognition.

Be that as it may, the majority of surviving Norwich silver was made for the church, and the only two known pieces, marked with the 'A' in a square of 1565, are communion cups. These, the first to bear the castle over a lion of the city, are also stamped with the orb and cross in a lozenge for William Cobbold, who definitely jumped the gun by two years. In most parts of the country the expense of converting the old Massing chalices was undertaken only when it had to be. In Norwich this was in 1567, when Bishop Parkhurst got on the warpath and 350 parishes in his diocese conformed by commissioning new communion cups that year, all marked with a 'C'. Twelve parishes, with surviving cups, also foresaw this need and own plate marked with the 'B' for 1566; yet the job was so thorough in 1567 that only eighteen exist with 'D'; six with 'E'; and two with 'F'. After that, no more church plate was made until 1627, except for one by Christopher Tannor engraved with the date 1585. Cobbold may have persuaded the rector of St Mary's, Diss, and St Saviour's, Norwich, to let him make their new cups sooner, before the inevitable rush got under way, than later, but whatever the reason, these two churches own the prototype of all that symbolises Norwich-made communion cups, so distinct from the nation-wide conventional Elizabethan type.

Not that all are exactly the same. These two, and in fact the majority made by Cobbold, are bell-shaped on a spool-shaped stem which has a central flange-like knop, so slender that it appears more like the joining point of two symmetrical, slightly flaring spools. They make a comparatively short stem that lives in perfect harmony with the bell of the bowl, and the low domed foot. These two have no paten cover, but where this survives, as in the lovely 1567 example at St Mary Coslany, Norwich (illustration, p 33), it completes the symmetry beautifully, the foot, or knop, again taking the spool shape which was also used in Holland.

Shape and size of Norwich-made cups vary enormously, but it is a fair generalisation to say that they are larger and wider in proportion to depth than those made elsewhere. Cobbold's cup at Diss, for instance, is 7½in high, and 5¼in in diameter; Valentine Isborne's at St Swithin's, Bintree, 5in high with a diameter at the rim of 3⅜in. It is also possible to generalise over weight, for the majority give a real impression of solid worth.

Most of Cobbold's cups are decorated around the bowl with a central band of stylised foliage between raised, reeded borders, which

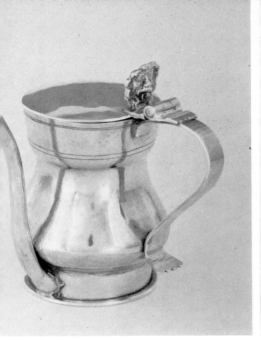
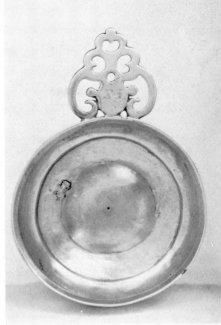

103 (*above left*) A rare and controversial spout cup marked with the 'TS' previously believed
[h]ave been Timothy Skottowe of Norwich, and a fleur de lys device, but now thought to be the
[wor]k of a Bury St Edmunds maker; (*above right*) the bleeding bowl is probably by Katherine Mangy,
[Hul]l, c 1685; (*below*) the Aberpergwm mazer, made entirely of silver, with parts dating from the
fifteenth century

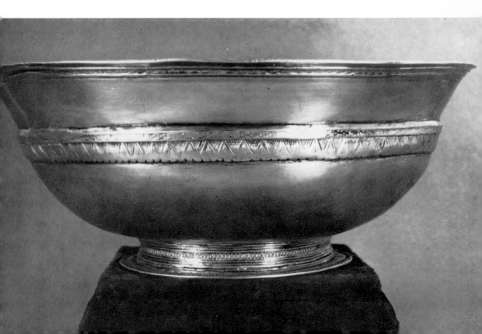

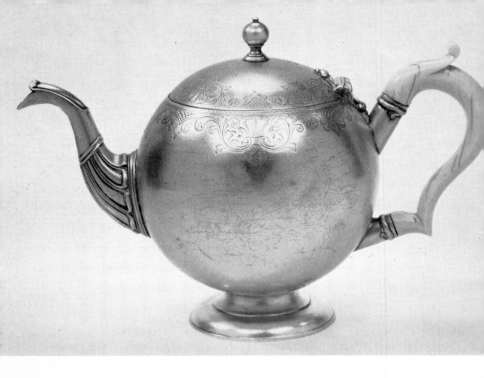

Page 104 (*above*) A silver gilt teapot by Edward Penman, Edinburgh, 1725. The way the b
sits on its pedestal is typically Scottish, although a straight spout was more unusual; (*below*) anot
bullet-shaped pot, by Sampson Bennett, 1759, a Falmouth maker stamping his work in Exe

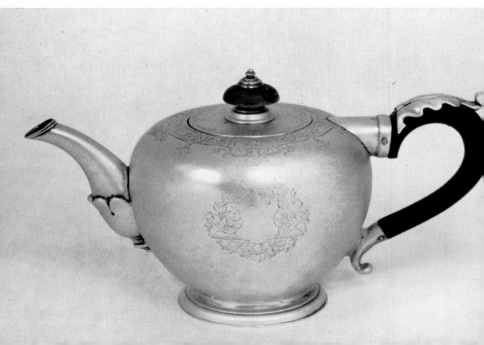

gives the engraving immensely more importance than that on the conventional cup. Nevertheless, an inscription is more usual in this place than other decoration. The St Swithin's, Bintree, cup, for instance, which has a bucket-shaped bowl, is engraved round the centre 'THIS. FOR. DE. THON. OF. BINTRI.'. Some have both. That at St Bartholomew's, Heigham, marked with the flat fish in an oval of Thomas Buttell—one of his two best cups, which were not all of equal worth—is engraved on the bowl with a central band of strapwork, forming four panels of stylised foliage, and also on the foot of its paten cover with 'SENT. BARTELMEVS. OF. HAYHAM', encircling the date of 1567. The beautiful St Mary Coslany example of Cobbold's also has 'A.G..I.K.' on the foot, and 'SAYNCT/MARYE. OF/COSLANYE/A° 1569', within a cartouche, on the foot of its paten cover, which also has three flat-chased scroll and foliage motifs. Around the bowl is engraved a central band of strapwork, forming six panels of stylised foliage. Another of Cobbold's, at the glorious church of St Peter Mancroft, Norwich, is engraved below the rim of the bowl with a narrow dotted border from which depend formal leaf and arabesque motifs. This also has his central band of strapwork forming panels of stylised foliage, between raised borders, and 'SANCT. PETER. OF. MAN/CROFTE A° 1569' below that. The permutations go on, and although all are not of equal merit and others vary the shape, none could be called the conventional Elizabethan style. The cup at All Saints, Horsford, marked with the trefoil slipped, for instance, has a long, slender bell-shaped, bowl on a spool stem, with stamped billet moulding at top and bottom. This bowl is engraved below the rim with a band of strapwork made up of three panels containing stylised foliage, a pendant of foliage being carried down from each of the intersections. It is a beautiful thing, as are all the fifty or so cups marked by this craftsman who devoted himself exclusively to church plate.

The gouged, zig-zag assay groove, which appears near the marks on many of these early cups, is a definitely Dutch feature, replacing the normal English scrape. It certainly indicates Dutch influence in the city, but while the zig-zag was usual in Holland until well into the eighteenth century, it was used in Norwich only in its earliest years. Nor was it consistent then, for although it appears more often than not on surviving communion cups in the first five years, the exceptions include all the makers, and all the years marked 'B', 'C', 'D' or 'E'. The two surviving cups with an 'A' both have it, but such a tiny proportion can prove nothing. It is strange that this zig-zag is so rare on secular plate, of which only a little exists, but nothing has turned up to show us why. Obviously, it was not the work of a Dutch assay master, which would have made for consistency in his year of office; nor can it be an indication that the craftsman came from the Netherlands, for the same reason. It remains a fascinating puzzle.

For years another riddle surrounded a plaque marked with the un-identified device of a maidenhead, the Norwich hall mark, and date letter for 1567. This small oval plaque, only 4½in high, depicts the head of a man, full face, wearing a cap with a feather and an ermine collar and ruff, standing out from a proportionately wide, plain border, a raised rim forming a frame. Purists cast doubts upon it because the man's costume was not correct for 1567, making the whole thing highly suspicious. But purists are apt to forget the broader concept of history.

In this case the story goes back to when King Henry VIII, in one of his more generous moments, promised the Great Hospital, Bishopsgate —the King's Hospital till about 1624—to the city, instead of selling it for the benefit of his own pocket, when he dissolved the cathedral priory. This exceptionally lovely place, also known as St Helen's, had been built for the care of 'poor and decrepit chaplains' in 1249, but Henry, naturally enough, wanted the world to know a little more than the truth, and an inscription was placed on the outer wall ascribing the foundation of the hospital to 'King Henry VIII of Noble fame'. But, thankful for small mercies, the hospital probably felt it expedient to adopt him as their master, and it was presumed, without proof, that the plaque was intended to be his portrait. In fact it is, but assumption is not sufficient to satisfy the pedantic. Then Mr Levine, as always, found the answer by discovering an early etching of a young King Henry VIII from which this portrait in silver had obviously been copied, so creating an interesting and most unusual piece.

Tigerware jugs were also made in Elizabethan Norwich, the majority of them lacking the elaborate repoussé decoration of Exeter and London examples. A jug supposedly mounted by Cobbold, for instance, 1571, but with marks that Mr Levine considers suspect—too large and un-believably sharp—has a wide silver lip band extending inside the neck and engraved with strapwork forming panels of stylised foliage, its lower border beaded. The handle mount is missing, and one might be tempted to assume that both lid and foot mounts have also disappeared, were it not that so many Norwich examples are found without these features.

Nor does the existing adornment in any way match the elaborate work found on Exeter jugs of the time, many of which also had bands of connecting strapwork, beautifully ornamented. In Norwich, considerably less silver appears in the mounts, and the lids, which are rare, are lower and less impressive. The finest Norwich tigerware jug, complete with all the usual mountings including a twin dolphin thumbpiece, was made in 1568, yet even this is simply engraved and lacks the usual high relief of the early years. It is believed to be the only surviving piece of silver made by a craftsman who stamped a five-petalled rose as his mark.

For some reason, date letters seem to have been dropped when the great days of Norwich-made communion plate were over. The letter 'G' marked on Cobbold's tigerware jug is the last recorded before a new cycle started in 1624. Christopher Tannor, free 1571 (although Jackson gives the year as 1562), was just too late to show his worth in communion cups, but he made many spoons—slip top, seal top, and at least one apostle—stamped with his monogram and the Norwich city mark. Nevertheless, with the exception of one bearing the date letter 'F', these, like all else in those years, had the date indicated, if at all, by a pricked out inscription, such as '1586 DIES NUPTIALIS/13 NOVEMBRIS' on the back of the fig-shaped bowl of Tannor's St John spoon. There is only one other Elizabethan Norwich-made apostle spoon known; c 1635, it can be seen in the Castle Museum.

More than half the known Norwich silver was made in the first five years, when craftsmen worked really hard and possibly grew rich. Nevertheless, silver continued to be made on a lesser scale, William Cobbold producing a fine jug and cover in about 1575, and his son Matthew a wine cup, c 1615, to take but two examples. The covered jug, now belonging to All Saints, Crostwight, but obviously first intended for secular use, is parcel gilt and decorated with all the fine varieties of applied and chased ornament associated with his work, as indeed is his wine cup. These are lovely objects to which no words of description can do justice, any more than they can to a glorious standing cup and cover, made in about 1600 for Thomas Lane, mayor of Norwich in 1603. This has a lovely thistle-shaped bowl set on an elaborate baluster stem, low domed foot, and a double-stepped domed cover with a rounded knop finial. Every part of this cup, 11½in high, is magnificently worked with fruit, foliage and other decoration, and is worthy of the highest honours. First used in the home, it was later given to St Peter Hungate church, and while such silver is hardly collectable, a visit to Norwich to see it is really an education. Although somewhat rubbed, its mark is clearly a bird, also seen on the cover of a cup at Bittering Parva.

With so many churches in and around Norwich, the city's few craftsmen could not supply the whole of East Anglia with new communion cups when the necessity arose in 1567—yet all required furnishing. In fact, Norfolk and Suffolk were particularly rich in their own craftsmen and, before leaving the Elizabethan era, it will be interesting to glance at the church plate made elsewhere in those counties. A few pieces, for instance, have been found bearing the marks of Kings Lynn, three dragon's heads erect, each pierced with a cross crosslet.

A very fine cup belonging to Middleton church, near King's Lynn, bears three marks, the first unrecognisably rubbed, although Jackson has managed to draw a fairly spritely bird from it; the maker's mark, a capital 'H' over a 'W', and the town mark. The date of 1632 is known by the inscription running around the centre of the tall, bell-shaped bowl between two triple bands of laurel leaves, broken by an upright row of three rosettes, reading 'Elizabeth Willton gave 40 s. and Mari Griffin gave 10 s. touered this bowle for the Parish Church of Middletun in Norfolke Anno Dom 1632'. Poor Mari! This has a paten cover with additions to the type made in Elizabethan Norwich, such as acanthus leaves engraved on the spool knop used there, which is itself surmounted by a reel-shaped collar stamped with ovolo ornament above an edging of foliage in relief. It is a lovely and most unusual cover to a beautifully made bowl, plain except for its central band, allowing the eye to focus on the finely decorated foot, leading through a series of steps—engraved in turn with ovolo decoration, reeded moulding, engraved flowers, and a narrow band of foliage in relief—to a fine vase-shaped stem, with flutings radiating towards a knop, decorated with interlacing strapwork and surmounted by a spool decorated with small oval hollows. Again, no stylised description can really do it justice, for this cup, 7½in high with another 2⅛in in the paten, is an exceptionally fine piece.

Jackson has recorded one other cup bearing this maker's mark and the three dragons of King's Lynn, dated 1635, but instead of the bird, the third mark is a 'T' with a reversed 's' entwining it, set in an urn-shaped shield, yet another version of the 'TS' in monogram which presents a puzzle later in this chapter. This cup is inscribed with the words 'The Quest of Thomas Clarke to the Church of Barmar', which is part of the living of Bagthorpe, near King's Lynn.

In the Lincoln Cathedral treasury there is a tiny communion cup, most unlike that at Middleton, slim and dainty, which is believed to be by William Howlett of King's Lynn, although it was marked in London in 1642. This would be explained by the fact that Howlett was a Parliamentarian, and King's Lynn was a royalist stronghold. His initials tally with those marked on the Middleton cup.

A slender cup on a baluster stem, dated 1640, belonging to St Etheldreda's, Southgate, Norwich, and a paten belonging to St Nicholas Chapel, King's Lynn, stamped with a different maker's mark, also bear the very rare King's Lynn punch.

A great deal of intensive research has been done recently on the marks found on Suffolk church plate, but the subject had become of general interest when a survey of the county's plate was made in 1893. This revealed that, apart from London- and Norwich-marked silver, a considerable quantity bore the stamps of local Elizabethan makers. Henry C. Casley broke these down in 1904, showing that forty, marked with the Roman letter 'G', were found within a 25-mile radius of Ipswich; of thirty-seven with a fleur de lys, all bar three were within 20 miles of Bury St Edmunds; seven with four hearts in the form of a cross, in north-east Suffolk; eight with a 'W' beneath a crown, within 8–10 miles of Ipswich; three with a cross wavy within a 5-mile radius of Woodbridge, or 12 of Ipswich; twenty with a sexfoil between Lowestoft and Woodbridge, while eight other marks are not analysed. Undoubtedly many more examples and yet further marks have since been found and names apportioned to them, but to us the clear inference is sufficient. Many goldsmiths worked in Suffolk, possibly in Woodbridge and other places, but certainly in Ipswich and Bury St Edmunds.

In fact it had always been so, for although the town had never apparently formed a guild, Casley had already found the names of nineteen goldsmiths working in Ipswich, starting with 'Agnes the

Goldsmith', taxed in the town in 1282, and ending with one William Whiting, mentioned in a will of 1611. These old records, for those with the patience to peruse them, are a never-ending source of discovery and can reveal some fascinating side-lights on social history in addition to the information being sought. Casley found enough medieval wills to prove that it had been very much the 'done' thing to leave one's silver plate to the church in early times. As a result, some Suffolk churches owned up to 1,000 oz of silver. The Rev James Gilchrist draws the same picture in his book *Anglican Church Plate*, quoting from old manuscripts found in Norfolk and Suffolk. Such lists gave a picture of an ordinary little church laden with the type of plate one had imagined to be the preserves of abbeys and cathedrals. More, he tells us that Archbishop Winchelsea (1293–1317) 'had made it obligatory for the parishioners to provide a chalice, a processional cross, a cross for the dead, a censor, a lantern, a small bell for carrying before the body of Christ at the visitation of the sick, a pyx for the body of Christ, a paxbrede and a candlestick for the Paschal Candle'. Obviously, if this was the basic minimum, well-to-do churches would have had considerably more and, indeed, other inventories quoted prove this to have been very much the case.

This was the greatest period of the provincial goldsmith, and in Ipswich one name stands out, Geoffrey Gilbert, c 1530–79, one of many Gilberts but undoubtedly the craftsman who marked his work with the Roman 'G'. Ipswich, which does not appear to have yet bothered with town arms, had had a royal mint since King Edgar's day, marking its coins with 'Gip', 'Gep', or a plain 'G', derived from its original name, Gippeswic; the 'G' Gilbert used could, therefore, have come from his home town, Ipswich. It was not, however, a town mark and Gilbert, who had been apprenticed to Matthew Garrarde, an Ipswich goldsmith, may have chosen this letter as his own maker's mark for all its associations—town, master, and personal initial.

Study of his life might make good romantic reading, but records show him, apart from his philandering, as an important goldsmith marking his work, in all probability, with the plain 'G' when alone, and in various shields in conjunction with his sons. There were a few other goldsmiths working in the town at the time that Bishop Parkhurst required the new communion cups to be made, most of those dated being 1567 or 1568, but Gilbert, undoubtedly, was the important man.

In the deanery of Bosmere, for instance, all the marked plate bears the 'G', and where 'G' appears in other deaneries, it predominates. The study of silver marks was in its infancy in Casley's day, and while he seems to have enjoyed researching Gilbert he took less pains over his references to other craftsmen. His entry for Martyn Denys, 1575, for instance, reads: 'born at Duysburghe, Duke of Cleves country, aged 84'. That is all!

Gilbert's communion cups, with bell-shaped bowls, were basically more inclined to the Norwich pattern than the conventional, but had a higher bowl in proportion to width than those, for example, of William Cobbold. A few of these were set on a conventional stem; others were of cone shape, sometimes set on a splayed foot with a decorated knop immediately below the bowl. Most have a band of foliage around the centre between plain bands, usually in quite individual designs but occasionally, as at Nacton, with armorial bearings added. The paten covers, a little lower than average, have a Norwich-type spool knop with the distinctive feature of letters taken from the village name engraved on top, such as 'H.G.' for Helmingham, which has the most lovely cup.

There are also a few contemporary spoons marked with the 'G', and at least one plain standing tazze belonging to the church of Charsfield in Suffolk. Nevertheless, the need for communion cups created the opportunity for Elizabethan craftsmen, and they form the majority of such men's known work.

Gilchrist's book illustrates two communion cups stamped with the sexfoil, both dated 1570 but sufficiently different to show a versatile mind. There is an unusually shallow bowl to the cup at Wickham Market, Suffolk, which is beautifully decorated on bowl, foot and paten cover. The band of leaf decoration, engraved centrally, is nevertheless of normal depth, occupying fully one-third of the surface, with sprays reaching both to bottom and top, where another lovely narrow band is placed just below the rim. The high, spool-shaped stem, the foot and the paten cover are all similarly engraved, but the high spool-shaped knop to the paten remains plain.

The same goldsmith's cup at Thwaite, on a truncated cone stem and with only a little decoration around the foot, supports a bowl of champagne-glass shape, surrounded just below the rim by a band of interlacing strapwork filled with foliage. The paten cover fits flush, is almost flat and is surmounted only by a plain knop. Two most unusual and really effective cups, obviously made by a fine craftsman.

Nevertheless, of all East Anglian work, that from Bury St Edmunds must be the most discussed, if only for the controversy that has raged over the years regarding the particular fleur-de-lys mark found in Suffolk, now pinned down to the Elizabethan, Erasmus Cooke of Bury St Edmunds.

Luke, the first recorded goldsmith in Bury, was mentioned in deeds of 1270, and there were many others through the centuries until, in Elizabethan times, the city is said to have had almost as many gold-smiths as Norwich. In fact, when wardens from London visited Bury in 1568, they administered the oath to thirteen craftsmen, more than Norwich can show at the time with surviving marked plate. Secular plate does not seem to have been made, and many of these goldsmiths may have been mere opportunists, but their work has been researched because of the interest taken in the many communion cups and patens marked with the incuse fleur-de-lys. These cups, well enough made, were more of the Norwich type than the London, in that they did not have the conventional stem with a central knop, but there similarity ends. One, at All Saint's church, Beyton, is only 4¾in high, and although a few others of this size exist, they average about 6¼in with a few up to 7½in. Mostly they are straight-sided, or have slightly bell-shaped bowls with a single engraved band just above centre, either of simple foliage or plain dots. Their patens were usually of the conventional type, but occasionally lacked a knop; some were of the old dish form, which rested on top of the cup rather than fitting it as a lid. Almost all were made in 1568, and were it not for their mark they would not have attracted much publicity.

No doubt an expert on marks will one day publish a book on the fleur-de-lys, after having spent a lifetime researching it. The beautiful gold pre-Reformation chalice of Bishop Foxe, London hallmarked for 1507, is stamped with the maker's mark of a fleur-de-lys, which also appeared in various forms for other London makers. It was variously the town mark of Odense, in Denmark; part of the York mark; certainly had some connection with Lincoln, and appeared on the coin of France, to mention but a few. They are not for us, but one such mark appears in conjunction with the letter 'G', and a 'TS' conjoined in monogram, which is of intense East Anglian interest. A most interesting spout cup bearing this mark is displayed in the Museum of Fine Arts, Boston, which Mr G. Levine recognised as having previously belonged to his father's collection. Spout cups, common in the United States, are very rare in England, but this one is of most unusual shape, plain except for a fine lion mask thumbpiece. It has a flat lid, a broad handle on which initials are engraved, and a slender spout rising to lid height from the skirted base. (Illustration, p 103.)

'TS' in monogram is the mark of Timothy Skottowe of Norwich, 1617–45, and this cup, together with a tankard in the Victoria and Albert Museum and a few other pieces so marked, have always been assumed to be Skottowe's work. Jackson, who ascribed virtually all fleur-de-lys-marked work to Lincoln, suggested that Skottowe worked in both cities, and in his Lincoln tables illustrated these marks found on Puritan spoons, a beaker, a mug and a tankard. Nevertheless, it is now believed that this version of 'TS', despite its similarity to Skottowe's mark, was not stamped on his work, as the majority of known examples were punched on trifid spoons. These did not appear till the 1660s, whereas Skottowe died in 1645. Quite possibly the 'TS' was another unknown maker's mark, or it may simply have denoted sterling standard. The 'G' must be a date letter, as at least one piece similarly marked exists with a 'T' replacing the 'G', and the whole combination is believed to have been stamped in Bury St Edmunds, where the majority of these pieces have been found. The fleur-de-lys, in itself, may have had some extra meaning in the town for, apart from Erasmus Cooke, bells made by Stephen Tonni, a bell-founder of Bury from 1559 to 1587, were marked with this device.

Possibly, like Peter Peterson, Skottowe's name is better known than it would otherwise be because of these errors of ascription. He was, nevertheless, an important name in the Company of Norwich Goldsmiths, re-formed in 1622, and was its warden in 1624. That year the new date cycle started with an 'A' in a shaped shield, changing yearly until the 'T' of 1642. Books were kept, and the names of wardens, apprentices, etc were properly recorded. But, alas! makers' marks do not appear to have been registered, so that those who preferred a device such as Pegasus, the pelican in her piety, or the lion rampant, continue to present a puzzle. The Norwich town mark continued to be the castle over lion, but now in a somewhat longer shield than before, and a new mark of a crowned rose was added, making four stamps.

This punch, undoubtedly used as a standard mark rather than the more usual lion passant, is yet another feature that has kept the experts arguing through the years. The rose and crown was used as a city mark in Dordrecht, Holland, and traffic between that port and Norwich makes it reasonable to presume that kinship had something to do with its adoption. The Netherlanders even used the same type of maker's device, and date letters were somewhat similar, so obviously Dutch influence was strong. But poor old Jackson really got in a tangle over it, and his ideas are best dismissed. The important fact is that the Dordrecht crown was open, with daylight showing between its points; that above the Norwich rose is closed.

It was also believed that this rose and crown was a second Norwich town mark, and H. D. Ellis, writing in the *Burlington Magazine* in 1908, declared that the assay master's oath proved this to be so 'beyond all cavil and doubt'. With two official hallmarks in the same city, he concluded that one was for native-born craftsmen, and the other for aliens. The oath read: 'You shall sweare that you will well and truly execute the office of a Say Master to the Company of Silver Smithes within the City of Norwich, *and not sett the stampe of the Rose and Crowne upon any Plate but what is according to the standard.*' The italics are mine, but the words, to me, prove, beyond any cavil and doubt that the mark was proof of standard, duly tested by assay. This was sometimes stamped across a joint to prevent malpractice, the three other marks being placed together elsewhere.

The rose crowned in Norwich was never stamped alone, and a large group of apostle spoons, c 1600–40, bearing an extra large crowned rose in the bowl and on the stem, were probably made in Taunton; they bear no other marks.

During this period a certain amount of church plate was again made, and a flagon, made for St Gregory's church, Norwich, and stamped with Pegasus in 1628, is particularly attractive. This flagon, with its globular bowl, waisted cylindrical neck and conical foot, depends on line for its beauty, and succeeds admirably. It has a knop at the top of the stem, a domed cover with baluster finial, and a delicate handle; the only decoration is a pricked-out inscription. (Illustration, p 86.)

Church plate at this time favoured simplicity, and the craftsman using the pelican in her piety as a mark made several communion cups of the old Norwich shape, without much adornment. A bell-shaped bowl on spool-shaped stem, for St Peter's, Tunstall, for instance, is pricked out with an inscription below the rim and engraved round the centre 'FOR. THE. TOUNE. OF. TVNSTALL. ANO. 1632'. Several are almost identical with it, but in 1640 the same craftsman added a new bowl to an old foot that Thomas Buttell had marked with his flat fish in 1567 for St Andrews, Lammas, using billet moulding at the top of its bell-shaped bowl to complement the egg-and-dart moulded border of the Elizabethan foot. Such cups lacked the importance the old raised borders gave to the central pattern of decoration, but Arthur Hasel-wood, a warden in 1628, revived this feature on his bucket-shaped cup with cover, 1633, for St Mary of Grace, Aspall, giving it an everted rim and a cylindrical stem flaring at the base. The lion rampant man also used raised reeded borders around the inscription on his bucket-shaped bowl for a communion cup and cover, 1634, belonging to St Simon and St Jude, Norwich.

Several communion patens, presumably replacing lost Elizabethan covers, were made alone at this period, and spoons appear marked with the devices of almost all the makers, although the tower incuse appears only on a coconut cup made as a marriage cup in 1641. There are several nice wine cups, one by Timothy Skottowe, 1639, 5in high, and another by Arthur Hazlewood, 1638, 6⅜in high, both having a round, funnel-shaped bowl on a slender baluster stem with a conical foot. The cup at St Laurence's, Beeston, however, is really superb. Eight and a quarter inches high, it is of the same shape, the conical foot being single stepped, with stamped billet and ovolo moulded borders. Three applied recurved scrolls appear above the lovely stem, and fabulous animal head terminals support the bowl which, like the foot and stem, is covered with repoussé decoration of fruit and formal scroll motifs with cockatrices. This elegant silver gilt cup, marked with the pelican in her piety, was presented to the church in 1744.

Although it is rare to see Norwich silver for sale, an exquisite wine cup, c 1595, marked with the orb and cross of Matthew Cobbold, was sold in London in 1954, showing him to be worthy of his father's name and mark. It is interesting to note that, at that time, Cobbold had not yet been discovered, and this beautifully decorated cup, 7in tall and far less ornate than the Beeston cup, was catalogued as 'by Peter Peterson'. At that time, long before the fantastic rise in silver prices, appreciation of this piece, one of the loveliest I have ever seen, was reflected in a bid for £600. The bowl of another wine cup, its stem and foot missing, by Arthur Hazlewood junior, c 1665, was also sold in 1969.

Such events are rare, but buying Norwich plate is not impossible. Among pieces seen for sale in recent years has been a small Charles II tapering cylindrical tankard, also by the second Arthur Hazlewood, c 1673. This, following a pattern that was almost invariable in Norwich, is quite plain, on a moulded base with a flat-topped cover with a plain rim and a double lobed thumbpiece, the scroll handle pricked with initials. All appear in the second half of the seventeenth century, the thumbpiece alone showing slight variation.

Other pieces to have appeared include a beaker, c 1695, only 3in high, but with a foliate band of strapwork marked 'P.R'; a pair of heavy plain tumbler cups by Elizabeth Hazlewood, widow of the second Arthur, 1697, and a really fascinating silver travelling spoon by Thomas Havers, c 1690. This spoon is 12in long, with a fine tubular stem of the type usually associated with basting spoons, tapering towards its rat tail joint with the spoon bowl.

On the whole, however, interest in Norwich silver stems mainly from its fascinating connection with local history and its superlative quality. The date cycle begun in 1624 ended with the 'T' of 1642, and thereafter silver bore no date letter until 1688, when a new cycle started with a Gothic 'a' in a plain shield. Why? The fact was that the marking of silver was a secondary consideration during the Civil War, and Cromwell's firm grip on the city kept life at its drabbest throughout the Commonwealth period. Timothy Skottowe, a member of a noble family who had been established in their Norfolk manor by the Saxons, must have been a man of character, for he alone remained staunchly royalist—but died poor as the result.

The rose crowned became separated, appearing as a rose and a crown in different punches at the same time that the date letter was dropped, and this can probably best be explained as an attempt to maintain four marks, which people trusted, whereas only three might arouse suspicion that something was lacking. Many strange marks were stamped during this period, Arthur Hazelwood I, for instance, using his own mark twice and a quatrefoil twice, in place of the usual castle over lion, on a communion cup and paten for St Mary's, Blundeston, 1647. Another of his patens bore his own mark, 'A.H.' in a shaped shield, a seeded rose, a small crown and a strange device described as a pineapple, a poor attempt at the Norwich town mark. He also used these same marks on a tankard of typical Norwich style in 1656, and on a most attractive serpentine jug, c 1650. This greenish jug, with a marbled grain was mounted in silver with a deep lip band, with reeded lower edge, another band of silver encircling the body connecting with a vertical strap from the spout. The scroll handle with a bifurcated thumbpiece, the flat, single-stepped lid, and a projecting foot mount with a scallopped border, are also of silver. A pleasant thing to look at, and most unusual.

Mr Levine thinks it probable that the Norwich assay office never closed, and certain that goldsmiths were not responsible for their own marks—an explanation that could well dispose of some of the anomalies of the time. For how else can the stamp of a castle over lion be explained on a 1650 beaker by William Haydon, made in the same year (probably) as Hazlewood's serpentine cup? Mr Levine suggests that the official punch was broken and makeshifts used while waiting for replacements, but this would not account for the use of the castle and lion in 1650, with other devices in 1647, 1656—and 1650.

An unknown maker, marking his work 'E.D.' in a shaped shield, also had a mug, 1660, stamped with the castle over lion twice, which was hardly correct, a seeded rose as the fourth mark, and no crown. This mug, 3⅛in high, had a globular body with a reeded cylindrical neck, a lip, and a grooved loop handle, giving it more the appearance of a small jug.

Arthur Hazlewood's son, of the same name, free 1661, certainly had more opportunities in his craft, but a large proportion of the small quantity of silver surviving from the Commonwealth days was marked by his father, who also made several seal-top spoons, marked with a seeded rose struck twice, and a crown, either once or twice, in addition to his own mark.

When the monarchy was restored in 1661, the castle over lion came back, but the rose, now sprigged in a shield and with the crown in a shield, remained separate. All over the country the ending of the drab days was celebrated by an exuberance of silver of all sorts, which in Norwich mainly concerned itself with the church, as it had always done. An exceptionally fine communion cup and cover, belonging to St Edmund's, Southwold, was probably made by William Edwards in conjunction with another craftsman in 1661. This was 8¾in high and in the old traditional Norwich shape, the superb decoration including pendant fleur-de-lys motifs. One can imagine this lovely piece on the drawing-board for years, its makers just waiting for the opportunity to show their skill.

More dependent on line was Arthur Hazlewood's complete communion set, which he made for the chapel of the Bishop's Palace, Norwich, in about 1662. The communion cup of this set, complete with its low domed cover, is $9\frac{1}{4}$in high, the flagon $10\frac{1}{2}$in and, like the shallow alms dish of the set with its wide rim and reeded border, they are engraved with the arms of Bishop Reynolds in lovely feather mantling.

Arthur Hazlewood, who died in 1684, made a large amount of the church plate in the period leading up to 1688, and like Thomas Havers, free 1674, they were always good and conventionally marked. Nevertheless, Robert Osborne, free 1665, stamped his own version of the Norwich town mark long after any reason for independence had passed. This tiny castle, hardly visible above a large lion, appeared both on a beaker, c 1665, and a trifid spoon, c 1670. On the spoon he marked a leaf, without rhyme or reason, in addition to the queer town mark and a small crown, decorating its oval bowl with an attractive crest. On the beaker, which was too good to require gimmicks, his third mark was a fleur-de-lys; $4\frac{1}{4}$in tall, and 3in in diameter, this nice beaker was flat chased below the rim with a band of interlacing strapwork with pendants of fleur-de-lys falling from its intersections, the band filled with hatched roundels. Arthur Hazlewood also used the fleur-de-lys motif in the same way on a beaker in 1670.

Hazlewood and Thomas Havers both also made secular plate, producing spoons, tankards, mugs, saucepans and beakers, all very well.

Beakers were so much a part of the silver produced in Norwich that they sum up its whole history. As old as the country of the North Folk itself, these drinking-vessels had originated in Scandinavia in Saxon times or earlier, but were brought to Norwich by the Dutch, who had been trading with the city long before settling there in Elizabethan times. They served very well as communion cups for the Low church, which is why so many were made in Scotland and America, usually dual-purposed, but the first important, surviving examples made in Norwich were the gift of Mr Rychard Browne of Heigham to the Dutch church of Black Friars in the city. These famous beakers, made by William Cobbold possibly in 1577 or '78, were stamped with the orb and cross in a shaped shield (his mark after 1574), the Norwich hall mark, and a wyvern's head erased, for which no explanation has been found. They are 7in tall, an unusual height, cylindrical with slightly everted lips, and are engraved with strapwork forming three panels filled with stylised flowers and foliage, a large spray, trefoil in design, being carried down from the intersections of the strapwork. Stamped ovolo and reeded moulding decorates the base, and the gift inscription surrounds the body, between rope-twist bands.

Beakers in Norwich, usually less than 4½in tall, were invariably of plain cylindrical form with everted rim and reeded moulded foot; decoration was rarely more than a simple band of strapwork filled with arabesque foliage, and pendant sprays were refinements above average. It is a pity that the Heigham set has been divided; only one beaker now remains in the Castle Museum, Norwich, another is in the Rijks-museum, Amsterdam, and two more in the Ashmolean Museum, Oxford.

Most of the surviving Norwich beakers were made in the seventeenth century, and one by Timothy Skottowe, 1637, was sold at the start of this century to the United States. The First Church, Boston, possesses a similar Dutch example, and because they were so very popular and New England craftsmen produced them so well for church and home use, it is fair to assume that some of those sold from the Dutch church in Norwich several years ago may have found their way to the States.

When Arthur Hazlewood II died in 1684, his widow Elizabeth kept the family name going, marking a wide variety of silver with a crown over her initials 'E.H.'. When Queen Elizabeth II opened the new County Hall, Norwich, in May 1968, Mr G. N. Barrett, of Hethersett, was asked to find a suitable Norwich-made beaker to present to her. One of Elizabeth Hazlewood's was chosen, c 1685, plain, on a moulded base, and only 3½in high.

This was no precedent, for when Elizabeth I visited Norwich in 1578 she was presented with a beaker. Unfortunately, her retinue brought infection to the city, where 5,000 people then died of the plague, one reason for the paucity of silver in the years that followed.

Thomas Havers, who lived till 1734, divided the lion's share of Norwich-made silver with Elizabeth Hazlewood in the closing years, both of them producing a wide variety of wares, with secular pieces, for the first time, predominating. But after the third date cycle started in 1688 a new name appears, James Daniel, who marked his work 'I.D.' in monogram; a Queen Anne type porringer, 1696, in the Castle Museum is possibly his best-known piece. His working life was cut short by the unfortunate Act of 1697 which precluded provincial marking of silver; nevertheless, two trifid spoons have come to light from this period, marked 'ID' three times, and then 'F. N SIL.' in an oblong stamp, denoting 'fine silver, Norwich'. Thomas Havers is also known to have marked some silver during this period.

In 1701, Norwich was one of the cities granted the right once more to use its town mark, along with the figure of Britannia, the lion's head erased, the new date letter, an old English capital 'A' in oval, and the maker's mark, which was to be the first two letters of his surname. Nowhere was the dubiety of this form better demonstrated, for the three pieces of Britannia period silver marked in Norwich, all that are known from a city where the craft was dying, are all stamped 'Ha.' This, with equal likelihood, could have been the mark of Arthur and Elizabeth Hazlewood's son, described as a goldsmith but more concerned with the retail side of the business, Robert Harsonage, assay master for 1701, or Thomas Havers, who proved that he was still working by marking his old stamp in 1706 without other marks. And so the craft in Norwich died as it had begun, clouded by uncertainty regarding its craftsmen's identity.

# Six

# Chester

No town or date letter was used in Chester until 1687, just fifteen years before Norwich stamped her last, yet the history of silver in the area is as old as Chester itself, where the Roman legions built a fortress and laid the cornerstone for one of the most beautiful and unusual cities in England.

Whether or not the Romans used local silver from the lead mines of North Wales, the city certainly had a thriving mint by Athelstane's time (925–40), when twenty-seven men were already employed in making money, an industry that continued intermittently until 1698. There is a magnificent collection of coin minted in Chester in the Grosvenor Museum there, but no evidence that these men also made other objects. Yet to me it seems likely, for with the material to hand, would not the creative spirits among them have felt an urge to try something different? Silver trinkets found nearby could be the work of men who were not satisfied merely with the constant churning out of coin.

Although no craftsmen's names were recorded in Chester before 1225, the probability is that goldsmiths worked there even earlier. Why then, was the city not given her 'touch' in 1423, when seven other provincial towns were granted the right to stamp their own silver? Why no Chester town mark, when unofficial stamps tell us that silver was made in countless unimportant places all over the country and identified by marks, generally derived from the town's own arms?

The fact is that Chester was very much a law unto herself, both the county and the city being ruled by her own earls rather than the Crown from the time the earldom was created in 1071. The Earl of Chester, one of the titles of the Prince of Wales since 1254, doubtless controlled the goldsmiths, as he did all things; Chester did not even send a member to Parliament until 1553.

This lack of a town mark has made early Chester silver more difficult to trace than in most places, but Canon Maurice H. Ridgway in his book *Chester Goldsmiths from Early Times to 1726* has made such a thorough job of research into it that every piece and every maker has been described and we have but to turn to it for detail.

Yet all this research, and all the records, have not been able to bring plate to light, for the work of centuries was lost to the ravages of wars and other destructive forces. Just one thirteenth-century chalice and paten, possibly made in Chester, have been found, buried near Dolgellau in Merionethshire. Nevertheless, were the museums overflowing with early Chester work, this pair would still have thrilled all lovers of beauty, for they are truly magnificent and cannot fail to excite all who enjoy the detective story that silver has to tell. Discussion has continued ever since the chalice and its wonderful paten were found in 1890 because of the inscription under the foot of the chalice, recording: 'NICOL'US ME/FECIT DE HER/FORDIE'.

Old records show goldsmiths living in Chester, witnessing deeds, buying or selling land, being fined or taking oaths, but nothing is said of the silver they made. Yet among a family of four, one, c 1270, is described as 'Nicholas The Great'. The chalice inscription, however, mentions Hereford, not Chester, and scholars, still arguing the matter, suggest that the reference may be to the donor who could have come from Hereford, that Nicolas might have been born there, or even that the cup was made in Herford in Germany. Certainly no goldsmiths are recorded in England's Hereford, yet the workmanship of this chalice is undoubtedly English. It was produced by the hand of an exceptionally fine craftsman, probably called Nicolas, at much the same time that Nicholas the Great was working in Chester. There is more than a case for wishful thinking in this, giving rise to a theory that standards in Chester may have been of the very highest. Because it has been fully described so often and is thoroughly discussed in Maurice H. Ridgway's book, this chalice calls only for brief reference in my chapter on Wales, but a journey to Cardiff would be well worth while if only to see this treasure, the property of Her Majesty the Queen, displayed in the National Museum of Wales. (Illustration, p 33.)

Two hundred years pass before another piece of possible Chester silver survives, years in which goldsmiths are known to have worked. Later references are made to the goldsmiths' guild in the city, as for instance in 1531 when the dyers and vintners agreed to share a carriage with them for the Whitsun plays, or when the goldsmiths provided a horse and a boy rider for the traditional races. Then, in about 1555, the first surviving minute book records that no brother should deliver plate without having first stamped his maker's mark upon it, and there are the usual regulations concerning apprentices, admissions to the company and the election of stewards. All would appear to be re-iterating long-accustomed habit, but regulations laid down in about 1585 regarding underselling must have had a basis in this practice at the time.

By comparison with the wealth of surviving Elizabethan church plate to be found all over England, there is a notable paucity in Chester, where the work of only two or three craftsmen survives. Yet the diocese was enormous, stretching to the Lake District and Yorkshire, and the city's goldsmiths were also supplying new vessels for the dioceses of Bangor and St Asaph in North Wales. However, itinerant London craftsmen following in the wake of the bishops looking for work, got precious little in Wales because they could not speak Welsh —a good reason for believing that much of the unmarked Elizabethan communion plate in North Wales was probably Chester made.

William Mutton, who marked his work with a somewhat odd sheep's head facing to the right in a shaped shield, is responsible for the earliest silver known to have been made in Chester. Four of his communion cups and covers made in 1570 were, according to church-wardens' accounts, for Cheshire churches. Others made in 1574 or soon after are in North Wales, mainly Anglesey, and one, rather surprisingly, in Dorset. These came in such a variety of shape, size and decoration that none can be described as typical; the majority are either decorated with interlacing strapwork filled with arabesques, some having sprigs carried above or below at the intersections, or with plain bands of 'hit-and-miss', while others have bands of both forms.

Bowl shapes vary enormously, but most have a stem with a central knop, a collar above and below, set on a high domed foot, sometimes with additional adornment. It is surprising how widely these stems and feet can vary within that basic description. One of the most graceful cups belongs to Great Budworth parish church, in Cheshire, c 1570, and has a well-splayed bell-shaped bowl opening from a rounded base, with an unusually broad flat rim enhancing the dainty engraving of foliage and sprigs in a way the more solid bucket-shaped bowls never do. This is one of the largest known cups by Mutton, being 8½in tall without a cover, and its stem and well-decorated foot are in perfect harmony. It makes some of his other cups look positively clumsy, though this word could certainly never apply to his cup at Holy Trinity, Chester. This is known from churchwardens' accounts for 1570 to be his earliest surviving work, and is also larger than average, at 7⅜in. The bowl is deep and beautifully proportioned, set on a less rounded base than the Great Budworth cup, but too well splayed towards its everted rim to be described as bucket-shaped. The stem is decorated with six ovals and small dots on the knop in a particularly open, attractive design, and geometric ornament also appears between mouldings, just below the bowl and on the top step of the foot. Unusual though these features are, it is the decoration on the bowl that strikes the eye, for in place of the normal filled strapwork there are two bands, one immediately below the rim and the other centrally, both containing large capital letters, a leaf between each word, spelling out 'DRINKE YE AL OF THIS FOR THIS IS MI BLOVD OF THE NEWE TESTAMENT' and in the lower band 'WHICHE IS SHED FOR YOU AND FOR MANE'. It is most effective.

William Mutton was fiercely Protestant, and it is understandable, in that time of change, that religious feelings should have run high. Nevertheless, the excessive fervour with which he set about destroying holy crosses and other emblems of the old church was not to everyone's liking, and the suggestion that his sudden and unaccountable death was due to poison may have been well founded.

It would appear that he and one J. Lingley divided their enormous 'parish' between them, for their cups do not appear in the same areas. Lingley, one of a family who marked their work 'IL' in an involved shield, produced one cup in Anglesey, but the majority were either in the Lleyn peninsula of Caernarvonshire, or in different parts of Cheshire and Denbighshire, with one in Lancashire. There is not a great deal of 'IL' silver, even counting a few unmarked 'possibles', but it has been found in such widely separated places that one must assume a quantity to have been lost. It is strange, for instance, that none appears in the city of Chester, and while a total lack of any marked silver in the mountainous parishes is understandable, a similar absence along the coast is not. Two pre-Reformation chalices dating from about 1500 found near Colwyn Bay are mentioned in the chapter on Wales, but there is nothing marked by the Chester craftsmen who made almost all the Elizabethan church plate between them. Nor does any evidence appear that London supplied those areas, for the majority of London-made Elizabethan cups appear in Anglesey and the Lleyn peninsula, where the Chester-made pieces predominate. We can only conclude that these remote areas were lucky when disaster struck elsewhere.

It seems likely that the three cups and paten covers on the Lleyn peninsula, 1574–5, were made by the first John Lingley, but definition is difficult because there were four Lingleys known to be goldsmiths, two Johns and two Josephs. These not only shared the same initial but the same mark, except that on the earlier pieces the 'I' is taller than the 'L', while the 'L' outgrows the 'I' later on. The first Joseph appears to have been written out of the story, but we know for sure that John I was active in the craft, for he was fined by the London goldsmiths in 1573, while the younger Joseph hit the headlines when his apprentice, Silvannus Glegg, bolted for Dublin, leaving some wretched girl to face life alone with his illegitimate twins. The second John became a freeman in 1592, but died six years before his father, and his brother Joseph, free in the year their father died, 1615, carried on the work alone. Not that this helps identification much, for the only known piece that would *appear* to have been made during this period is the fine cup at Wood-church, Cheshire, the date '1625' appearing in the inscription running below the rim; however, Maurice H. Ridgway thinks this inscription may have been added later, leaving the question of maker still open.

Lingley-marked cups are pleasant without being distinctive, although the one at Bottwnog parish church, in the Lleyn peninsula, almost certainly by the first John, shows considerable craftsmanship, the domed foot being beautifully decorated. Its conventional paten is engraved with the date '1575 ANO', the two figure 5s for some unknown reason being upside down; the inscription is enclosed in a circle, with a sprig below. At the nearby parish of Bryncroes, the paten of another Lingley cup has the date 1574, again with the figure 5 upside down, and all these cups are on the small side, that at Bottwnog being under five inches high.

Probably the most interesting piece by a Lingley, and the only one not made for the church, is the small mace at Holt, in Denbighshire. It seems incredible that this village with a population of only 1,038 in the 1961 census should own civic plate but, in fact, the Lingley mace and another by Benjaman Pyne, 1709, a great London Huguenot, are kept on trust at Kenyon Hall, Holt, together with a charter from Queen Elizabeth I confirming a grant made in 1411. By that time Holt, which had been a flourishing pottery town in the second century, was already more than 1,000 years old. Only 20in long and weighing a mere 8oz, the mace made by Lingley is dated 1606, and so was probably the work of a John. Though known as the Queen's Mace, it nevertheless bears the royal arms of James I on its head, complete with 'I R' in an attractive twisted rope border, the head having a scalloped rim. Below this is a fence which Maurice H. Ridgway describes as consisting of 'coiled dolphin-like creatures placed back to back', and the slender shaft ends in a silver ball capped with acanthus leaves. How this piece survived the Civil War, when Holt Castle defended the ancient bridge across the river Dee, is something of a miracle, for most plate, both for church and home, was given over to the king for conversion to coin at that time—and not always entirely voluntarily.

Mystery surrounds the mace given to the city of Chester by the Earl of Derby in 1668, for the marks found on it do not tally with the date. Continual refashioning seems the only answer to this puzzle, for some of the silver parts bear the mark ascribed to Chester's Richard Gregorie, free in 1594. A new mace had evidently been made in 1509, and it seems probable that this was remade by Gregorie, and that his mace was the one captured during the siege of Chester in 1645. This mace was believed to have been melted down, but if the marks upon silver sections of the shaft, and quite possibly on the head, are really Gregorie's, this could not have been the case. Yet the embossed decoration of the 1668 head was obviously the work of a Charles II craftsman. Moreover, had this mace been made for Lord Derby in London it would have been fully hallmarked, whereas it bears only one mutilated punch which appears to resemble those on the shaft. This looks as if Richard Gregorie's old head was refashioned, which could account for damage to the mark. Records show him to have been keen on signing the book, even in apprentice days, indicating that he was an avid supporter of his craft, yet this mace is all that remains of his work.

The Civil War was, of course, responsible for enormous losses of plate all over the country, but the lack of Chester-marked church work goes deeper than that, for after the Elizabethan conversion period, virtually nothing surviving was made locally for many years, nor do many Chester goldsmiths appear to have been working then. The bishops of the three dioceses most concerned were ardent supporters of Archbishop Laud, and whether their allegiance to Goldsmiths' Hall was the cause or the effect of the decline in Chester is unimportant. Undoubtedly the two Griffith Edwardes, father free 1585, and son free 1607, made more during this period than remains to be seen, but their chief claim to fame is in founding a family line that eventually restored Chester to its ancient and proper place among the provincial goldsmiths of England.

Although only one piece of church plate survives from each of these elder Edwardes, it is recorded that Griffith Edwardes junior made a silver-gilt cup for Chester races in 1634, weighing 23oz. Such cups had long been a feature of the Chester goldsmith's work, a silver bell having been recorded for a race in 1512, most probably similar to the Carlisle bells mentioned in the Newcastle chapter. These bells resemble those that adorned harness in those days—as they do a complete set of sleigh bells from the harness of my American grandfather's horses of some hundred years ago—except that the racing bells were inscribed with names and dates commemorating the race.

The first races on Chester's Roodee, with a properly laid-out course, took place on Shrove Tuesday, 1540, and continued to be the highlight of that day's celebrations until 1609. Shrove Tuesday, in fact, had long been a great sporting occasion, with shooting and football matches as well as running races, long before this date. While it is difficult to be precise, it would appear that the 'broad arrows of Shrovetide' were made in sets of six for these events and presented by the Shoemakers' Company, while silver bells, given by the Saddlers' Company, were the prizes for horse races. Hundreds of arrows and bells must have been made by Chester craftsmen in those far-off days for the traditional sports under the Roman walls. What a prize they would make if any were to be found now!

In Roman days, the Roodee had been Chester's harbour and all over the farms of the neighbouring Wirral great posts appear, with mooring rings, for all was once part of one vast inlet, with Chester and the river

Dee at its head, Liverpool growing up on the far side only centuries later. As the water receded and great areas of the estuary became good grazing land, Chester gradually lost her position as a port, and with it her considerable trade with Ireland, to the great detriment of the demand for silver that her previous prosperity had created.

In 1609, the horse races changed their date to St George's Day, 23 April, presumably disassociating themselves from the Shrovetide sports, with the City Corporation giving every support; in fact, Griffith Edwardes's cup of 1634 was made for them to present. By that time bells were no longer given, but members of the goldsmiths' guild were obliged to contribute towards the prize list, and of course still made the cups and arrows.

The races have continued ever since, except in troubled times such as those of the Commonwealth and the two world wars, and many cups originally won on the Roodee now appear for sale. One of the finest was the Chester Gold Cup of 1765, a magnificent gold tumbler cup, 3⅜in high, made by an unidentified maker. This is engraved with the full achievement of the Grosvenor family, and the inscription 'The Gift of The Right Honourable Lord Grosvenor to the City of Chester, 1766'. As principal landowners, the Grosvenors gave the Gold Cup each year during a large part of the eighteenth century, and several have come up for sale at various times. Many other such trophies are stored away in the vaults of racing families in the area and these would now make a particularly good subject for collection.

By the time Chester established a full hallmarking system in 1687, she had once again become an important centre of the craft. This was largely due to the efforts of Peter Edwardes, son of the second Griffith, and his uncle, Gerrard Jones, to whom he was apprenticed. Jones gained his freedom in 1632, and the majority of what should have been his working life coincided with wholesale melting down of plate for coin. Yet somehow he managed to train several apprentices and to keep the dormant goldsmiths' company alive throughout the Civil War by preserving its minute book. Peter Edwardes was sworn-in in 1654 and, one must assume, went to work at once, although only his communion cup and cover, 1685, at Caerwys survive. This is the village where Queen Elizabeth I presented the already old Mostyn harp to the winning bard at their Eisteddfod in 1568.

The gay atmosphere of the Restoration was speedily reflected in a less drab fashion in silver, and the demand for it knew no legal bounds. All over the country coin was melted down wholesale to provide the raw material, leading eventually, as we have seen, to the introduction of the higher, Britannia standard.

In Chester, Peter Edwardes upheld the city's good name in the craft, and produced sons to ensure its continuing high standing. Samuel was of no great importance, but Peter junior is one of those craftsmen who make the loss of Chester silver such a tragedy, for what remains of his work is of the very highest quality. The fourth generation to follow the craft, he gained his freedom in 1680 and so saw the beginning of hallmarking in Chester and its all too sudden curtailment with the Britannia Act of 1697, after which he disappears from the scene. Only four of his pieces appear to survive, all fully marked, and the greatest of these is a Montieth type of punch bowl, 1687, bearing the 'A' of their first date cycle. The rim is indented with eight notches and surrounded by applied acanthus leaf decoration. Looped flutings fall from each side of the notches, dividing the lovely bowl into narrow and broad panels, one of which is engraved with the arms of Holland in a foliate cartouche. There is no detachable rim to spoil its lines, a feature introduced in about 1690, when the notches were found to be inconvenient for balancing the lemon strainer when mixing the punch at table.

The bad years had left the goldsmiths' company devoid of ordinary members, its officers—and full strength in 1662—consisting of Gerrard Jones, Thomas Chapman, also an apprentice of Jones, and the elder Peter Edwardes, alderman and stewards respectively. To make good their depleted numbers, the goldsmiths amalgamated with the watchmakers in about 1664, and many of the mistakes made by Jackson can be attributed to the fact that these men, as officers of the company, were able to sign the minutes and to stamp their watch-cases with the proper Chester marks. In his second volume on the work of the later Chester goldsmiths, to be published shortly, Maurice H. Ridgway refers to more than one thousand such marks, those stamped on the inside of watch-cases being particularly valuable because of their clarity.

Likely lads were leaving Chester to be apprenticed to Dublin goldsmiths throughout this time, yet some new names, later to become famous, joined in the next few years: Nathaniel Bullen, 1669; the first Peter Pemberton, 1676; Thomas Robinson, 1681; and Ralph Walley,

1682. Others were working in Manchester, Liverpool and other places, yet the company still felt insecure, and new laws were continually introduced in attempts to regularise their position. The demand for plate was enormous and still stronger control than their existing framework allowed was necessary to maintain their high reputation. After a great deal of thought had been given to the matter, the officers decided to reorganise their company on lines which had proved successful elsewhere, with standards proved by assay and shown by marks.

The new company was to have an assay master and two wardens, the first master being Peter Edwardes, with his son Peter and Ralph Walley as wardens. Silver was to be marked with the old arms of the city of Chester, a dagger erect between three wheatsheaves, sometimes described as 'gerbes'; a sword wreathed in ribbon, the crest of the city presumably used as standard mark; the variable date letter, and maker's mark, which were to be recorded on a copper plate at the assay office. This made four marks, but the date letters changed only with the officers instead of yearly, the original object, after all, having been the identification of plate with the men who marked it. The Gothic 'A', therefore, remained in use until June 1690 when, under something of a cloud, Ralph Walley was replaced as warden by Timothy Gardner.

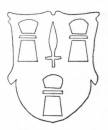

Old Chester mark

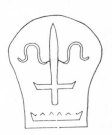

Chester crest

The Chester town mark of three wheatsheaves had first been seen on a Charles I coin of 1645 but, to me, the crest is so unlike its description that I cannot help wondering whether the fleur-de-lys described by Chaffers and explained away by every subsequent writer was not, in fact, this same mark badly punched. Nevertheless, it is considered likely, if it existed at all, to have been a plume of feathers, misinterpreted by Chaffers. Jackson mentions this mark on a spoon by Alexander Pulford, free 1690; unfortunately, the spoon cannot now be found and scrutinised by modern methods. The plume of feathers, however, makes sense for it was stamped on Chester coin during the Civil War, reminding us that the Prince of Wales was, and is, the Earl of Chester. This is Pulford's main claim to fame, but he did make a very nice, slender, baluster taperstick on an octagonal base. Marked only with his initials three times, it was probably made about 1700 and, like candlesticks generally, is very rare in Chester although not unique. Richard Richardson, for instance, made a taperstick for Magdalen College, Oxford, in 1704.

The marking of Chester silver had seen some queer irregularities in the preceding years. Ralph Walley marked his exceptionally beautiful plate paten at his family church, St John the Baptist, Chester, c 1683, with the word 'sterling' in two lines, $^{STER}_{LING}$, between his own mark, 'R.W' in a shaped shield stamped twice. The word 'sterling' was to recur, but its use when the maker's mark alone sufficed might appear as a measure of stress within the company at this time. The plate paten was a magnificent piece of silver, nearly 9in wide, with exquisite engraving on its broad rim and around the inscription in its centre, and its maker had every right to be proud of it. Why should it not be known to be of sterling standard, when all other craftsmen throughout the country had their silver stamped after assay to prove this point?

This dish showed Ralph Walley's high standard and it is tragic that he found it necessary to disappear from the scene a mere nine years after attaining his freedom. Only eight pieces are known by him: a jug; two spoons, one marked in the same way, and four tankards, two of which have recently appeared for sale, one 1686–90 fetching £4,000. (Illustration, p 52.) So few tankards were made in Chester that this constitutes a high proportion, particularly as one by Peter Pemberton, 1703, was also sold in 1965. All are of the plain cylindrical type, perhaps a little less wide in proportion to height than those made elsewhere. They are set on a plain reeded base, with a flat stepped lid with a serrated front edge, and all have a scroll handle with a corkscrew thumbpiece and beautifully engraved arms on the front of the bowl.

Chester silver before about 1730 is hard to come by, but a look at Maurice H. Ridgway's book will show that a large proportion of the secular plate has passed through the salerooms at some time. Walley's lovely mead jug, marked with the 'B' of 1690–2, was another to have done so, in 1963. This is much less plain, for in addition to arms engraved on its baluster body, its lip spout is decorated with an attractive rat tail of seventeen graded pellets. The sockets joining its wooden handle, set not quite at right angles, are also lightly engraved on their shaped edges.

Although Ralph Walley had six sons, three of whom became freemen of the city, none appears to have been a goldsmith. Yet in 1773 Joseph Walley is listed among Chester craftsmen and made several nice pieces, including a fine dish cross, 1786, with pierced sliding supports, floral centre and beaded rim. It is worthy of the family name, and Joseph could, presumably, have been a descendant of Ralph's, even though he worked in Liverpool.

Nathaniel Bullen, contemporary with Ralph Walley, used an abbreviated version of the sterling stamp, 'sterl', at least once, probably during the closed period when many of the Chester goldsmiths found this a sensible answer to their dilemma. But Bullen, whose work was rather ordinary, somehow got himself the job of making most, if not all, the new punches in 1701. He is described as having had a flair for engraving, but of all his known work, mostly communion cups and spoons, only one piece appears to have been engraved at all, and that, an oval tobacco box in the Victoria and Albert Museum, with simple arms. To cast aspersions on Bullen's integrity is possibly unfair, but a man who could take a good piece of another's work and punch his own mark over that of the true maker, as he did on Ralph Walley's Mostyn tankard, leads me to suspect his moral standards, from which anything can be deduced.

The sterling mark, and its variants, was also used during the close period by several of Chester's neighbours, in Liverpool particularly, in Manchester, Whitchurch, and elsewhere. One who used it at least once, on a marrow scoop, was Benjamin Brancker of Liverpool, who requested the privilege of becoming a freeman of Chester. His earlier mark was 'BB' in an oval, but on his better-known punch his initials are capped by a 'liver' bird, taken from his city's arms. Liverpool Corporation own a collection of his silver, including a tankard, coffee pot and jug, and he also made a fine flagon for St Nicholas church, Liverpool, all of which show him to have been a considerable craftsman. His small brandy saucepan, c 1700, only 1¾in high and marked with the 'BB' and bird, passed through the salerooms in 1967, a rare little treat.

More silver was made in Liverpool than Jackson ever guessed, and a particularly fine coffee pot, c 1700, by Robert Shields realised over £7,000 in a 1970 New York sale. Coffee pots of that date are rare enough in any case, and for a Liverpool example of such superb proportions to turn up in America was indeed an event. This cylindrical pot, with a swan-neck spout set at right angles to an attractively shaped, wooden handle, has a gadrooned domed lid, held by a chain, identical with chocolate pots of the period, with the important exception that the finial on the lid is not hinged. The cut card foliage fanning out around the junctions of handle and spout is particularly effective.

Two rather plain communion cups and a tumbler cup by the first Peter Pemberton show that Ralph Walley was not alone in pursuing his own ideas on marking before it was necessary. These, the only known examples stamped with the 'PP' in a shaped shield with a crown above as used by Peter Pemberton between 1677 and 1687, also bear the word 'sterling' in two lines, his mark again, and then a single wheatsheaf. Use of the wheatsheaf, taken from the city arms, would appear to have been with the object of showing place of origin in addition to standard, yet such laudable motives were disproved in 1687, for he stamped neither of the city punches when they became official but continued to use the word 'sterling' in two lines, or 'sta', in various permutations with his own mark, now a larger 'PP', without the crown, often twice, and the correct date letter. With a full hallmarking system in operation, no sense can be made of such individualism. During the closed period, between 1697 and 1701, he carried on in the same way except for changing his own mark on one known example, a beautifully fluted porringer, to a smaller 'PP' in a rectangle. Timothy Gardner also used the same 'sta' mark on his only known work, a communion cup and cover at Llansadwrn, Anglesey.

Yet when the assay office reopened in 1701, Peter Pemberton conformed, and proved his worth in a particularly fine chocolate pot, 1703, which went to America after a London sale in 1958. The knop on the lid of all chocolate pots is removable, allowing a swizzle stick to be inserted to beat the chocolate to a froth, but on this fine piece both the acorn knop and the high stepped lid are fastened to the wooden handle by robust chains, an unusual feature. There is a pleasant serrated strap of silver superimposed on the handle, set at right angles to the sweeping swan-neck spout, but the baluster bowl itself is plain, adorned only with reeded mouldings around the neck and foot. At that time the majority of chocolate, or coffee pots, were of the tapering cylindrical, or 'lighthouse' form, and this shape was distinctive.

When Chester and several other provincial assay offices officially reopened in 1701, the higher, 'Britannia' standard of metal was obligatory and all plate was stamped with the seated figure of Britannia and the lion's head erased, after assay. New makers' marks consisted of the first two letters of the goldsmith's surname, and a new date letter cycle was also begun. The town mark now had to be taken from the official arms of a city, which in Chester meant changing to those granted in 1580, a rather untidy halved mark with three lions passant on one side and one and a half wheatsheaves on the other. This, however, was only used until 1779, when Chester reverted to its old, clear stamp of three wheatsheaves, with sword erect. The office remained active until 1962, and a look at the silver on many dining-tables today will show how prolifically this mark was used during the next 180 years, particularly on salts, peppers, etc, for flatware was not common; an exception was John Sutters of Liverpool, who made a quantity of it in the first half of the nineteenth century.

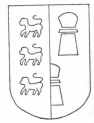

Chester mark between 1701 and 1779

When, in 1720, the sterling standard was restored at the option of the maker and the maker's mark reverted once more to his initials, Chester, for some reason, continued with the first two letters of the surname for another four years, so creating havoc. Peter Pemberton, for instance, had a brother, Thomas, who had been his apprentice, three sons and two grandsons, and while all were not working at the same time the name of Pemberton could create sufficient muddle to the unwary without this further complication—'Pe' for Pemberton.

Apart from reverting to the old town mark in 1779, now in a simple shield, other dates affecting marks in Chester were 1784, the year the sovereign's head was first stamped everywhere to show duty paid, and also the year that new punches were made for all other marks in Chester, noticeably smaller than those previously used, possibly because of the space needed for six marks. In 1823, the leopard's head lost its crown, a funny, barefaced little object, which was dropped altogether in 1839, reverting to five marks; the sovereign's head was also abandoned in 1889, and these four marks continued until the office closed in 1962.

Only three members of the old brigade registered their marks on Chester's new copper plate in 1701, headed by Thomas Robinson, then Peter Pemberton and Nathaniel Bullen. Robinson was another to have confused past experts on marking, for he not only used the word 'sterling' in two lines on an otherwise correctly marked porringer, 1690–2, but the word 'sta' appears twice, with his initials, 'TR', also twice, on a plain somewhat squat jug probably made in 1720, when his fellow craftsmen would have marked it 'Ro', with the proper marks of the newly restored sterling standard. Yet a mug bearing the same date letter as the porringer, 'B' for 1690–2, is correctly marked, as is the majority of his plate made during the Britannia period, mostly consisting of tumbler cups and spoons. There is nothing outstanding about his work, which conforms to the times, but it is too good to need gimmicks to attract notice.

New names during the Britannia period were few, mostly those of watchmakers, but although Thomas Maddock is first mentioned in 1717, he is best known for having used insulting language to the wardens when rebuked for 'obstinately refusing to observe and obey the Lawfull orders of the Company'. Nevertheless, he became warden himself only two years later, in 1723, when Thomas Robinson died, and mayor in 1744. His working life was long, but not particularly illustrious.

Throughout the century, the scene was dominated by one Richard Richardson or another, for when the first of this name gained his freedom in 1703 a new era of assay history was begun. Whatever the date, silver marked 'Ri', or after 1725 'RR', is sold as 'by Richard Richardson', and it will simplify matters to give dates for these three identically named men. The first, born in 1676, was given a grant by a city charity fund soon after completing his apprenticeship under Ralph Walley, which enabled him to set up his own firm. This passed, soon after his death in 1729, to his eighteen-year-old son who died in 1769, and then to his grandson who worked until the firm was taken over by J. F. Watthew in 1823, the name eventually changing again to Butt & Company. It would be interesting to establish a connection between this family and the Richardsons of Philadelphia, where Joseph, 1711–84, in particular, produced such really lovely work. Unfortunately, this is not possible, for Francis, the first of them, was already working in America in 1700.

All the Richard Richardsons made tumbler cups which, as we have seen, were very much a speciality of Chester, reaching their heights in the hands of the second Richard Richardson in about 1750. Originally conceived for the man who could not wait to finish his journey before taking a drink, they were raised from a single circle of silver in such a way that the weight of metal at the rounded bottom made overturning impossible—an excellent cup to use in a moving carriage.

Tumblers were made in the seventeenth century, but Chester makers had begun to specialise in them well before its end, and although they were also made in most other places these goldsmiths were supreme, balancing them to perfection. They came in many sizes, some quite tiny, but in Chester and other northern centres they were inclined to be rather lower in proportion to width than those of London. Normally, they were totally plain, engraved with arms only, or with an inscription or motto added; a pair by the second Richard Richardson, 1748, shown at the 1970 Antique Dealers Fair, for instance, weighed 2oz each, cupping nicely into the hand. Both were engraved in script, one reading 'The Sheriff's Office', the other 'The Foreman's Oath'. Most of them had a gilt interior and some, including one by Benjamin Pemberton, 1725, son of the first Peter, were engraved only with contemporary initials, another usual form. These cups did not evolve, the slight variations of size and decoration appearing in any era, although one, made in 1783 by an unidentified maker, had a slightly everted lip. Often presented as racing trophies, such as the large one already mentioned which does not look as if it were locally made, they were also used as prizes for cockfights, one by the second Richard Richardson presented for this purpose in 1757 being inscribed 'Drink and be sober'.

The first Richard Richardson, whose workshops still exist in Eastgate Row, made more church plate than any other craftsman since the Elizabethan era, and at least one of his cups appeared before he gained his freedom, indicating that this was delayed by the closed period. Nevertheless, none was decorated in any special way or showed the initiative of which he was capable, doubtlessly at the will of the bishops. He did, though, make a considerable quantity of miniature communion sets for the sick, mostly in the last years of his life, following the styles of the larger cups normal in the diocese.

Chester's civic plate is largely London made, but Richard Richardson, who was assay master for many years, was responsible for most of the remainder. One of the earliest of his pieces in this collection is an oval tobacco box which, according to an entry in the corporation

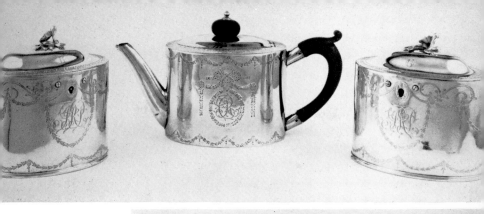

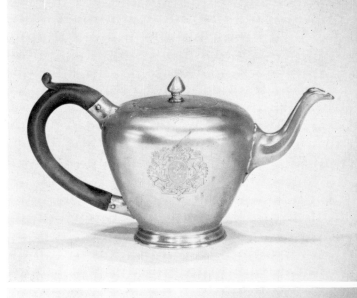

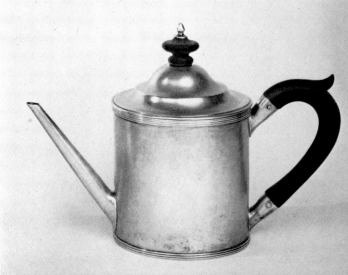

137 (above) Teapot and two caddies made in York, 1780, soon after the assay office there had reopened; (centre) teapot by Isaac Cookson, Newcastle, 1745; (below) single cuppa teapot by H. Prince & Co, York, 1801

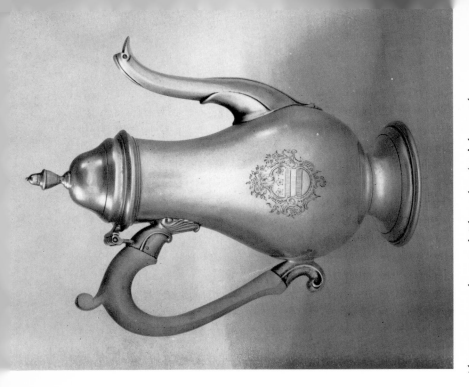

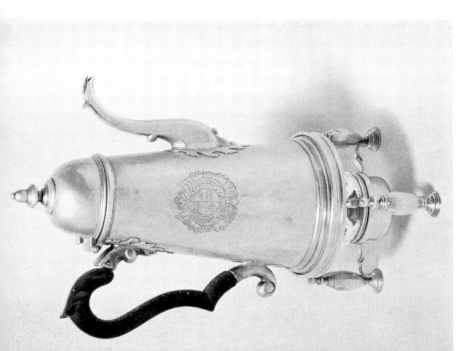

*Page* 138 (*left*) An Exeter chocolate pot of the lighthouse type, 1729, with contemporary lampstand. The maker, 'R.F.', has not been

minutes of 1704, was made from melting down the city's old tobacco box, obviously too small, and a tumbler cup. This box, engraved on the lid with the city arms that all seemed to prefer—the three wheat-sheaves with sword erect—is most unusual in that it stands on four ball feet. Sometimes referred to as a snuff box because it was later used as such, it has two features that distinguish it from such containers: a lid that lifts off, whereas snuff boxes, often used one-handed on horseback, had hinged lids, and a pipe stopper, attached by a chain, inside. This, used for tamping down the tobacco, belonged to the original box, and although unmarked, is engraved 1673.

Also in the civic collection are two long, rat-tail spoons, dated 1712, with a bull's head crest on their rounded necks. These crests are lightly engraved, a sign of good early work, for later engraving was more deeply cut. There is also an unusual, wooden-handled spoon and a tumbler cup, inscribed to the Holland family.

The Chester City Oar was also of Richardson's making. It is 14in long with a plain blade and a square shaft. One side is engraved with the city arms and 'Rd STUBS' 1752'; another carries a shield of arms and the motto 'EITHER FOR EVER', and a third side the inscription 'James Meakin 17 March 1812'. Presumably the fourth space still awaits an occasion worthy of inscription, for the oar is hallmarked for Chester, 1719.

In 1721 Richardson mounted the mayor's porter's staff with a fine silver head, one of the more elaborate examples of Chester craftsman-ship. This round head is more than 5in deep and embossed with both the old and the new city arms, as well as representations of the city mace and sword, all within elaborate frames and the inscription 'Thomas Edwards Esq., Mayor 1721'.

But the greatest of Richardson's civic work was undoubtedly the pair of identical maces he made for the Corporation of Caernarvon, where they can be seen in the town hall. These maces, measuring just over 2ft 5in long, have beautifully balanced heads really more attractive than many a more elaborate piece. Each head has a bowl set on a ribbed knop at the top of the shaft, similar in shape to the local tumbler cup, and surmounted by an engraved border between two strong ribs, and then an upstanding decorative frieze, which includes the Prince of Wales's feathers. A fine crown of high looped straps arches over this, coming together at their lowest point in the centre, from which rises a magnificent orb and cross. The bowl itself is exquisitely engraved with an inscription proclaiming them to be the gift of Capt George Twistleton of Ilyon, 'TO THE ANCIENT AND LOYAL CORPORATION OF CARNARVON, 1718', and two delicately engraved coats of arms.

These were made from an earlier London-marked mace, c 1650, and Richardson has incorporated a part of it on one of them showing the old stamps, almost indistinguishably worn but relevant. Each section of the shaft, however, bears his own 'Ri' mark within an oval, one of several used during the Britannia period and, on the head of each mace, the letters 'stirl' stamped in a rectangle. He was assay master at the time, and it seems strange that he did not mark this great work correctly.

There is also another wooden-handled spoon in the civic collection, very like Richard's but made by William Richardson, his youngest brother, in 1722. The marks on this are distinguished by a small crescent over the 'Ri', and, of course, the five Chester marks of the sterling standard, where the earlier one, 1713, was in Britannia times. Both spoons are about 18in long with large silver bowls, 4in × 3in, a rat-tail and a silver socket for the wooden handle.

Spoons, however, never were a feature of Chester, where only one Elizabethan seal top, c 1580 by William Mutton, is recorded, and where no apostle or other distinctively knopped spoon survives—if they were ever made. Yet from the end of the seventeenth century a certain number of spoons were produced, mostly of the long, reeded rat-tail variety usually with a trifid end. Peter Pemberton, for instance, made several, many of which had graded pellets on the rat tail. None had the lacy pattern engraving around the tail, normal at the time, but well-engraved crests usually appeared on the back of the broad end. One of Pemberton's, 1694 or 1695, was chased all over the front surface, a less usual practice since the spoon was generally laid at table face downwards. More exciting was his basting spoon of 1705, with a tapering cylindrical handle, crested with a balloon knop finial.

In the 1720s the rat tail continued, but the ends were rounded and ridged in the Hanovarian style without engraving other than crests. Benjamin Pemberton made one of these, including the gift initials which appeared on most, and a rat-tailed ladle, 16in long, of which 7½in was wooden handle in 1724; another variation of this was a rat-tailed spoon, 1728, with a marrow scoop handle. Marrow scoops were made on occasion for a long time, and three described in catalogues as by 'Richard Richardson' illustrate a previous point, for one bears the date letter for 1724, another for 1736, and the third, 1787—three generations.

Another item missing from the Chester lists was the large type of two-handled cup and cover, although they made the smaller type, usually called porringers. None survive prior to that of Thomas Robinson, 1690–2, already mentioned for its $_{LING}^{STER}$ mark, and all lack the cover, often found with fine finials elsewhere, which completed these vessels. But the shape of Robinson's conformed, with its ornate moulded 'S' scroll handles, its moulded base ring and rim, and the fluting on its lower half. Peter Pemberton's delightful little porringer, only 1in high and possibly made as a sample during the closed period, 1697–1701, has plain 'S'-shaped handles and thirty-six spiral flutes around its lower half. An added refinement is a floral, or wheel-type decoration above each flute, composed of five triangles each. He also made two other porringers, one of them nearly 5in high, in 1702, and the other a mere 3in in 1706, with alternate flutes and gadroons in true Queen Anne manner. George Walker was one to show how little these changed through the years with a tiny porringer in 1776, bell-shaped and punched with foliate motifs. But he had also made one in 1769 that was taller proportionately, with a well-everted rim and flat reeded handles. This utterly plain cup, weighing nearly 9oz, was decorated only with initials that had been punched rather than engraved.

More of a rarity in England was an American type of porringer described as a cupping bowl when it appeared for sale in 1929. This shallow bowl, 5in across, with the one flat, pierced handle so usual across the Atlantic, was made by Alexander Pulford in about 1690. English lemon strainers, used in the making of punch, had similar handles, although rarely was full use made of the opportunities they offered. A few were made in Chester later, including one by Joseph Walley, 1780. Another rarity reminiscent of the American spout cup was a tiny feeding cup, only 3½in high, with a spout issuing from its plain, cylindrical body and a lid joined to its 'S' scroll handle, made by Robert Green in 1790.

In Georgian times, mugs were quite a feature of Chester, where the lidded tankard was so rare. Usually small, up to half a pint, they were ogee-shaped and continued being made until the assay office closed in 1962. The earliest example, made by Thomas Robinson between 1690 and 1692, is more like a cup and less than 3½in high. The slightly bulbous, fluted lower part has ring mouldings above and below, and one flat, ribbed 'S' scroll handle. Later these mugs became more severe, and an example by the first Richard Richardson, 1721, now in Carlisle Museum, is typical. This is just over 2in high, with almost straight sides and a sharply everted rim. There is no decoration, doubtlessly because the inscription left no room, and the 'S'-shaped handle is plain, except for side ridges. One would expect such a mug to have been a christening present, but the inscription proclaims it to have been the gift of Joseph Sewell, son of Jon Sewell, to the fraternity of shoemakers at Carlisle, 4 May 1722, which seems strange. Another, very similar and only fractionally taller, was made in 1725 by Benjamin Pemberton, and bears an inscription which probably refers to a child—'IANE IONES, MARCH YE IST, 1726.7'.

The tradition for minute mugs continued, and of a group of four by Richard Richardson II in one sale, the tallest was 3in, and weighed 3oz, 16dwt, which was heavy by comparison to some. This little mug was completely plain, with a spreading rim foot, double scroll handle and gilt interior. All four were made in 1751 or 1767 and were significantly described in the catalogue as 'of typical local ogee shape'.

Chester makers obviously favoured the plain, slightly bulbous form of good solid workmanship, and this is seen again in their brandy warmers, or saucepans, which spanned the whole century. The Liverpool example of Benjamin Brancker, 1700, already mentioned, sums them up, for the baluster bowl with straight turned wooden handle at right angles to the lip, and very small size, was usual. Inevitably Richard Richardson enters the picture, and while the handle of one of his made in 1722 ends in a drop, and the body is a little more everted at the lip in another of 1741, solid worth remains the keynote of both. Their straight wooden handles fitted into a silver sleeve, 1½in long in the case of Benjamin Pemberton's 1726 example, and while later they became a little larger—George Walker in 1790, going up to 6oz, 7dwt, and Robert Green, 1794, just 1oz less—the only real difference was that the extra space allowed for armorial engraving. Small size in these was not confined to Chester, but an identically shaped saucepan by Hester Bateman, 1786, weighing 30 oz, 7dwt with a flat lid, emphasises the extent to which Chester specialised in the very small and quite plain object.

The same story is told in jugs, most of them from the time of Ralph Walley's 1690 example being very nearly taller editions of the brandy warmers, with, of course, a different handle. Yet Benjamin Pemberton made a cream jug in 1725, in itself a rarity, that really got away from this. Of inverted pear shape, it was described by Sotheby's as 'chased at the shoulders and foot with diaper scale ornament, scrolls and leafage, the narrow neck chased under the lip with a shell motif and at the upper handle terminal, capped with a satyr mask and a leaf at the lower end of the serpent, on spreading circular base, 5in high'—quite one of his more ambitious pieces. Strangely, Chester seems to have become less rather than more decorative over the years, largely ignoring both the rococo and Adam styles.

But all was not entirely stylised during this period. George Walker, who gained his freedom in 1772 and, like so many before him, founded a continuing family of goldsmiths in the city, produced a lot of silver, some of it quite distinctive. An oval cream boat on three shell and hoof feet, with a long lip and fine flying scroll handle capped with nice leaf ornament, has a beautifully scalloped rim and is really very attractive, though personally I would have described it as a sauce boat. (Illustration, p 190.)

George Lowe also founded a family line, and a firm that still continues in an honoured position in Chester. He gained his freedom in 1791 and, inevitably, most of his work was in the small table wares—sugar tongs, skewers, marrow scoops, salt, pepper and teapots to name but a few—of which later work largely consisted. These, particularly skewers, which were made prolifically and well, are an excellent subject for collection and surprisingly varied.

But Lowe also did more individual work, including a lovely chamber candlestick, always a rarity in Chester, marked for 1823. This has a plain, circular pan, engraved like the extinguisher with initials, which also appear below a crest on the sconce, with its detachable nozzle. There is a simple handle with a leaf top, and the extinguisher has a most attractive, rope twist, circular handle. (Illustration, p 190.) Two pap boats of Lowe's, 1828 and 1837, were also sold at Sotheby's in 1968. Somewhat like a sauce boat but without either handle or feet, they were used for feeding infants, and it seems surprising that the gorgets—silver bibs—largely made in Scotland, were not produced to go with them as feeding a toddler from them must have been a messy business. Both these pap boats were perfectly plain in design, though one had a crest engraved below the moulded lip.

Beakers, at their height in Elizabethan times, were not made in Chester until well into the eighteenth century and were then quite distinctive. Almost entirely of tapering, cylindrical form, they were made to simulate barrels, with staves and reeded hoops above and below. An early example by Richard Richardson, 1748, is typical, being only 3in high and weighing 4oz 16dwt. (Illustration, p 190.) He, as might be expected, made several, and the only really significant difference in a pair he made in 1765 is that the two fitted together, one reversed above the other, to make a total height of 6¾in. Like most of these beakers, they are gilded inside, and each is engraved with a small crest between the staves, and initials. George Walker made two, exactly like them, and great encouragement is given to the inexperienced collector when he recognises such Chester work at a glance—sitting unlabelled on a shelf. The first slight difference noted appeared in 1802, when Robert Boulger made a pair of beakers, identically shaped, without the staves, plain except for mouldings at rim and base. (Illustration, p 190.) He was one of many Liverpool goldsmiths, free 1787, to have his work stamped in Chester.

He was in good company, for in the years leading up to the great inquiry of 1773, Matthew Boulton and James Fothergill of Birmingham sent their work to Chester for assay in preference to London. It was largely Boulton, with his excellent business sense, who set the 1773 search in motion, for his efforts to get separate assay offices for Birmingham and Sheffield led to London's objections and the subsequent inquiry which showed that, while London might pass silver a fraction below standard, Chester never would. Led by their most efficient assay master, Mr Scasebrick, Chester goldsmiths came through this ordeal with full honours, and if the silver they made was not always exciting in its variety, at least it was certain to have been of the highest standard, both of workmanship and silver.

But Boulton, father of the machine age, eventually brought about the downfall of the provincial craftsman, for few could compete with the productions of Birmingham once the era of hand-made silver was over. One by one they closed down, only Chester, producing as always the smaller type of silver, managed to keep going until 1962. Then a craft which the city had fostered for more than a thousand years came to an end, and its records were removed for safe keeping to Birmingham assay office—the youngest of them all.

# Seven

# Wales

The only evidence that silver was ever made in Wales is circumstantial, for other than those in the Chester lists the names of Welsh goldsmiths do not appear to have been recorded, and without such record, proof cannot exist. Yet the silver of Wales is rich in interest, and conjecture about its origins adds to the fascination. Silver- and, to a lesser extent, gold-mining was a considerable industry in many parts of the country, particularly Cardiganshire, and it is easy to establish that Welsh metal was used in plate. But did goldsmiths make the best of their opportunities, as they did, for instance, at Barnstaple where the local mines at Coombe Martin supplied a flourishing guild? Some of the plate to be found in Wales bears the stamp of Chester makers, and a quantity is London hallmarked, but there is much, particularly in the churches, that bears unknown marks or is without any mark at all. Some of this, especially in the north, was obviously made in Chester, but the rest could well be the work of local craftsmen and, because history makes this plausible, it is my belief that it was.

The Romans worked the argentiferous lead mines of Wales but just how far they went in extracting silver from them is uncertain. Nevertheless, Roman coins have been found in the north, and village names that mean the 'place of the fiery furnace' are evidence of lost smelters. The upper layer in a lead mine is the richest in silver, and a law of AD 79 limited the annual production because it was so easily come by. In fact, the silver-bearing lead was almost on the surface at that time.

These mines were worked spasmodically throughout history, the next surge of activity coming with the Normans when the lead, probably with silver intact, was used for roofing the great castles and abbeys which sprang up like housing estates. Welsh silver pennies of both Norman and Plantagenet times were, nevertheless, found during excavations at Rhuddlan, Denbighshire, proving that at least some was smelted.

By this time, gorgeous plate was being made and the question of where the metal came from has never been satisfactorily answered. The Dolgellau chalice, one of the most beautiful pieces of medieval work surviving, was found in 1890 in Merionethshire, and poses many such questions. It was undoubtedly British made, despite suggestions that it might be German (see the chapter on Chester), because its broad bowl, the broadest known, has an outward curved lip which was peculiarly English, as was the leaf pattern on a hatched ground of the foot.

With the exception of only two, this lovely cup is the tallest known, and its superlative workmanship suggests the hand of a master craftsman. Entirely gilded inside and out, it has a beautifully ornamented twelve-lobe knot, alternatively beaded and plain, on a stem that draws the eye outwards and down to its exquisitely engraved twelve-lobed foot, accentuating its lovely symmetry. Its finely engraved paten is the largest known in Great Britain and of the same high standard of workmanship as the cup itself.

That these superlative treasures were hidden near Dolgellau when trouble came, does not, of course, prove that they were always used there, but it seems perfectly possible that their history was entirely Welsh. It is one of those fascinating puzzles which are unlikely to be solved, though, conceivably, the precise methods of modern research may one day uncover details of their maker.

Edward I allowed any adventurer to dig where he liked for gold and silver, provided only that he compensated the owner for any damage done to his land. The owner himself could claim no further interest until 1426, when one-twentieth part of the spoils was granted to him. By this time a European shortage of silver had developed owing to the demands of commerce and, despite similar needs at home, so much was being exported from the port of Chester and to a lesser extent, Flint, that laws were passed prohibiting the precious metal from being sent out of the country.

The Mostyn harp personifies all that is romantic in history, known and unknown, as portrayed in silver. No one knows when it was made or by whom, but the chances are that the silver was mined on the

Mostyn estate in north Flintshire and the harp possibly made by a local man. This tiny replica of a Welsh harp, only 4in high and with its nine strings representing the Muses still intact, first came into known history about 400 years ago, when Queen Elizabeth presented it to the winning bard at the special Eisteddfod held at nearby Caerwys in 1568. Lord Mostyn does not know how long it had already been in his family then, nor quite how the first Elizabeth happened to present it, but its value is wrapped up in its romantic history and in its utterly Welsh background.

The Aberpergwm mazer in the National Museum of Wales also poses fascinating question marks, for all its known history is Welsh. This extremely lovely piece is most unusual in that it is made entirely of silver, whereas mazers normally had polished wooden bowls, mounted in silver for the rich. They were the most common drinking-vessels in medieval times, and it would appear that the silver bowl of this unmarked piece was an Elizabethan replacement of the original wood, for it is of the normal shape, with its gilded rim fixed over the top in the same old way. This rim, and possibly the foot, were earlier, probably fifteenth century, and the arms, once enamelled, of the Glamorganshire family of Aberpergwm, known as Williams since the seventeenth century, are shown on the boss inside. (Illustration, p 103.)

The mazer bowl of about the same date which somehow survived the dissolution of the monastery at Clynog, Caernarvonshire, is a beautiful bowl of dark maplewood, surmounted by a gilded band engraved with a Latin inscription meaning 'Jesus of Nazareth, King of the Jews, Son of God, have mercy upon me', each word divided by exquisite decoration. This has been used as an alms dish in the ancient church there, and is of extraordinary beauty and interest.

Such treasures, of course, are rare, but unmarked silver is a fine breeding-ground for fascinating theory. The tiniest churches have their silver, often forgotten, and a survey of it might yield most interesting results, although there are not many pieces of pre-Reformation plate known in Wales. Two funeral chalices in St David's Cathedral, both rather roughly hewn in the plain, round style of the age, were taken from bishops' tombs, the one from that of Richard de Carew (1256-80) being in a much better state of preservation than the chalice and fragment of its paten found in the tomb of Bishop Beck (1280-93). Crozier heads of remarkable interest were also found in these tombs, but little is known of their history.

There are two other chalices, somewhat alike and both dating from about AD 1500; one is at the church of Llanelian yn Rhos, near Colwyn Bay, an area in which silver was mined. Unfortunately, its bowl has been restored and the toes broken off the hexagonal foot. The other, at Llandudwen in Caernarvonshire, is in much better condition and has a large ornate knop with six diamond-shaped projections and an engraving of the Crucifixion in one of the compartments of the foot.

There is no proof that any of these, or the few other really ancient pieces known, were made in Wales by Welsh craftsmen. Equally, there is no reason to believe they were not, although it may eventually be proved that some, if not all in the north, were made by Chester goldsmiths, many of whom were Welsh.

Throughout England and Wales the majority of Elizabethan communion cups were made from the old Massing chalices, with extra silver added, and in Wales the chances are that even those hallmarked in London used Welsh-mined silver. There are, however, a great number of cups tending to differ from the normal which bear no marks at all, or an unascribed maker's mark only. The bowl is rarely of the simple, inverted bell form, varies in height and even shape, and frequently has a flat base. More often than not, particularly in the south and west but rarely in the north, there are two bands of decorated strapwork, the upper one enclosing the usual arabesques, or woodbine foliage, sometimes with a sprig carried above and below each intersection. The lower one, around the centre, invariably carries the name of the church in an inscription that reads: ✠ POCVLVM * ECLESIE * DE * AMROTH, or any other village name. Sometimes there is the addition of a date, although this is more normally shown on the knop of the cover, which is otherwise plain. The stem usually conforms to the normal, but not always, and 'hit and miss' decoration is frequently added.

The main interest in the cups, however, is the prolific work of the local craftsman, possibly working in Carmarthen about 1573–89, who marked his work with the four ovals—OOOO. Communion cups by him are common throughout the vast diocese of St David's, including the majority of those in Pembrokeshire and Carmarthenshire, while in Cardiganshire all bar two are stamped only with his mark. A delightfully slim little cup and paten cover, its inscribed central band proclaiming it to have belonged to the Welsh church of Meline, is displayed in the Museum of Fine Arts in Boston. This has the date 1577 engraved on the knop of its cover, and bears the four oval mark. Were the name of this maker known, it would be well respected; it is a pity that records were not kept for, in finding his history, no doubt others would also come to light.

Many unmarked communion cups in Wales, particularly in the south, follow the same general pattern, and it is worth looking into any little church in hopes of finding Elizabethan cups. Sometimes this proves of great general interest, for a search for facts about their silver can reveal some fascinating local history. The little church at Eglwyscummin in Carmarthenshire is a prime example. Known to have existed since about AD 500, and with an Ogham stone to show its early connection with Ireland, this church has an Elizabethan cup which is not mentioned in *The Church plate of Carmarthenshire* (J. T. Evans, 1907) because it had then been missing for more than a hundred years. In 1920, the cup was found in a London pawnshop and its rightful ownership established by the Latin inscription around its centre. It was probably stolen originally, though some such cups were given less importance, as, for instance, the old chalice at the little church of Llandefaelog, Carmarthenshire, which was pawned for 13s 4d in order to buy a copy of Erasmus's *Paraphrase*. King James I made things very difficult for such poor parishes when he decreed that each should be provided with a copy of this work, in addition to the Bible and Prayer Book.

There was never enough silver to be had at this time for all its uses. Queen Elizabeth set about getting more silver from her mines by bringing in foreign experts to show the way and then claiming all mines as 'royal', which meant that the silver gained had to be sent to the Tower of London for minting. The amount yielded was still not very great, but when the mine at Cwmsymlog, near Aberystwyth, was discovered, things improved, the Welsh mines alone in 1590 sending more than double the 871lb which had come from the whole of Britain in 1575. A special mark was struck on coins made from silver mined at Cwmsymlog, which yielded 40 oz of silver per ton of ore.

In view of the dangers involved in the long journey from Wales, it is difficult to believe that all the silver mined there was really sent to London, particularly when Sir Hugh Myddleton took over the Cwmsymlog and other lead mines in 1617. For Sir Hugh, who made a great success of the venture for fourteen years, was himself a goldsmith and entered his mark in London in 1600. Did he perhaps keep some metal back for his own use? King James, convinced that Cardiganshire was really rich in silver, had given him every support, and may well have turned a blind eye to irregularities. In any case, the chances seem extremely high that it was Welsh silver that Myddleton used for his work. A few spoons of this period are known, marked with an 'AB' and castle, at one time believed to have been used by an Aberystwyth maker. Unfortunately, the theory has been impossible to prove as no records have been found, but quite a number of spoons have appeared for sale without the nimbus normal on apostle spoons.

After Sir Hugh's death, the mines were idle until Thomas Bushell drained and ventilated the flooded shafts, making them infinitely more workable. Having convinced the king of the national advantages of minting silver obtained locally, he set up his mint in Aberystwyth castle in 1637, and coins struck there were stamped on both sides with the Welsh feathers, as well as the mint mark of an open book. This immediately stimulated production, for local miners, smiths, and other workmen were employed and paid in their own coin. How many of those smiths, one wonders, kept some silver back to fulfil commissions for plate, delivered unmarked? There is some church silver from the reigns of James I and Charles I that could come into this category, although in the north several Charles I cups are known to have been made in Chester.

The mines were captured by Cromwell towards the end of the Civil War, ending a period that had promised great things. Bushell had had six mines in full production when he moved his mint to Shrewsbury and then to Oxford in support of the king, the London mint having been lost early in the war. There he supervised the vast melting-down operations that turned much of the country's finest plate into coin, supplementing it with £100 worth of pure silver per week from Cardiganshire, so that a large part of the coin of that time consisted of Welsh silver.

The Civil War left the mines in a parlous condition which was to persist for many years to come, until the Act of 1701 so regularised the marking of silver that the great uncertainties of the past were largely done away with. In fact, the one piece of silver declared to be of Welsh origin was made after this date. It is a jug, now in the National Museum of Wales, made by John Smith, hallmarked in London in 1710, and inscribed as having been made from silver from the mines of Bwlch-yr-Esker-hir in Cardiganshire. The interest shown in this piece is not so much for itself as for its local associations, which would appear to me to be less rare than is generally believed. For when silversmiths were crying out for metal after the Civil War and the melting-down process was reversed, a great deal of coin made from Welsh-mined silver must have found its way back into plate. Equally, it is perfectly possible that unmarked silver found in Wales, like that bearing only unknown marks, could have been made in the Principality.

# Eight

# Birmingham and Sheffield

At a time when men must seize their opportunities Birmingham and Sheffield enter the story of provincial silver. In 1743 Thomas Boulsover, a Sheffield cutler, had discovered that a thin sheet of silver fused on to a thicker piece of copper would expand equally as one metal when flattened out. This became known as Sheffield plate and, since it was cheaper to produce and subject to none of the restrictions surrounding the manufacture of silver, its effect upon the craft can be imagined.

Boulsover guarded his secret jealously and was soon using the process for making buttons and buckles, undercutting those who were still using solid silver for the manufacture of these fashionable 'toys'. His business flourished so that he was soon making other small trinkets, bringing the making of snuff boxes to a high art by 1750. Toys, incidentally, had nothing to do with playthings. They were the small objects which had been the mainstay of Birmingham silver production since the end of the Civil War.

Then Joseph Hancock of Sheffield, who had been Boulsover's apprentice, discovered the plating process and in 1751 he set to work with considerably more enterprise than his master had shown in the medium, producing all the larger articles most popular at the time, particularly those which displayed only their outer side, such as tea and coffee pots, for the silver was fused on to only one side of the copper at first. His creations graced Georgian tea tables at only a fraction of the cost of solid silver, which it so closely resembled.

So obvious a winner did not lack eager followers and production of Sheffield plate was quickly taken up by others. Silversmiths, visualising a rosy future, made tracks to Sheffield from London and elsewhere, while the city's own cutlers changed jobs in droves, many of them poor-quality workmen who were to cause endless trouble.

London was not amused. Birmingham had been a thorn in the capital's side ever since the Civil War, for the types of goods her goldsmiths made were suitable for production by the machines Birmingham engineers had already invented. These rolling machines, stamps and presses were, of course, hand operated, but were none the less capable of producing goods so much more cheaply than by traditional methods that they could be sold in London at prices well below those of the capital's own craftsmen. Now the platers had taken this undercutting a stage further.

Midlands goldsmiths, too, were getting a taste of the same medicine and found it increasingly difficult to keep their heads above water in face of such competition. Many of them, in consequence, worked in both mediums, tooling Sheffield plate in the same manner as they had been taught to do with silver.

During the inquiry of 1773 it was stated that upwards of forty licensed silversmiths were working in Birmingham, but by no means all of those who took up production of Sheffield plate came into that category. Matthew Boulton, for instance, had been largely concerned with the steel side of the family business of toy-making, producing buckles, corkscrews, watch chains, sugar nippers and a host of other small objects in steel. Having raised that art to a surprisingly high level, he then went to Sheffield to learn the art of fusing plate and, in 1762, set up a department for it in his already famous Soho factory in Birmingham, the first and only maker of Sheffield plate outside Sheffield until 1770. It was after this was well established, in about 1765, that he turned his attention to silver. Doubtless many others also took it in that order, for the wheel was fast turning full circle; so many platers had made a fortune that they could now afford solid silver.

Birmingham had always been more progressive than any other city in England, applying for three times more patents than Manchester, her nearest rival. Mass production methods were already being introduced and Boulton, by taking John Fothergill, the salesman, into partnership, was setting the pattern of modern commercial practice. New industries to produce materials for others to use were also starting up, and Hancock was among those who gave up craftsmanship to go into the business side. Fusing ingots and rolling them down to usable sheets had

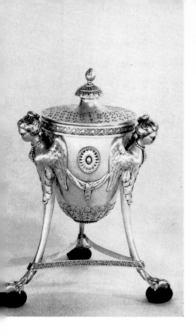

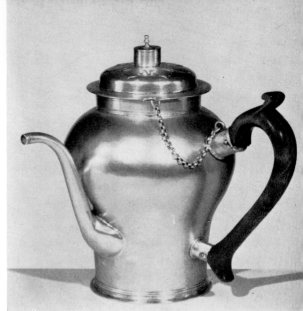

age 155 (*above left*) A unique perfume burner, or cassolet, by Matthew Boulton and John othergill, now in Temple Newsam, near Leeds; (*above right*) very rare Leeds chocolate pot, c 1685, y R. Williamson; (*below*) this elegant shallow bowl, by 'CB', Edinburgh, 1822, demonstrates the sense of proportion maintained in Scotland in the early nineteenth century

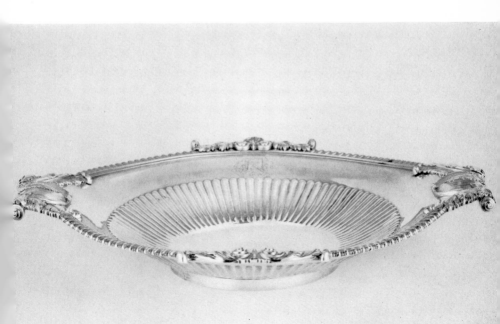

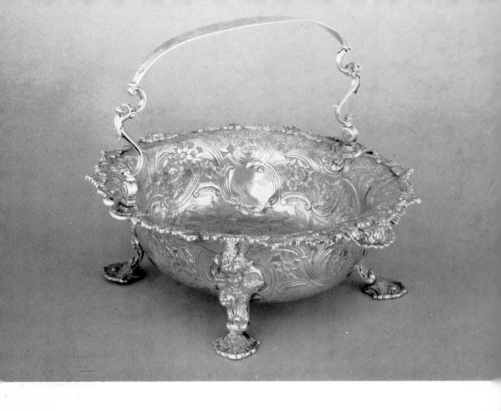

*Page* 156    Two of the author's favourite pieces, both by John Williamson, of Dublin. The cak
basket, 1755, (*above*) and bowl, 1760, (*below*) are worthy of long scrutiny

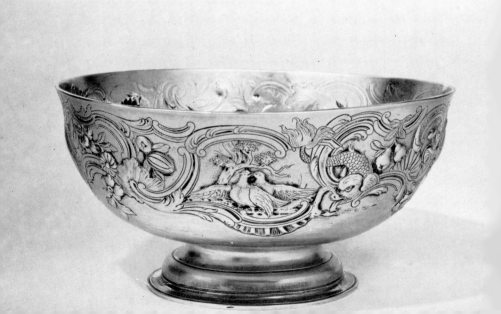

not only taken up the plater's time, but had been fraught with many difficulties that could easily ruin the sheet. Now Hancock, using water power, produced ready-fused sheets for them and, in a different medium, the firm he founded produces metal sheets to this day.

Inventions and new ideas for easing work and improving results followed one another quickly, and each new development, each new success, hit the silversmith squarely between the eyes. Who would pay for silver when Sheffield plate was so much cheaper and virtually indistinguishable from it? Even the designs were largely copied from the silversmiths.

Once double plating arrived in 1765, covering the silver on both sides, only hallmarks remained to distinguish this new work from the old. In this lay another bone of contention, for many platers were stamping their initials and other marks on their work in such a way that deception was complete, at least at first glance. Which is probably why the cutlers of Sheffield punched the word 'Sterling' on the silver handles of their knives in the five years preceding 1773. It, at least, held no ambiguity.

When Boulton considered adding silver to his productions, he thought big, as always. He was the largest single manufacturer of Sheffield plate in the country, and sizeable pieces, notably with shell or gadroon borders, from his Soho works were already raising the standard well above any yet known. He perfected the art of covering bare copper edges with silver thread, invented by Samuel Roberts and George Cadman, and brought it to a fine art, marking such work 'silver borders'. Everything he did was designed to be of the best. But he also thought commercially and the disadvantages of sending sterling silver to Chester, seventy-two miles away, for assay, included danger to the work itself and to his designs, expense and waste of time. From that time on his energies were directed towards the establishment of an assay office in Birmingham. Determined to be a great silversmith, he also wanted to remove the stigma, already noticeable, from the term 'Made in Birmingham'. He had the designs, the workmen and the belief that he could produce finer silver more cheaply than his competitors, but he let it be known publicly that he would not do so 'in the Large way' until a local office for marking silver had been established. Sheffield was glad to hear this and joined him in the fight. Meanwhile his work frequently suffered serious damage as a result of careless packing for its return journey from Chester, and there were intolerable delays.

The work he was having marked in Chester included candlesticks, coffee pots, tureens, vases and other major pieces. The earliest of these were substantially different from the work by which he is best known, for the classic revival or 'Adam style' did not come into full force until about 1770. There is, for instance, a pair of candlesticks by Boulton and Fothergill in the Birmingham assay office collection, marked in Chester in 1768, which are decidedly rococo, with husks, scrolls and flowers decorating its pear-shaped column, and separate, removable nozzles repeating the pattern in Sheffield plate. As one might expect, they are superbly done.

The changeover to the Adam style began with architecture, then spread to interior decoration, and finally plate to harmonise with it. Boulton and Fothergill naturally followed suit, at first adorning the elegant lightness of the classic outline with somewhat heavy applied ornamentation, but still within the prescribed limits of the style. A tureen of theirs in the Victoria and Albert Museum, dated 1776 and bearing the Birmingham marks, shows how quickly the perfect balance was achieved and how skilfully flat fluting was employed. After 1790, when bright cut engraving came in, the overall lightness became more marked, particularly in the smaller objects such as tea caddies. Nevertheless, some of the loveliest work from the Soho factory bears very little decoration at all.

It is strange that so little of Boulton's Chester plate seems to have survived, yet but for his exertions it is doubtful whether the official period in the Midlands would ever have been launched. Sheffield set the ball rolling when they sent in a petition to Parliament in February 1773, strongly backed up by another from Birmingham the following day, requesting the establishment of an assay office in each town so that goldsmiths might mark their own goods and compete with their rivals on equal terms. These requests were referred to a committee whose members were circularised with a well-phrased memorandum by Boulton, setting out their position clearly. In it he said, in effect, that no other town had anything to fear from them, except for their ability to work harder and their 'Excellence in Design and Workmanship and moderate prices'. Yet perhaps this was just what London did fear, for it is easier to compete with shoddy work than excellence. Birmingham also took the opportunity of this enquiry to influence the passing of a law preventing the assayers from defacing work by stamping marks without consideration, often over fine engraving or chasing.

The London goldsmiths as we have seen (Chapter One) jumped at this chance to air their long-felt grievances against the provincial offices generally, but their counter-petition against the granting of any privileges to these midland towns merely led Parliament to set up an inquiry into the workings of all offices, including London. Goldsmiths' Hall then put in a further petition, drawing particular attention to abuses and frauds committed in and near Birmingham and Sheffield by workmen who covered base metal with silver and impressed marks upon it. Yet it was not London but the midlands silversmiths themselves who suffered most from the platers, who were not obliged to spend time and money on having their work assayed, whereas goldsmiths were liable to a fine of £500 for counterfeiting marks on wrought plate, while the transposition of genuine marks was punishable by death.

London came badly out of the inquiry, where it was established that

Birmingham
anchor

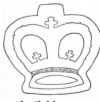

Sheffield crown

a great deal of abuse could and did take place unless the maker protected his work by buying the scraper a drink. It also disclosed that London had been in the habit of marking work as much as 2½dwt below standard, while Birmingham and Sheffield had always worked to the exact standards which Chester had always insisted upon.

The outcome was that both towns were granted assay offices on 18 May 1773, and established companies known as 'The guardians of the standard of wrought plate within the town . . .' of Birmingham or Sheffield. Silver in Birmingham was to be stamped with the lion passant, the town mark of an anchor, the maker's mark, and the date letter. This began at once with a Roman 'A', changing yearly through the alphabet, excluding 'J'.

For Sheffield, the variable date letter began with an old English 'E', possibly in honour of the Earl of Effingham, their first chairman, and proceeded without rhyme or reason, the letter, its type, and even its shield being chosen by the guardians at their annual meeting, although the lion passant and maker's initials were as elsewhere. The town mark was a crown, popularly believed to have been won by tossing a coin with Birmingham, as so many preliminary meetings had been held at the 'Crown and Anchor' inn, in the Strand.

At the same time it was laid down that no letters were to be punched on any metal article, 'plated, or covered with silver . . .'. As this precluded any signing of Sheffield plate and was a disadvantage to the top platers, another Act was passed in 1784 allowing plated work made within 100 miles of Sheffield to carry the maker's name and any figure or device that did not resemble any already registered for silver. Some 75 per cent of all Sheffield plate now to be found was made in Sheffield, but the number of platers registered in Birmingham outnumbered them.

The imposition of a tax of 6d an ounce on silver in that same year, 1784, gave further advantage to the fused plate industry, for sixpence in those days was real money, and when multiplied by 200 oz or so, not an uncommon weight for a large article, buyers were inclined to prefer the cheaper wares. In an attempt to counteract the effect of the tax with lighter metal, goldsmiths took to rolling their silver ever thinner. The platers promptly copied them, so that even in this respect their work, which already followed patterns used for silver, looked much the same.

Nothing could halt the platers' prosperity, which reached its heights in 1785; even the outbreak of the French Revolution in 1789, which initially halted export to France, failed to do more than dent the boom, which continued until 1815.

This is probably one reason why Boulton and Fothergill lost money on the silver side of their business, though fortunately the Soho factory was such a large and complex industry, employing many hundreds of workers, that its various other enterprises were able to carry the loss on this fine work. The whole concept was interlocking. Fothergill, the salesman, took no part in production but was constantly travelling and found no difficulty in marketing his silver through the agencies he had set up at home and abroad. Apprentices in the accepted sense, which could be a dead loss, were not taken on, however much the reward offered; instead, the boys Boulton employed started in the 'toy' department, and were given every opportunity to develop their skill. Those who showed promise were then given specialist training. It is possible that Boulton, who had a hand in most things, may also have been instrumental in setting up the city's famous art schools. Certainly he arranged for boys with artistic leanings to be taught to draw.

Design was always one of his strong points, and in his role as a 'captain of industry' he saw to it that the standard maintained by his firm was of the very highest. His eye and taste must have matched his ambition for in 1770, when Sheffield plate and ormulu were his main products, the Adam brothers, then at the height of their fame, suggested a liaison tantamount to a partnership under which Boulton would supply plate and ormulu in an elegant and superior style. Though this eventually fell through, it illustrates the esteem in which he was held, and his close association with the Adam brothers, who actually designed some of his finest silver, and his friendship with Josiah Wedgwood, no doubt influenced Boulton's taste and helped to inspire new ideas.

Design in silver at this period was restricted in scope, the same classic outlines, decorated in different permutations of the same set of decorations, being used by all. Boulton, however, wanted everything turned out at his Soho factory to be superior in every way, not only to Birmingham's normal but to the work of all other manufacturers, and he took steps to secure the finest artists for his work.

Technically, too, he kept Soho in the forefront, and his partnership with Watt (1775), which led to the installation of the steam engine at his works long before it became general, was of the greatest benefit. Machinery is not within the scope of this book, and technical advances at this period were continual, but the wire draw bench he perfected, which allowed wire to be drawn of uniform thickness, was an invaluable aid to a style that relied on symmetry. A basket made in 1778 and now to be seen in the Birmingham assay office collection, shows how he took this further, producing a most graceful piece on classic lines made entirely of wire.

There is no denying the quality of the work which, after Fothergill retired in 1790, was marked [MB] alone. Yet this, strange to say, is another reason why the firm failed to make money, for it turned out that London rather than Birmingham was the best market for plate of that high standard. Birmingham was geared more to small wares, and of the 841oz of silver Boulton and Fothergill had saved up to have marked at the new office at its opening, some was in really large pieces.

161

Having reached the artistic heights he had set himself, it is not surprising that a man of Boulton's temperament should then have tended to lose interest. It was the establishment of a standard that had really interested him and there were other fields to conquer. With so well-trained a staff, beautiful silver bearing his mark continued to be turned out from the Soho factory and its quality was never allowed to fall appreciably during his lifetime.

After his death in 1809, his son continued to use his mark, but he never showed the same interest as his father, nor any real appreciation of design, his craftsmen following fashion, rather than leading it, into the Romanesque stage of classic revival. From 1834 the work produced at Soho was marked 'R.E.A.' for Robinson, Edkins, and Aston, three men who then ran the silver department, a shadow of its former self. Nothing worth mention emerged, and the factory closed down in 1848.

There was never a craftsman in Sheffield comparable with Boulton, and of the nineteen who registered their mark in 1773 none really stands out above the others. It is a sign of the times that, from the beginning, the domestic wares they produced were virtually all in company names. The commercial side of production was an intrinsic part of their policy, which was to produce goods more cheaply than the traditional craftsmen. Everything within their works dovetailed, and every job in the hands of specialists increased the savings of both time and materials which could be gained by the use of machines and the thin rolling of silver. And in this way they made their fortunes.

Machine-assisted silver could not, of course, match the traditional for beauty or strength, but it was not yet being mass-produced and a great deal of individual skill was still required. If industrialisation and thin rolling give an impression of shoddy work, it seems only fair to point out that throughout the history of both these offices the silver assayed was always up to the full legal requirements—which is more than many assay offices could boast. More, in 1889 it was proudly claimed that these two cities by their constant insistence on full compliance with the law had raised the quality of the silver standard throughout the entire country. It is doubtful if the old, traditional craftsman, undercut in price by his machine-assisted rivals, would have seen it quite in that way, but it is a point of view.

Bright cut engraving, perfected in Birmingham, with its bevelled cut which automatically polished as it scraped, was best suited to the plain surfaces of the tureens, tea caddies, salvers or jugs of the period, and was well employed on a cylindrical argyle that appeared for sale recently. Made in Sheffield in 1777 by J. Hoyland & Co, it is most attractive with its swan-neck spout and lid with a pyroform finial.

Pierced work also suited the Sheffield methods, for parts were often stamped out by specialist firms for use by individual makers. A pair of snuffer trays, made by Tudor & Leader in 1776, had pierced lattice-work galleries, possibly bought in for the purpose, and beaded rims. These two craftsmen were among the pioneers of Sheffield's silver history, Henry Tudor having been one of the first guardians at the new assay office. In fact, the first entry in the book, dated 20 September 1773, is for a goblet by Tudor & Leader weighing 1lb, 8oz, 7dwt, 18gr of higher standard silver, while a chased cup weighing 2lb, 5oz, 14dwt by Fenton, Creswick & Co was the first entry for standard silver. Thirteen pairs of candlesticks were also marked that day, and it does not sound as if silver was skimped in any of them.

Tudor & Leader worked both in silver and Sheffield plate, and while they devoted their attention to it and adopted every new development as it came along, they thrived. A look through a selection of London sales catalogues will show the wide variety of important work they produced.

An excellent example of craftsmanship in pierced work is the fine 'Adam' breadbasket by John Younge & Co, 1779, presented by J. F. Rigaud to the Royal Academy in 1784. This, being the whole thing rather than a galleried part, was in an altogether different class from any machine-stamped pierced silver. On election, Royal Academicians were expected to pay a fee of 5s 3d and make a handsome present of plate for the use of the council, and Rigaud certainly lived up to expectations for his gift is a particularly pleasing work, decorated with all the dainty devices of the Adam style. Another cake basket by Luke Proctor & Co, 1790, depends more on its evenly drawn wire loops for effect, but in 1791 Fenton Creswick & Co produced an oblong inkstand which had a pierced and lightly engraved gallery with a beaded rim. This contained two cut-glass bottles with silver holders and rims. Early in Sheffield history, a quantity of wine coasters were made with pierced galleries, sometimes on rollers, but during the nineteenth century these became rare and were then usually embossed. True pierced work was much more of an Irish speciality, but in Sheffield it suited the system well.

It is an interesting sidelight on the subject that, at about this time, the guardians of the Sheffield office bought some premises in The Farr Gate, Sheffield, for £70. The land had been on lease, but they were able to buy the freehold of the site for a further £75. Pulling down the old building and erecting their own office and dwelling house cost a further £900, and the resultant premises suited them nicely until 1881. One wonders what such a site in Sheffield would cost today.

Changing fashions dictated production in Sheffield as elsewhere, though the reasons for the changes are sometimes obscure. The fall from grace of scales, used to weigh money, or buckles for knee breeches or shoes, is easy enough to understand, but why should salts be a major item in 1773 and then fall right away? There is no obvious answer, as there is with drinking accessories which were always changing in fashion, or the introduction of gas, which brought the candlestick makers to their lowest ebb in 1832.

Nevertheless, Sheffield's main claim to fame was candlestick making, and these were turned out in profusion in fierce competition with the fused plate industry. In fact, of some 5,000 patterns for Sheffield plate listed by Watson and Bradbury, 1,134 were for various forms of candlesticks, the remainder covering the ninety-five other articles made. In the face of such competition the silversmith had to produce as economically as possible and the silver they used for their candlesticks was often rolled so thinly that without 'loading' with solid material, poured in in molten form, many could not have survived. They also made a practice of die-casting various parts in as few sections as possible, soldering them together before loading.

All the shapes popular in successive periods were made by them in quantity. Some had classic columns mounted on a weighted pedestal which was more often round in Sheffield than the square shape favoured elsewhere. These were often stepped, but sometimes had beaded borders. Others had beautifully fluted, tapering stems on circular, fluted bases, with vase-shaped sconces, like an inverted bell or tulip, reflecting the same design. But to attempt to describe the candlesticks of Sheffield is to go through the book from 1773, for the differences lay in methods of production rather than of design.

Candelabra were also made in quantity. Pleasing and restrained to start with, their styles became a rare jumble in the massive age which followed, when size was of more importance than grace. This fashion for enormity was hard on the craftsman struggling to show his worth with a large display of silver, and the thinly rolled products of Sheffield solved his problems. Quite frequently the branches of silver candelabra were made of Sheffield plate.

Perhaps the most important contribution that Sheffield made in this field was the telescopic candlestick, although this was really more a speciality of old Sheffield plate. In silver, they appeared from about 1790 onwards, and the manner in which the stick can be extended, the nozzle rising as smoothly as a well-oiled piston rod, is a creditable example of workmanship. A set of four, seen recently, by John Roberts & Co, 1805, are plain except for a beaded rim, and would be quite suitable for table use today. It would be difficult to distinguish them from the very best that London can provide.

As the nineteenth century continued to unfold, ornamentation generally became more and more florid, until at length the basic object could hardly be discerned beneath the elaborate portrayals of nature. In this general departure from standards of good taste Birmingham and Sheffield did not lag behind, and their names became a by-word for horrid exhibitionism in their domestic wares. Luckily their reputations did not rest upon such things.

Both cities are better known for their inventive imagination, and Birmingham gave evidence of this in a variety of small silver objects, as well as in the design and production of machinery. Wine labels, for example, were made in many places, particularly in London, Edinburgh and Dublin, but the standard in Birmingham was exceptionally high, and a great number that appear for sale today were made there. Fewer came from Sheffield, but at a recent London sale of wine labels an unusually high price was paid for one by Thomas Law of Sheffield, 1774. This has a feather scroll edge and is engraved with 'W' for wine. Matthew Fenton & Co, a little later, and Roger Gainsford at the start of the next century, were other notable Sheffield makers. Law, one of the original silversmiths of Sheffield, was more particularly a worker in fused plate, yet curiously enough very few wine labels were made in Sheffield plate and virtually never appear for sale. Unfortunately, the fact that they do exist gives the unscrupulous rogue an opportunity to try and pass off electro-plate in this guise to the unwary collector.

Wine labels do not rank as important silver, yet all the finest crafts-men took infinite trouble over their delicate and intricate workman-ship. Originally known as 'bottle tickets', they first appeared around 1730, and by 1750 had become general, along with wine drinking in much greater variety than previously. At first they were usually marked only with the maker's initials, but full marking became com-pulsory in an Act of 1790. From 1860, all bottles of wine had to bear descriptive paper labels, and the making of silver tickets virtually ceased. (Illustration, p 207.)

At first these labels, entirely made by hand, were of extremely deli-cate workmanship. Beautiful little things of infinite variety, they are a never-failing source of interest to the collector, who is continually surprised not only at the extraordinary versatility displayed in the design of such small pieces of silver but also at the variety of wines and other drinks for which they were made. 'Noyeau', for instance, was a cordial made from brandy, celery and prunes, flavoured with the kernels of apricots or peaches. 'Shrub' was a very fashionable drink made from rum and fruit juices, and 'arquebuscade' was a healing lotion applied to gunshot wounds. (See E. W. Whitworth's book on wine labels.) Imagine a silver ticket on such a bottle!

Their production allowed the craftsman so much opportunity to use his imagination even when conforming to the fashion of the moment, that there are few small items better suited to the modest collector. In fact, one could easily specialise in the work of Birmingham alone, for the city was well able to hold its own with the best. It has even been said that her workmen, conscious of the challenge they presented, put special effort into their making. One of the finest makers of all, Matthew Linwood, was a Birmingham man, and it was he who first produced die-stamped wine labels in 1794. This was a most important advance, and the casts he made were superbly cut, raising the standard well above any known by the old method of hand tooling. His methods were soon copied, but his skill was not surpassed and the many attempts to take casts from his designs all failed to match the sharpness of the original.

These die-stamped labels were generally thinner than the hand-beaten ones, but it would be a mistake to consider them in any way 'factory' produced, for the cutting of the pattern in reverse in hardened steel is very much a skilled job. In about 1810 the process was somewhat debased by the use of a mould in many cases, and results were not of the same quality; nevertheless, it was not until about 1840 that the workmanship really deteriorated.

Joseph Willmore also did much to keep the Birmingham mark in high repute, but in wine labels the honours must go to Matthew Linwood, not only for his inventiveness, but for the invariably high quality of his work. Both these names recur in all the small works that were such a feature of the city, and Matthew Linwood produced many —caddy spoons, snuff boxes and vinaigrettes—in the shape of a shell, a snail's being a particular favourite. A well-modelled shell wine label of his, 1811, was sold quite recently in London, and he used the same motif in many other ways.

The earliest caddy spoons were made in Sheffield and were of shell design, the most popular motif generally through the years. The vogue for tea drinking began soon after the Restoration, when tea was packed for transport in chests accompanied by a selection of large sea shells, useful as scoops (or to make up the weight!), and some porcelain containers capable of holding the Malay measure of a 'kati' of tea. These rather attractive, blue and white jars, either pear-shaped or octagonal, were the forerunner of today's endless 'give away' attractions, and had lift-off lids into which a measure of the precious leaves could be placed. The first silver caddies, in Queen Anne and George I days, copied them almost exactly, and any spoon could be used to put the tea into the lid, which was itself the measure. The 'caddy spoon' had not yet arrived, though George Smith of London did make short-stemmed medicine spoons for this purpose after 1739.

The canister itself changed its form many times, and we note one from Tudor & Leader, 1777, which was plain oval, with beaded borders and a flat lid, a type often found adorned with bright cut engraving. This was the year that the first fully hallmarked caddy spoons appeared in Sheffield, and although London took up the form and produced more shell bowls than anywhere else, those from Sheffield are quite distinctive as the handles spread from the shell in one piece whereas the London ones were mostly soldered on. The Adam style had, of course, arrived with the shell as one of its major motifs, and while it is probable that the caddy spoon was following this vogue, it is possible that it was intended as a reminder of the shells given away in the original tea chests.

Birmingham silversmiths, as usual, were not slow to follow the fashion and before long were showing their customary inventiveness in producing new styles, and more enterprising versions of the old ones. In fact, the spoons they made were always more delicate and interesting than those of London. Matthew Linwood was not content with modelling fine shells, but also mounted beautiful varieties in silver, generally adding a plain, fiddle pattern handle, using a lovely variety of coloured, translucent or variegated shells. Nor did he confine his output to these, but produced something rather special in every form he attempted. An 1808 snuff-box of his, unfortunately later engraved all over, was double-lidded, a refinement typical of his work.

Like wine labels, caddy spoons appear in such enormous variety that it is not possible to describe them all, and fakes are common as it is all too easy to take a cut-down handle, complete with Georgian marks, and use it with a modern bowl. Nevertheless, they are an ideal subject for the wary collector, and the workmanship on some is magnificent. Obviously, too, they were fun to make, which is why they soon ceased to be really practical. One form that shows this up particularly well is the 'eagle's wing', which originated in Birmingham. Joseph Willmore, a craftsman who gloried in fine detail, made most of these, and the feathers he chased on the back of the bowl, as fine as a lady's fan, continue most realistically on up the neck to end in a sharp beak. His work was always good, and was produced by die casting. Joseph Taylor, another fine Birmingham specialist, made one such spoon, and Matthew Linwood also made a few, but the form was rare.

Less well known was Joseph's father, Thomas Willmore, but he made a unique caddy spoon in the form of a harebell in 1791. This was hand-raised, the wide, bell-shaped bowl being embossed with a whorl of petals and the wire stem ending in a small leaf. It really looks like a flower. Most of his productions were fairly original and well made—a snuff box, dated 1810, was inset with an oval bloodstone—but though they covered the range of small wares, they were less plentiful than those of his son.

The jockey cap caddy spoon was made prolifically, and though the majority came from London, the design was conceived in Birmingham, where a large number were made by Joseph Taylor. Anyone who has ever gone racing will know what a variety of different designs jockeys sport in their headgear, and so it is with these caddy spoons. Yet it is possible to break them down into different types. From Birmingham, (and largely Taylor), came the plain segmented cap, which might be translated to my own 'orange, green stripes', but often with bright cut engraving on the peak and frequently a star motif on the crown. Taylor's workshops were largely responsible for caps with geometric designs, and at least one filigree cap which has never yet graced a racecourse. This was unusual in that Taylor had punched his initials, whereas filigree work usually goes unmarked. Yet he frequently omitted his own stamp on otherwise fully marked jockey caps, which had plenty of room for it. Samuel Pemberton often used filigree panels, while several other Birmingham makers simulated filigree in die-stamped caddy spoons. By and large, one could say that Birmingham examples were generally die-stamped, while those from London were heavier and either plain or lightly engraved, but there was a fair degree of give and take in it.

Little boxes were another feature of Birmingham, but those for tobacco, which always had lift-off lids, were a much earlier form. The ritual of smoking involved sitting at a table, when both hands were available; because snuff might be taken anywhere the lids were hinged. Smaller boxes with lift-off lids were probably patch boxes, and though some were made in Birmingham in the early nineteenth century, notably by Samuel Pemberton, and Cocks & Bettridge, they were not really of importance.

Snuff-taking also had its origins long before the days of the Midlands assay offices, but the habit continues today and the vogue is to keep it in antique snuff-boxes. Thomas Boulsover developed their production in Birmingham, and they came in many shapes and styles. A great number were engine-turned, and Francis Clark, who made them virtually throughout this time, seemed particularly to favour this method. The variety of ornamental styles, and of interpretation within those styles, was endless. Nathanial Mills, one of the best of their makers, sometimes engraved, but generally used die-cast tops in highly pictorial form and of great variety. Many of his boxes were of the popular sporting scene type, and would make excellent presents for hunting or shooting men, though fishing scenes were less common. (Illustration, p 207.) Joseph Willmore made a wonderful box in 1838 decorated all over with rocaille motifs, including, among others, flowers, leaves, a running fox and a group of exotic birds. It would be possible to specialise in collecting these boxes, perhaps creating a series of, for instance, English cathedrals, castles and stately homes; for the railways were by then opening up the country and interest in it was being reflected in almost every art form.

Other small containers were made for all forms of personal possessions, and the Birmingham assay office recently acquired one they believe to have been made for toothpicks by Samuel Pemberton. Their main interest in it is that it bears the date letter 'M' for 1784, so all but completing their collection of the marks in the city's first date cycle (with the exception of 'I' for 1781). This most interesting collection not only shows really representative silver, but also such items as the Boulton papers and pattern books, and the Chester records.

One more type of toy of prime importance to Birmingham was the vinaigrette, and Samuel Pemberton provides a link between objects with his little silver combination of snuff box and vinaigrette, the box being divided to serve its dual purpose. Vinaigrettes, or 'body fresheners', started life in Roman times as pomanders, but the custom of using perfumes to counter the smell of unwashed bodies or to fumigate against infection goes back to about 1800 BC. Some thousands of vinaigrettes were produced in Birmingham from the close of the eighteenth century onwards and their shapes encompassed the widest conceivable range. From acorns and strawberries to miniature guns; hearts and crosses, bellows and bottles and books, anything and everything was realistically produced, though the decoration on those which remained basically boxes followed the all-embracing pictorial lines of the snuff boxes. The same names stand out, but the manufacture of vinaigrettes involved an additional and intricate factor—the grille.

These little containers, which could be worn hanging from a belt, concealed in the bosom, or held in the hand, were heavily gilt inside to prevent tarnishing by the spiced vinegars they held, and to allow the scent to do its work a hinged grille was placed inside them. At first these were plainly punched, but the inventive Birmingham manufacturers soon pierced these grills with all the pictorial imagination at their command. Dainty, light, with a tightly fitting and equally well-hinged lid, they really were a source of pride, and never-failing surprise, far outclassing the somewhat prosaic types made in London, virtually the only other centre of production.

These are but a sample of the small wares of Birmingham, but they are good examples which took the city creditably through a period of elaborate silver, and perforce, restrained exuberance in the large way. Sheffield, without this major influence, really enjoyed the general jumble of ornamentation, but one of her designers, James Dixon, showed that good and simple silver could still be made. Unfortunately, such work was rare.

Meanwhile, G. R. Elkington, of Birmingham, had been working out a new process for electro-plating, and in 1842 his firm took out a patent for this work. Just as fused plate had caused a revolution by its new and simplified method of coating copper with silver before use, so Elkington's development of electrical action for applying silver or gold, evenly and firmly, to base metals after they had been made up, once more upset the accepted standards. By this time the use of the spinner for silver was normal; piercing machines could produce galleries by the mile, and machinery generally could perform most of the necessary actions quickly and easily. To produce the best work still required added fine handwork, but other objects could be stamped out whole. The new process was able to reduce costs still further by using a cheap material instead of precious metal, before hanging it in an electrical bath. At the end of a specified time it was removed and, hey presto! all was silver.

Initial reluctance to take out licences to use the new process was short-lived. The savings made possible were enormous, particularly in the monumental sculptural works then in vogue. Firms produced gargantuan centrepieces in electro-plate as proudly as craftsmen had previously shown silver.

The vogue for naturalism, in all its vulgarity, gave way after this exhibition to a more Romanesque form of classicism, and although ornament was on the whole still too much and too heavy, the improvement in taste and workmanship was marked. At this stage Elkington, who considered himself the rightful heir to Boulton, really justified his claims. In 1851 his work had been unsurpassed, even by London, but that was a time of exceptionally low ebb in English art. Now, employing the best designers wherever they came from, he showed work at the International Exhibition of 1862 that displayed an elegance missing from the heavy, self-consciously Roman work of many of his rivals. He was not alone, for Dixon & Sons also produced fine work, some of it in silver, as did Thomas Bradbury & Sons of Sheffield, and many others. Yet none of them was incapable of heavy, over-ornate work, which was just as bad in London.

But this is a book on antique silver, and although Birmingham and Sheffield carried the provincial flag through the Victorian period and are now demonstrating a new era of fine workmanship and design, these more recent products have no real place here. Birmingham had shown that silver need not be in the grand manner to be of the very best, and there can be no city where more was made that is within the range of the modest collector, or which is so well worth collecting.

Through the years there were a few idiosyncracies in the marking of silver in these assay offices. In Sheffield, between 1780 and 1853, small wares often incorporated the crown mark and the date letter in the same stamp, oblong, or oval, either alongside, or one above the other. From 1815 to 1819 the crown was often placed upside down, a useful aid to dating when the date letter is rubbed. Even more exact, from July 1797 to April 1798, the duty mark of the sovereign's head was struck twice to show the increased duty. For the first two years, 1784 and 1785, this mark was stamped in intaglio instead of relief, giving more the impression of a seal.

The double use of the sovereign's head was also a feature of Birmingham marking. In Sheffield, from 1798 to 1810, the punch followed the outline of the sovereign's head. Birmingham might strike its anchor vertically or horizontally, according to whim, and when the higher standard was used, they struck Britannia without the addition of the lion's head erased.

# Nine

# Ireland

A mere glimpse at the work of Ireland's Celtic goldsmiths is as tantalising as a guided tour with no time for browsing. But what is the alternative? To wax lyrical? Or to indulge in stylised description? Either would fill a book, and the craft in Ireland was of continuing richness, sufficient for many volumes.

An organised farming community in the Bronze Age led to a prosperity that allowed gold to be mined in the Wicklow mountains and tin to be imported from Cornwall to blend with their native copper to make bronze. They used this magnificently in bronze artefacts which demonstrate the high standards of early Irish culture as clearly as do the gold torcs, earrings, bracelets, collars and other ornaments dating from 2000–1500 BC which have been dug up, often in bogs, all over Ireland.

By the time the Tara brooch was made, probably about AD 800, thousands of years of perfecting the goldsmith's art and its techniques had gone by. This gold brooch was dug up on the beach near Drogheda, on the Boyne estuary, in 1850. Reminiscent of the magnificent Irish manuscripts of the time, with an elaborate design worked out in minute detail, it is unique in being as carefully decorated on the back as on the front and pin. Ireland had been left in comparative peace, an atmosphere conducive to art, until a large Viking fleet arrived on the Boyne in AD 837 and fanned out inland on foraging expeditions. It is easy to imagine one of these marauders dropping the Tara brooch on the sand as he struggled towards his ship, laden with loot; this may have been one of many, for several other such brooches survive.

Silver entered the story about the fifth century AD for the decoration of sacred vessels, and at first was often used in conjunction with other

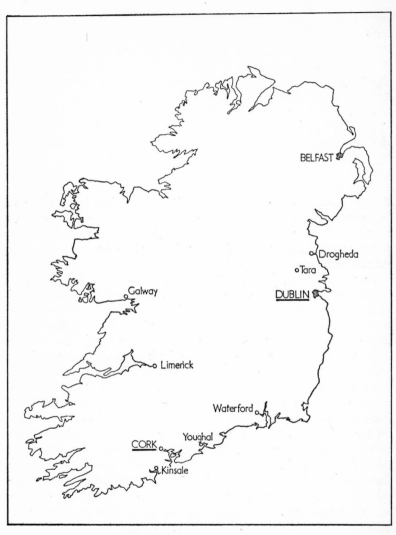

Silver-making centres in Ireland

metals. The early eighth-century Ardagh chalice is the first and finest such vessel to survive. This is a magnificent two-handled silver bowl, richly decorated with a band of interlacing gold filigree punctuated with blue and red glass with inset silver grilles, the names of the apostles being lightly incised below against a stipple background. Other studs of silver patterned coloured glass drop below the wonderful handles, while exquisitely decorated gold roundels on the side of the cup carry the eye down to the intricate spiral and interlacing patterns of the gilded, cast bronze stem which separates the body from the cone foot set on a flat, richly decorated rim. Full description of any elaborate piece clouds the mind's eye, yet this chalice is so perfectly balanced that it gives an impression of simple, uncluttered lines, and is one of the first things to look for when visiting the National Museum of Ireland in Dublin. Yet its full glory cannot be appreciated within a glass case, for underneath the foot a crystal knob is set among zones of further elaborate decoration. The wealth of metals used, particularly on the rim of the foot, is astounding and includes patterned silver foil, coloured glass, and woven silver and copper wires.

The centuries fly by, and almost everything for the church was made in glorious profusion. The Irish craftsman at his best could teach the world, with his unmatched ability to transfer all that he felt to metal, elegant but strong, stylised and sometimes formal, yet capable of expressing wit, fantasy and mystique with equal clarity. Reliquaries of every sort were made, so detailed in the story they tell that a long scrutiny is like reading a book. Naturally enough, one such shrine was made for all that remained of St Patrick—his bell, and when this patron saint died, that symbol of his life's work was buried with him. Later, because people wanted something to touch which had belonged to the saint, it was removed from the tomb. Many other such bells were housed in beautiful shrines, but this one, made in about AD 1100, if not necessarily the finest was the most precious because of its connections. Basically of brass, with silver, gold and enamelled plaques riveted to it, the front is richly decorated with thirty-one different gold panels with interlacing scrolls, knotworks of golden filigree, and sparkling coloured gems. The sides show scrolls of elongated animals, and the back is overlaid with silver plate of cruciform pattern.

The Cross of Cong, c 1123, is one of the earliest known processional crosses, with fine gold filigree work on basic copper and brass. It shows fine workmanship, but some of the croziers made at that time were even more intricate, for the Irish, who had not abandoned their old Celtic techniques lightly, also clung to Anglo-Saxon ways after the passing of the period. And why not? They were their own masters, beholden to no one for patterns and styles, and had no reason for giving up their own specialities which, in Anglo-Saxon times, included trumpet spirals of interlacing ribbon animals. The Limerick crozier of 1418, 7ft high and weighing 10lb, may have been the largest but, however magnificent, it was by no means the finest, for by that time early Irish craftsmanship had passed its peak.

Domestic silver had entered the picture with the coming of the Normans, but as none survives church plate alone remains to show the standards maintained. Several fine chalices exist and one the earliest, probably made in Galway, is in the National Museum of Ireland. This has a plain, bell-shaped bowl and an octagonal stem, with panels of Gothic tracery; a richly chased eight-lobed wrythen knop with eight projecting diamond-shaped knots, originally enamelled, and an in-curved octagonal pointed foot with concave, chamfered sides. The whole is silver gilt, and around the foot, in Gothic lettering, is an inscription that includes the donor's name, Thomas de Burgo, and the date, 1494, surrounding the sacred monogram 'I h c'.

An interesting feature is that while this and some other chalices in Ireland used the octagonal form, those of the same period in England favoured the hexagonal. The Irish were ever original: another from County Fermanagh, 1529, has an octagonal foot with a hexagonal stem and knot; the mixture is typically Irish but others, with the hexagonal foot, had round stems.

A chalice at the Augustinian church in Dublin provides an interesting connection with the earlier Galway cup, for its inscription also includes the name 'de Burgo', and the date 1648. It was by no means the last, for the de Burgo family, now called Burke, founded a friary in County Galway in the fourteenth century, which was destroyed by fire during the Elizabethan wars. Nothing daunted, the de Burgo family rebuilt it in the seventeenth century and continued donating cups until 1730.

Irish chalices changed little at a time when those in England did so radically, even the 'Burke' chalice of 1730 being of much the same rather disproportionate style as that of 1648, the tall, outspreading concave foot being larger than the small, bell-shaped bowl. This foot, with a rounded sexfoil base, is engraved with a crucifixion, and a fleur-de-lys above the angles of its base moulding, but the stem is octagonal.

Anglican communion cups varied in style, and were mostly very different from the English normal, often being very tall, with a stem almost as wide as the bowl and foot. For all their difference, there was nothing very Irish about them, but quantities were made, for the same reasons as in England, by makers otherwise unknown, as well as by the big names.

Chalices were more typical, and Richard Joyce of Galway made several which can now be seen in Dublin's museum. All of his were rather charming and inscribed by a donor, or in memory, a typical example being, 'Pray for Pat$^k$ Prendergas and his wife Mary Ann, who ordered ys to be made, 1725'. Such dedications alone date many of these pieces.

Hardeman's *History of Galway* refers to a goldsmith as early as 1500, but no marks have been found before the 'RI' in a square, standing alone, on the 1648 chalice at the Augustinian church. Richard Joyce sometimes stamped his 'RI' in a shaped shield, but on his Prendergas chalice it is punched twice in a square, identical with the earlier mark,

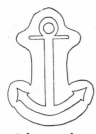

Galway anchor

the anchor mark of Galway in a shaped shield between them. Joyce, even then, was an old Galway name, and with goldsmiths long established in the town, it seems safe to assume that Richard's father, or grandfather, was the goldsmith who made the 1648 cup. That the museum describes the 1494 chalice as 'probably Galway', means that proof is lacking, but wishful thinking is permissible and it is just possible that a Joyce could have made it.

Hardiman tells us that Richard Joyce was captured by Algerian pirates in his youth and sold as a slave to a Moorish goldsmith, from whom he learned his craft. He was considered so good that the Moor, when ordered to release Joyce by William III after fourteen years captivity, offered him his only daughter in marriage and half his property if he would stay. Ireland was the richer by his refusal, but it certainly was an unusual apprenticeship. Like most Irish goldsmiths, his marking was somewhat erratic and he did not always punch the Galway anchor.

Joyce eventually took Mark Fallon into partnership and several chalices are marked 'MF', with or without the anchor, the last being for 1731. He had a brother, Bartholomew Fallon, whose initials appear on a particularly fine chalice dated 1683, but he is more notable for having made the only tankard with a Galway mark, c 1680, now in a private Dublin collection. This is very fine, with a scroll thumbpiece and well-engraved arms on its large body, which holds 3½ pints. His initials and the anchor mark in a shaped punch are stamped on the body and lid. A pair of Dublin tankards of 1680, decorated at the base with alternate acanthus and palm leaves, were referred to as 'tankers'; there were also fine Cork examples at the time.

The National Museum of Ireland also has a large and magnificent tankard and cover by William Wall of Kinsale, 1720, whose mark was a plain 'w', sometimes within a heart. The names of goldsmiths had been recorded in this County Cork harbour town intermittently from about 1687, including those of Joseph and William Wall, but very little of their work appears to have survived. Nevertheless, a fine mug made by one of the Wall brothers in 1710 appeared for sale in 1967. Beautifully engraved, a magnificent coat of arms surrounded by scrolling foliate mantling, with a helmet and crest above, fills the whole front of the tapered cylindrical body, which is set on a moulded base. It is not very big, 4½in high, and weighs only 8oz 14dwt, but its scroll handle has a beaded rat tail and initials, and it is marked on the body and handle. Jackson had found this 'w' mark from Kinsale only twice, on a punch ladle of 1700 and on wavy-ended spoons of 1710, but a rat-tail table spoon, struck with 'w' four times, appeared in the same 1967 sale engraved with initials and the date 1721 on its terminal.

Another very rare Irish mark was the single-masted sailing ship, known as a yawl, stamped on silver made at Youghal—pronounced like the ship—where goldsmiths probably worked from early times until about 1720. The mark Jackson gave for Belfast, very like the red hand of Ulster, was actually stamped in Malta, and if silver was ever made in the north it was probably sent to Dublin for assay.

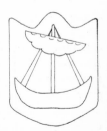

Youghal mark

Dublin certainly had goldsmiths working by AD 1200, and a guild by 1498; in 1555 they petitioned for a new charter, their old one having been

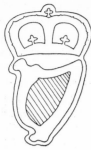

Harp crowned

burnt, but although this was granted it was not until 1605 that the use of marks was suggested. It is on record that these marks consisted of a lion, harp and castle, together with maker's mark, but there is no record of their ever having been seen. Dublin's assay history really began in 1637, when the city goldsmiths were granted a royal charter setting out laws stipulating the same standards as for London plate. This standard was to be shown by the mark of a harp crowned, the plate also being stamped with the maker's mark, usually his initials often in an involved form. The date letter was added a year later, 'Hibernia' appearing only in 1730.

Irish silver marked before 1730 is rare, and a communion cup in Trinity College, Dublin, is almost unique for its date letter 'A' of 1638. The reason is not hard to find, for in 1642 £12,000 worth of plate was melted down for coin 'to supply the exigencies of state', and this must have represented a very high proportion. Production picked up again in the 'nineties after yet another war, and a domestic porringer, Dublin c 1659, unique in its strange flat-bottomed style, is also unusual because the few items made in those meagre days were mostly for church use.

Fine work was done after 1690, and can occasionally be bought—at a price. A salver with a raised moulded rim, well-engraved armorials and a capstan foot, made by an unidentified craftsman between 1693 and 1695, went through the saleroom in 1967. It is interesting to note how little these salvers changed through the years. After about 1730 the central spreading foot gave way to three supports, very often in the form of hoof feet. Rims varied somewhat in the eighteenth and early nineteenth centuries, often being shell and scroll, gadrooned or something more ambitious, but the basic circular pattern (occasionally square) with central arms, rim and feet almost never took an additional ornament.

The great days in Dublin were approaching when Thomas Bolton, whose work is so well represented in the United States, was warden for the first time in 1690 and master in 1692–3; to be followed by David King in 1696, and Joseph Walker, both of whom made many salvers, in 1697. All went on to enhance reputations they had already established. Others were less well known. John Humphreys became a freeman in 1685, was warden from 1695 until he became master in 1698, yet never held office again and disappeared from the scene altogether in 1704. Something must have gone wrong, but between 1693 and 1695 Henry Sydney, Earl of Romney, who had achieved almost every conceivable appointment and honour, commissioned him to make a silver gilt ewer and basin in keeping with his immense importance. Together, these pieces weighed 350 oz, the largest example of Irish silver surviving, yet despite its size this enormous circular dish is simplicity itself, plain except for a moulded gadroon border and a central coat of arms. The helmet-shaped ewer, almost a foot high, is dwarfed beside it, and is also of uncluttered appearance with ample space for cut-card foliage below a moulded band near the base of the plain bowl, and another moulded band just below the neat little spout chased with a shell. The harp handle has leaf decoration and two beaded rat-tails, and there is a circular gadrooned foot and bell-shaped stem with a gadroon knop above. It is a magnificent piece, tastefully balanced, and was sold for £12,000 in 1969.

Thomas Bolton has magnificent ewers of the period in both the Metropolitan Museum of Art, New York, and the Museum of Fine Arts, Boston, while another of the same shape, 1702, was seen for sale recently, engraved on the front with the full armorials of Queen Anne. Bolton certainly was the master, but helmet ewers of the period by other makers do appear from time to time.

Another piece by Thomas Bolton, 1696, was sold in 1964, showing that a long purse has no date barriers. This was a baluster-shaped urn with a fluted baluster finial and stem on a bell-shaped foot. The decoration, well separated by unadorned spaces allowing its beauty to show, consists of alternate bands of acanthus leaves and spiral fluting, the foot having a gadroon border. The crest, engraved on the body, shows a cock, and there is a most amusing cock spigot standing out from the body. Such balance was an Irish feature, master craftsmen always allowing plain surfaces to highlight the quality of decoration.

During this period the goldsmiths of Cork were producing plate of at least equal standard. Some Swiss Protestant refugees, set up in 1784 at New Geneva, Co Waterford, by a government anxious to encourage them, were the only company outside Dublin ever to be authorised to run their own assay office, but lack of a charter never inhibited the craftsmen of Cork despite their repeated requests for one. It seems certain that silver had been wrought for centuries in Cork, which had rich silver mines not far away, but it was not until 1631 that King Charles I granted them the 'same privileges as those enjoyed by Youghal', the only recognition they ever achieved. Surviving records date only from 1656—some having been destroyed by fire in 1891—in which year they formed a guild with members of other trades. From that date, in theory, they stamped their work with a three-masted galleon between two castles, and the maker's mark. In fact, this was rarely used correctly but is seen occasionally, stamped twice, between the maker's punch, also twice. As a mark, it broke up well into varying

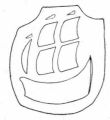

Cork galleon

permutations; the ship alone twice, with maker's mark, one, between them; the maker's mark only, three times; the maker's mark and a castle alone, both stamped twice, alternately; one castle, with one maker's mark; maker's mark, castle alone, ship alone, castle again. After about 1692, the ship drops out and the castle changes shape repeatedly until the word 'sterling' appears for the first time in 1710, with both the ship and the castle stamped separately. No wonder people thought it a good idea, and from then on the word, in endless forms, appears with the maker's mark alone. No date letter was ever used, and as the goldsmiths of Limerick also used a similar castle before changing to the word 'sterling', the situation is somewhat involved. Silver, often distinctive enough as Irish, had no regional peculiarities by which Cork or Limerick work could be known, but the word 'sterling' was spelt 'starlin' more often in Limerick. Kurt Ticher, Irish master detective where marks are concerned, has found the lion rampant in varying shields between maker's initials sufficiently often on mid- eighteenth-century Limerick silver to conclude that this was used there as a standard mark. Lack of it proves nothing, but when present it is a great help.

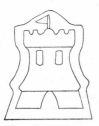

Cork castle

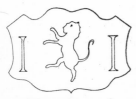

Lion rampant of Limerick

Records of goldsmiths in each place are the only other indication of origin providing that a maker remembered to stamp his work—but it is more likely to be Cork, where very much more silver was made than at Limerick, and generally of higher quality.

Even makers' marks were incredibly varied. Robert Goble of Cork, for instance, not only punched his own mark in six or seven different ways but also rang the changes with every conceivable permutation of castles or ships. Such a superlative craftsman, one of Ireland's finest, could afford to do what he liked, and if he was not the first to give Cork a name synonymous with the highest quality, he certainly did more than his bit to keep it there. Warden in 1672, he lived till 1719, and a surprising amount of his work survives, ranging through every type of silver even including teaspoons. The mace he made for the trade guilds of Cork in 1696, now in the Victoria and Albert Museum, London, would alone require pages of description to do it justice.

Richard Smart was one of the earliest to set Cork's standards, and the recent sale of a large porringer and cover, c 1675, was an exciting event. It is not an outstanding piece, but the truly Irish mixture of flowers, foliage and an elephant carrying a small castle, embossed on its bulging sides, is most attractive. Charles Begheagle (or Bekegle), a Dutch immigrant and warden in 1693, was considered by Jackson to have been superior to Robert Goble—if you forget the mace, which is impossible. Certainly the porringer he made about 1697, heavily embossed with fruit, flowers and foliage, is a magnificent piece typical of the period. A large eagle stands guard over the fruit; a high-domed lid continues the idiom until fluting and a baluster finial take over, and the harp handles draw the eye, diminishing the heavy effect.

The production of Irish silver increased all through the eighteenth century, the greatest quantity appearing in the last quarter and the finest quality in the first half, when Irish craftsmen stood second only to London—according to London. In 1810 the 70,000 oz stamped in Dublin were only fractionally below peak, but this had fallen to a mere 6,000 oz in 1835, and nineteenth-century Irish work was considerably less significant.

Marking was always somewhat haphazard, the date letter often being omitted and the maker's mark surprisingly so. In 1730 the mark known as 'Hibernia', showing a seated woman with a harp and olive branch, was also stamped to indicate duty paid of 6d per ounce. Recently, the vagueness surrounding dates on so many Irish pieces has been alleviated by a book which analyses the researches of Kurt Ticher on the harp crowned and Hibernia marks. Both were altered in detail almost annually, but this masterly summary places each shape in its proper year so that when both marks are clearly stamped dates can now be accurately deduced.

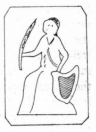

Hibernia mark

The Britannia standard was never enforced in Ireland, and there were no special marks at that period, though the sovereign's head was introduced in 1806 to bring Irish silver into line with English. Hibernia, serving the same purpose, should then have been dropped, but having become a symbol was retained. Nevertheless, neither the harp nor Hibernia, often thought of as 'Irish' marks, was ever used outside Dublin. Limerick sometimes used a trefoil mark on spoons between 1780 and 1820 but, again, absence of this mark proves nothing. An Act of 1807 reinforced the charter of 1637 which, in theory, had given Dublin full control of all silver marking in Ireland. No notice had been taken then, but circumstances changed with improved transport and by 1824 the craft in Limerick and Cork, the only survivors, had petered out.

Ireland, as a rule, was little influenced by Continental styles, generally following London, often in a distinctively Irish way, and when a form suited them they continued with it long after it had been dropped in England. Sometimes they mixed styles, adding a bit of their own, and occasionally they produced a style before London. An Irish candlestick in the Victoria and Albert Museum, by Joseph Walker, in 1704, has an octagonal faceted base little different from those made in England after 1715, its stem using the octagonal form usual in London at the time but in its own distinctive manner. Another pair by the same maker, 1706, had an identical base but was utterly different with its conventional octagonal stem, which London was then using on a round base. A set of four by John Hamilton, 1730, had a round base, by then long discarded in London, as did a pair of 1737, showing a distinct time lag. But this pair had detachable nozzles fully five years before such things were seen in London, and the identical marks on the sticks and on each of the strangely enclosed tubes proves them to be contemporary.

Looking closely at all the varying styles in candlesticks through the century, very few other distinctions emerge, except that English marks were usually out of sight, while Irish marks were generally placed in the well, or on the side of the base. In rococo and the Adam style, Ireland definitely lagged, and while it is tempting to describe outstanding exceptions, such as a set of six by Robert Calderwood, c 1750, in the Ashmolean Museum, Oxford, there are other items more specific in their national differences. Nor must we fall for the urge to describe things like the lovely wager cup, c 1706, in the Victoria and Albert Museum, exceptional though it is, or the Mead Cup in Irwin Untermyer's New York collection, for these, like many other products of Irish imagination, are unique.

Two-handled cups, generally without the covers usual in England, were very much an Irish speciality typical of their simplification of styles. Thomas Bolton made a conventional porringer type, 1693, now in Boston, with cut card work radiating from the base and on the lid, but David King took this form through its transition, producing a two-handled cup of porringer dimensions in 1696 decorating its lower half with narrow vertical convex flutes. Then, in 1707, he produced a cup from which the Irish favourite developed, a cup with two harp handles and a domed lid with a high finial. Harp handles, incidentally, were occasionally used elsewhere—by copyists.

The Irish Queen Anne two-handled cup had a bell-shaped bowl surrounded by an applied band, above which arms were engraved, often at a later date, to leaf-capped harp, or double scroll handles, and a rim foot. By 1720, the foot might be a little higher, and the applied band was triple moulded, or reeded. Styles changed little, and Limerick makers excelled, producing well-made cups of solid worth, pleasant on the eye and wonderful in the hand. Joseph Johns made several, one c 1720 and another c 1730, being a little larger but otherwise indistinguishable from a Dublin example of 1735. Size was the most variable feature, for although they evolved a little, older styles were still used occasionally. By the end of the century, the foot had become generally higher, often pedestal or even trumpet-shaped, and the body was often baluster. Matthew Walsh of Limerick made one of these in 1790, and Matthew West, of Dublin, another in 1787 using a gadrooned band, in addition. Nevertheless, the old form continued to be used, as a look at any exhibition of racing trophies will show.

England had abandoned this simple style by about 1720, and the typical Irish cup, with its lovely patina on a flat surface, was unfortunately an open invitation to later spoilers, who delighted in decorating them. Irish makers did attempt rococo on a few of these cups later on, and continued with it after the phase had passed in England, but such pieces were not typical of Ireland and should be viewed with suspicion. It is only necessary to look at a few catalogues to see how often the words 'chased later' appear. The form eventually changed and in 1795 George West, of Dublin, produced a pair that were normal for the time, with baluster bodies and no band, set on trumpet bases with reeded rims.

Further evidence of Ireland's preference for simplicity of design is clearly seen in their strawberry dishes, the larger ones intended for serving soft fruit, and the smaller ones for individual portions. The majority of those seen in London sales were made between 1710 and 1726 by a variety of well-known makers, including Thomas Bolton, David King, Matthew Walker, William Archdall and Philip Kinnersley. (Illustration, p 208.) These simple, round dishes with their upward curved fluted sides and a crest or full armorials engraved centrally, are simplicity itself, yet give a great feeling of solid worth. A few made in England at the time were similar except for steeper sides, but the majority are Irish. They vary from about 10in in diameter with up to thirty-two flutes, to small twelve-fluted dishes of only 4½in diameter. Sometimes the scalloped edge is wavy, often simply curved, but none is of the more ornate style found in England at a later date. A strawberry dish with twenty flutes, by Robert Harrison of Dublin, 1720, was given to the First Church, Boston, in 1905, the only piece of Irish silver in a New England church.

Dinner plates were usually of the same very fine, uncluttered quality. A set by Robert Calderwood, 1775, very similar to those of William Williamson, 1748, exemplify Irish standards and show how little a good thing changed. These plates, 9¾in in diameter, have nicely shaped gadrooned rims in perfect balance, with armorials beautifully engraved on the border, which is otherwise plain.

Beakers in the second half of the century were also normally plain, usually cylindrical in shape and sometimes with an everted lip and crest engraved. In America they did double duty in church and home, whereas in Ireland these small vessels were purely domestic utensils.

Nevertheless, it is the round bowl that personifies the plain idiom in

Irish silver, for these heavy bowls were so well made in Dublin and Cork in the reign of George I that they were still being copied in the nineteenth century, although in lighter form and lacking the planishing of hand-raised work. Some simply had a thick upper edge on a plain low rim foot, while others, such as Robert Calderwood's, 1729, used a simple moulded upper edge and similar foot. Dorothy Monjoy, 1730, deviated from this by using the moulded edge and plain rim foot, but variety generally depended on depth and width.

By mid-century these bowls had become wider in proportion to depth, and were set on a low baluster foot. They were still usually plain, but David King, who had made a montieth in 1715, always rare in Ireland, engraved arms and scroll mantling on one of these bowls in 1727. Even his montieth had been unadorned, except for scrolls and strapwork pendants outlining its detachable rim, until later spoilers set to work on it.

Engraving of arms became more usual, but the bowl changed little for years to come. One by William Townsend, c 1740, shows that the foot was lifting a little, while Andrew Goodwin, c 1748, gave more importance to the arms on a larger bowl, always well engraved in Dublin. By 1760 they were wider in proportion to depth, and this graceful shape, on a moulded pedestal foot, was perfected by John Williamson of Dublin in the truly Irish school of imaginative decoration, refuting any allegation that rococo was not understood in Ireland. This delight has repoussé and chased scrolls, flowers, fruit and dolphins standing out from clear spaces so that their beauty can clearly be seen, enclosing on one side a scene of two pheasants beneath a tree, and on the other a heron preening itself.

John, one of at least four Williamsons upholding the good name of Dublin's goldsmiths during the second quarter of the eighteenth century, was a master of Irish rococo. A cake basket of his, c 1755, mixes scrolls, flowers and leaves in exquisite taste creating an effect of light and beauty, despite its heavy weight and solid workmanship. Flowers of several varieties stand out on the body, left clear by piercing; they are moulded on the magnificent rim, chased on the feet, and even appear in the hair of the pretty faces that would officially be described as masks above them. Scrolls and shells are worked into the design in perfect balance, and the swing handle somehow gives an air of simplicity, despite a really complicated design. (Illustration, p 156.)

Cake baskets made a perfect compromise between the Irish speciality of piercing and rococo, a mixture incompatible with the heavy effect possible with over-elaboration on such things as coffee pots. A cake basket by John Hamilton, c 1745, with a shaped moulded rim, putto masks and shell motifs, pleases only slightly less than the 'flower' basket, but while actually less decorated, it gives a heavier appearance. Another, by Richard Williams, c 1760, pierced with diaper, flowerhead and scroll designs, gives a dainty effect but lacks the Irish imagination of John Williamson's gem, a basket that makes concentration on any other difficult.

Mr Charles Oman, late Keeper of Metalwork at the Victoria and Albert Museum and a leading authority on silver, names Stephen Walsh, who made a tea caddy in their collection, as a goldsmith with a deeper understanding of rococo than average in Ireland. Judith Bannister, in her popular book, *An Introduction to Old English Silver*, describes a fine covered jug by William Williamson, 1736, as exhibiting the flamboyance of rococo chasing in its restrained Irish form, with its beautiful contrasts of plain curved surfaces with chased decoration. But for me, John Williamson produced the most pleasing silver of all.

One of the delights of these makers was their ability to change to the plain style, relying upon line and good workmanship for effect. The coffee pot of Ireland was remarkable only for its large size and, like chocolate pots and everything to do with the tea table, they went through the gamut of styles, following on in their own leisurely way. Some of them were very fine indeed; some plain ones, unfortunately, were chased later, but others were a perfect medium for the craftsman with an insufficient understanding of his art. Rococo, descending in taste from not bad to appalling, can be seen on these objects, in which bad rococo is often confused with a little-understood classicism. Luckily such things are rare in a country known for its good work.

The same remarks could apply to jugs, but the average mid-century beer jug was normally of plain baluster form, with moulded lip and short spout standing on a pedestal foot. When they have harp handles it is not difficult to understand why the word 'Irish' springs to mind on sight, but with any other simple handle the effect is the same, and it seems impossible to explain why, for this type was also made in England. Armorials often appear boldly under the spout on both.

Earlier jugs had a lid, those in England showing contemporary decoration, while the Irish were generally plain. Thomas Bolton made a slightly baluster jug set on a moulded foot in 1704. A beaded rat-tail runs down the handle from the scroll thumbpiece, and mouldings fall in diminishing sizes from the spout; it is otherwise plain, with only a small crest.

It is quite fortuitous that the choice of an exceptional jug, photographed in Irwin Untermyer's New York collection, should again be by John Williamson, 1736. This slender jug is basically of the form described, but has a lid and an amusing devil's mask covering the spout. It is most beautifully chased and engraved on its lid and on the upper part of the back of its wonderfully made handle. The body is mainly left plain, but engraving surrounds the junctions of the handle, and just below the rim a glowering face unexpectedly appears amid the light and delicate strokes, the appearance of a bird here and there coming as less of a surprise.

The Adam period, beginning only in about 1780 in Ireland and continuing long after it had ceased in England, was very well expressed on later jugs, where the pendant drapes, festoons, flutes and scrolls found natural expression. There was nothing very different about the way this style was used in Ireland, but it was employed prolifically and well for a long time on tureens, candlesticks, teapots and all other forms suited to it. Much of it, however, was still distinctively Irish, and examples of this period of decoration are to be seen in almost every Georgian house in Dublin.

Mid-century Irish sugar bowls share one typical feature with creamers and some sauceboats—three feet—and while these are seen often enough in English work, there is no mistaking the origin of those made in Ireland. Round sugar bowls with a flaring lip, about 5in across, with lion's mask and paw feet, were generally quite plain to start with, but later took on a great variety of embossed decoration which rather detracted from the effect of the masks. Nevertheless, John Hamilton refutes generalisation with a bowl chased with scrolls, shells and flowers, which also appear on the rim, made as early as 1740. On this he confounds theory further by using female heads as masks for his three feet, a practice more usual in the provinces, particularly Cork, whereas Dublin craftsmen in the main preferred a lion's mask, or shells, above paw or shell feet.

By about 1760 sugar bowls, which occasionally took other less

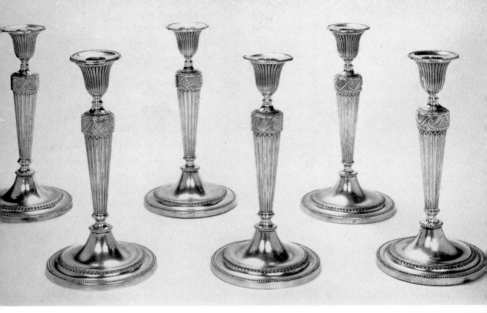

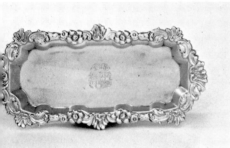

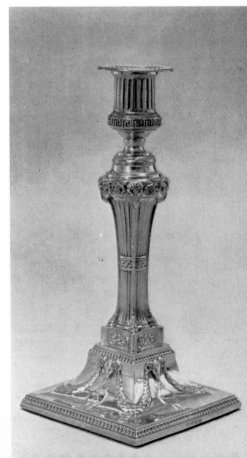

*age* 189 (*above*) Set of six table candlesticks, in high, by John Winter & Co, of Sheffield, 780; (*centre*) one of a pair of pen trays by John d Thomas Settle, Sheffield, 1825; (*right*) a ndlestick by G. Ashforth & Co, Sheffield, 1774, ne of the earliest to be marked with the crown, en on the base

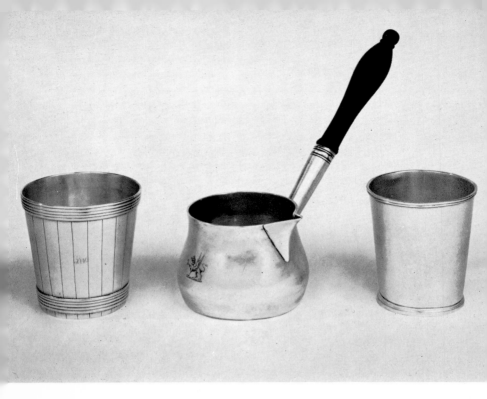

*Page* 190   Chester concentrated mainly on small objects. The beaker (*above*) 3in high, is typic?
Richard Richardson, 1748; brandy saucepan by George Walker, 1790, and plain beaker by R?
Boulger, 1802; (*below*) still all Chester. Chamber candlestick (*left*) by George Lowe, 1823; G?
Walker's oval cream boat, (*centre*) and a typical Chester mug (*right*) by Richard Richardson,

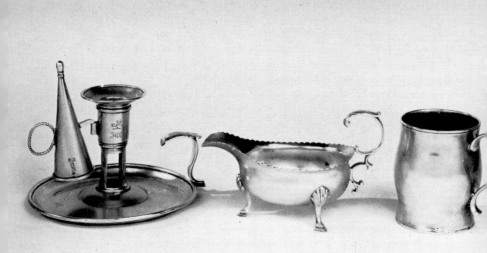

definable forms, often had deeply incised flutes, curved or straight, widely separated on the same shape bowl, and sometimes with beads on or below the lip. These were particularly favoured in Limerick, where Joseph Johns excelled. By 1775 these flutes, spiralling in the case of John Nicolson of Cork, also had foliate motifs between them; George Hodder, one of Cork's major Georgians, had used an upright line of 'v's' between flutes as early as 1750.

Helmet-shaped cream jugs are even more distinctively Irish, with their waved rim, double scroll handle, occasionally leaf-capped, three feet and triple encircling band. The feet appear with human masks in Dublin, as in Cork and Limerick, nearly as often as lion's mask or shell feet. Embossing, which appeared on some jugs, any time between 1745 and 1780, varied with the skill of its application and showed the usual shells, scrolls, flowers, dolphins, or more imaginative forms. Sometimes they were not so overwhelming as to hide the effect of the masks and band, one by Jonathon Buck of Cork, 1764, being of a particularly high standard.

These jugs were generally larger than their English counterparts, with particularly generous lips to control the flow of thick Irish cream, and are easy to recognise by their encircling band, which was used nowhere else. Around 1750, this was invariably triple moulded, but the size of both the band and the lip had diminished somewhat by 1770. At that time the incised curved flutes, already seen on the sugar bowls and found only in Ireland, occasionally appeared on the lower part of these lovely, very Irish, creamers.

The Victoria and Albert Museum has two of these with lion's mask and paw feet, one plain and the other nicely chased. Both were made in 1760 by William Hughes, one of the many Irish goldsmiths who later went to America, setting up his workshops in Baltimore. He had become a freeman of Dublin in 1767 and, like Philip Syng of Cork who emigrated in 1714, contributed to the American heritage both with the silver he made and the native apprentices he trained.

It is less easy to define the Irish characteristics of sauceboats, for while a boat with three lion mask feet, leaf-capped flying scroll handle and wavy rim is very likely to be Irish, c 1760, particularly if chased all over, it could equally have been made in London. A useful pointer is the fact that the third foot is generally set under the lip in Ireland, while in those made in England it is placed under the handle. Dolphin head

M                                               191

and similar handles were more often English but the Irish did break out exuberantly at times. Then handles might take any form, such as female busts, particularly in Cork where the most cherubic faces sometimes languish under the catalogue description 'human masks'. Irish silver has to be seen to be believed, for some of its features are too charming for cold description.

An exceptionally attractive sauceboat by Mark Fallon of Galway, c 1730, is quite plain, with a very wide lip similar to that on a Dublin example of 1737 which had delightful trefoil heads to its three scroll legs with hoof feet. Later examples frequently had punched beading under the rim, with or without chasing—a style favoured by Ambrose Boxwell, for one—while the lip gradually became longer and less wide. A pair of exceptional quality from Cork, c 1790, had this long lip, but the low bowls were themselves almost completely round, giving an utterly different effect despite the three lion's mask feet.

The Irish undoubtedly made a feature of feet, a circular salt cellar, c 1740, for instance, having four goat's mask and hoof feet joined by festoons of flowers. Another a set of three by Joseph Johns of Limerick, c 1760, with gadrooned rims, is chased with flowers and scrolls and has three scroll legs with shell heads and feet. Far more unusual is a coconut cup decorated with a rim and three lion's mask feet only, a design very different in appearance from the old mounted coconuts of England and made only between 1730 and 1750 in Dublin.

Such unusual pieces, though fun to find, are not really representative of Irish silver, whereas dish rings are. These, sometimes wrongly called 'potato' rings, were intended to be placed on the table to protect the surface from damage by a succession of hot dishes. They had been made in a small way in England earlier, but emerged as an Irish speciality after 1750, reaching their heights in the 'seventies. They were all that the Irish goldsmith could desire, spool-shaped circles of silver averaging about 9in across and roughly 3in high, the perfect outlet for his native inventiveness, whatever the medium in vogue at the moment. Generally pierced to give a light and delicate appearance, the spool itself was of perfect symmetry and the interior design, whether original or a copy of a contemporary engraving, was an entirely individual affair. One made by Christopher Haines of Dublin in 1770, now in the Untermyer collection, shows a Chinaman sitting fishing on a bank, in a position least likely to be successful but highly expressive of concentration and hope, with an urn beside him, presumably for refreshment. The scrolls, shells, foliage, bananas and trees that surround him are strongly embossed, yet the overall effect is delicate. Another of the same date by William Homer appears, on first sight, to be more straightforward rococo, with arms on one side and a crest on the other. Perhaps it was meant to be, but then a heron and a duck irresistibly wound their way in among the scrolls.

The general idiom was pastoral, with animals, birds, and buildings, people going about their business or herding cattle; milkmaids on their stools or carrying pails; even, at times, a touch of the 'little folk', all against a pierced background of trellis work, foliage or scrolls that showed up the main theme to perfection.

When the Adam style came in the craftsmen who made these rings adopted it without entirely abandoning the free hand they had enjoyed. William Hughes, still a Dubliner, produced a perfectly conventional ring marked on its lower rim in a pierced design with ovals and circles and scrolling leaves, all beautifully draped with foliate festoons. But then he put some birds in, flying above. The utterly conventional was rare. One, by Joseph Jackson, c 1780, attempted it with somewhat heavier effect, but an Irish setter, sitting expectantly, enlivened it. After stamping machines appeared in Ireland, however, inventiveness was curbed and pure neo-classicism, or plain geometric designs, appeared.

Wine coasters enjoyed the same treatment, a pair c 1770 being typical. In a way, these were a smaller version of the dish rings, with straight sides and a wooden, baize-covered base to protect the table when pushed across. The pair made in 1770, by an unidentified maker, managed to incorporate three crests on sides that were embossed and pierced in rural settings, with houses, windmills, trees and birds under waved gadroon rims. Most coasters were rather more formal in design, nearly all having the same rims, but a magnificent set of six with deliberately erased marks, c 1775, is pierced and chased with scrolls, flowers, sprays, foxes, setters, game birds and figures. How the maker must have enjoyed himself.

Sugar castors, beautifully made in the prevailing form, showed that conventional piercing had always been well done in Ireland. A Queen Anne baluster castor engraved with magnificent armorials, made by Thomas Bolton in 1704, had a tall, slip-lock domed cover, waisted and pierced in a lozenge design.

Lemon strainers and some gravy straining spoons, often halved for easy use, were not far behind, for although piercing of bowl and handles was inclined to be more conventional, one strainer, probably made by Thomas Slade in about 1723, was pierced with a flower head pattern. Fish or cake slices, might again be pastoral in piercing, as were baskets of all sorts at times, while other containers which would normally be solid, such as sugar bowls or salt cellars, were fitted with blue glass liners and pierced in the conventional Adam style.

Bright-cut engraving was also used prolifically in Ireland from the end of the eighteenth century, carrying on the Adam style in this difficult medium. Spoons were made from early days, but more were lost than in most places, so that any before the early eighteenth century are virtually museum pieces, as are some made later. One impressive set in the Metropolitan Museum of Art, New York, probably the work of Francis Williamson of Dublin, 1765, consists of a strainer spoon, sugar tongs and teaspoon, all in gold and exceptionally dainty. Obviously the Earl of Kerry, whose coronet surmounted by a 'K' is engraved on each, liked his tea carefully served. The strainer is quite small with a long, tapering handle, its egg-shaped bowl pierced with simple holes. The scissor-type tongs have shell grips, and the spoon is small and unadorned.

Spoons for the small collector cover all later types, together with the most beautiful ladles, basting spoons usually with hooked ends, gravy spoons and, of course, the ever-varied strainer spoons. The quality of bright-cut engraving on many of these was very high, particularly in Cork, but spoons were also made in several other places. Of all things these are the easiest to collect, and if they do not sound very exciting, a visit to Ireland to see them in all their styles will soon correct such an impression. Between about 1730 and 1800, one feature distinguishes Irish spoons from those of the same style elsewhere—a more pointed tip to the bowl, which in England was rounded. They were also flatter on the whole, and generally rather light.

Caddy spoons were also made and, like wine labels, showed originality of design and fine workmanship. Many took the form of letters, but the eye-shaped type, in the last twenty years of the century, was specifically Dublin. These were given a variety of borders: reeded, single or double beaded, bright-cut, gadrooned or chased, all of them quite delightfully.

Snuff boxes were also made, one of them by Robert Goble of Cork, but freedom boxes were so much more of an Irish feature, particularly in Cork, that they make a more interesting subject. In many ways similar to snuff boxes, they were of much the same size with either a hinged or detachable lid, and the decoration, which usually included a coat of arms, was similar to that often found on other little boxes. They were of all shapes but it is the stories behind these boxes that make them so interesting, for they were presented with the freedom of a city, often in recognition of some exciting deed or notable achievement. (Illustration, p 207.) A box by David King of Dublin, 1733, one of the earliest, bears the arms of Lionel Sackville, who is described as having the greatest dignity in appearance, coupled, in private life, with the greatest love of low humour and buffoonery. Another, an oval box by Aeneas Ryan, 1787, depicts a mechanical loom, flanked by a peasant girl throwing away her knitting, and a scholar in a cap and gown. It was presented with the freedom of the Corporation of Hosiers to Sir Frederick Flood, Bart, in recognition of his efforts in Parliament to promote trade and prosperity of Ireland. This imaginative box represented the end of hand weaving and the beginning of industrialised hosiery, but research into the life of Flood, a judge of the High Court of the Admiralty of Ireland, reveals him to have been considered 'but a second rate blunderer . . . possessed of the qualification of pure nonsense'. Ah well!

The silver of Ireland was great, but the machine age hit it doubly hard, for just when Elkington of Birmingham had reduced processes which had at least been hand-assisted to mass production, Ireland underwent one of the most disastrous periods of her history, 'the hungry forties'. That her assay office survived to return to a new age still marking silver is a tribute to the resilience of the Irish character and to the enduring artistry of her craftsmen in gold and silver.

# Ten

# Scotland

The earliest history of silver in Scotland is so bound up with that of Ireland that to prove it had one of its own is a matter of clutching at straws. Yet some of those straws are quite substantial. Large bronze armlets of a kind found nowhere but in the north strongly indicate that Scottish metal craftsmen had a high degree of skill and culture in the Bronze Age. Why, then, should we presume this to have been totally lost?

Very many fewer gold and silver relics have been found in Scotland than Ireland, but reasoning does not rule out the possibility that more of these were of Scottish origin than was previously believed. The Bronze Age in Ireland was one of settled, prosperous economy, and its craftsmen were able to indulge their Celtic genius to the full, using their native gold. The Scots, in no such happy position, were greatly influenced by the Irish, the very word 'Scotland' deriving from a north-eastern Irish tribe, the 'Scoti'. Their only other contact, a somewhat less happy one, was with Scandinavia.

Christianity, with all the impetus it gave to the creation of beauty in art, was strong very early in Ireland, but of only local interest in Scotland. St Martin, following St Paul, had first brought a Celtic form of worship to Iona in AD 335, and several others followed before St Columba landed there from Ireland in 563 to build Scotland's first abbey and strengthen an already established church. The teachings of this church had reached as far south as Kent by the time St Augustine landed in 597, but while Catholicism became a force in Ireland and elsewhere, Scotland, although accepting it after 714, retained a preference for the simple. This was later to be reflected in her church plate.

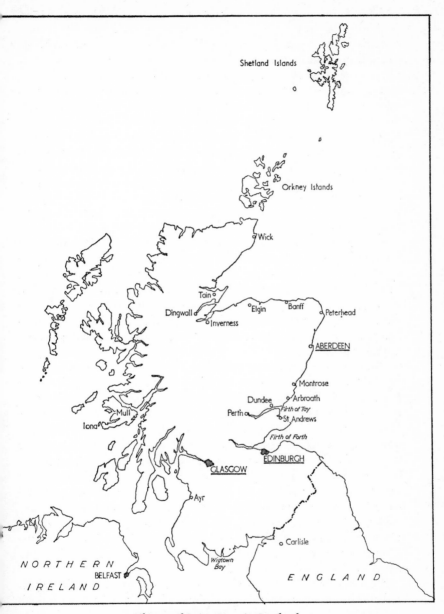

Silver-making centres in Scotland

Some of the belongings of these Celtic Christians have been found beneath the nave of a medieval church, probably built over an earlier one, on the island of St Ninian in the Shetlands. No doubt buried when Viking longboats were seen approaching in the early ninth century, they were dug up nearly 1,200 years later, in 1958. These twenty-nine objects, made of an alloy of silver and copper, may all have had ecclesiastical use, though only the spoon and ladle are familiar to the later church. Many of the objects appear personal: brooches, belt attachments, strap ends and a sword pommel, but the most important piece was a small hanging bowl decorated with a nice Celtic touch but simple compared with the work of Ireland. Experts believe the whole hoard to have been made in Scotland, but are still undecided about the purpose of the hanging bowls.

The church in the north remained as remote from Rome as an independent spirit, highlands, Alps, and seas could make it, and the whole history of Scottish silver shows a similarly sturdy individuality. Even later on, much less was made for the church in Scotland than elsewhere since neither the country's economy nor the number of Christians justified the expense. Why should they have paid Irish craftsmen rather than make themselves what was wanted to meet their own few needs?

The Monymusk reliquary may be an exception, for it is said to have housed the Psalter of St Columba, who came to Iona, previously sacred to the Druids, from Ireland. This little box, carved out of solid wood, is less of interest for the fine Celtic decoration on the silver and bronze plates riveted to its sides, than for the way in which its story illustrates how oddly paganism remained associated with the early faith. It was believed that if the box, worn on the breast of the cleric most nearly free from mortal sin, were first to pass around the army three times in the direction of the sun, that army would return home safe and victorious. By the time it had been deposited for safekeeping in the abbey of Arbroath in AD 1211, this had no doubt become mere superstition, yet the abbot of Arbroath is said to have carried it with the Scottish army at the battle of Bannockburn in 1314 with devastating effect. Such old beliefs died hard.

Brooches found in Scotland, contemporary with Ireland's eighth- and ninth-century masterpieces, show sufficient similarities for Irish workmanship to be presumed by many. Yet Ireland's brooches, including the well-known 'Tara', were basically of bronze, whereas Scotland's were mainly of silver decorated with gold. The Scots had their own supplies of both precious metals, but it is uncertain where Ireland obtained the silver she used at that time. Why should the Irish not have traded skill for metal, as has been suggested? It would be wonderful to prove this, for the lovely Hunterston brooch, for one, would put Scottish goldsmiths of that period into the highest class of skill and understanding.

The remote nature of the countryside kept prosperity at a distance, so that no great quantity of plate was made in the early middle ages. In fact, until discovery of the St Ninian hoard four spoons, found in the ruins of a Benedictine nunnery on Iona and believed to be twelfth or thirteenth century, had been thought to be the oldest in Scotland— though not of native make.

Very few spoons in all Britain exist from the period of the middle ages, but these few survivers, one totally undamaged, give a good picture of standards at the time. Probably intended for ceremonial use, they have a fig-shaped bowl engraved at the base with a floral design; the stem, starting in panel form, decorated by arches, curves and pellets, slims towards its end, which finishes in a mulberry or calyx knop. Although spoons of undoubted Scottish make appear in the late sixteenth century, others ascribed to Scotland from the thirteenth to fourteenth century were almost certainly made abroad.

In the early fourteenth century travelling tinkers made the first ring brooches, later to develop into a beautiful and distinctively Scottish feature, but these were quite simple and made of silver in octagonal form. Much more sophisticated is the boss of the Bute mazer, 5in wide, the subject of endless discussion and conjecture among experts. Whether it was actually made in Scotland or not, it appears to be agreed that this fantastic boss, with its strange monster and six superbly enamelled heraldic shields, probably dates from between 1314 and 1318, and is very much tied up with Scottish history. It is not certain that this boss was always a part of a mazer, but the bowl itself may be of much the same date, and has the unique feature of a carved whalebone cover. Covers at this time were most unusual, yet an inventory declares that Robert the Bruce, King of Scotland when this boss was made, possessed a mazer with a cover. Erudite interpretations of the monsters on the boss further connect it with the Bruce, making rather more than a case of wishful thinking. The silver mounts were added to the wide, shallow bowl in the early sixteenth century, the inscribed lip band being connected to the foot by scalloped straps, the only Scottish mazer with this feature which is more often seen on coconut cups.

Robert the Bruce brought some degree of law and order to Scotland, and during the various periods of prosperity which followed monastic land was well farmed and overseas trade established. In consequence, Scottish goldsmiths grew in importance so that by the time Mary, Queen of Scots, fled in 1567, 1,300 oz of her own silver were available to convert to coin, as well as quantities from the Palace of Holyrood. This included a gold font weighing 333 oz given by Elizabeth I for the baptism of Mary's son, James, the first Scottish king to rule England. Such records give a picture of the standard and volume of work created, but almost nothing survives, either for church or home.

Among the few exceptions are three magnificent Gothic maces belonging to the University of St Andrews, founded in 1412, the first in a great tradition of learning in Scotland. Of these three maces, only the one belonging to the Faculty of Canon Law is held to be Scottish, possibly made by a burgh or provincial craftsman, and is one of the four oldest ceremonial maces in Britain.

The geography of Scotland meant that goldsmiths did not seek the capital but fulfilled local needs, incorporating themselves with other hammer trades where numbers warranted. If this mace really was the work of a burgh craftsman, Perth must have the greatest claim, for although no records were kept the city is known to have had goldsmiths in the thirteenth century. Makers stamped their initials from the time minutes were first kept in 1518, but it is uncertain when the mark of a lamb carrying the banner of St Andrews was adopted, for no silver bearing it has been found before about 1675. Later the mark was changed to a complicated double-headed eagle.

The Dolgellau chalice, possibly the work of a thirteenth-century Chester maker, proves that the greatest artists in silver were not always

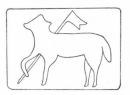

Perth lamb with banner

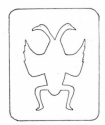

Double-headed eagle

200

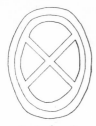

St Andrew's
mark

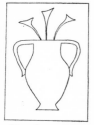

Dundee mark

found in the capital. St Andrews itself, a great seat of learning, could have possessed such a goldsmith, for although the only known silver bearing the saltire mark of this burgh was by one maker in the 1670s, nothing is impossible in fifteenth-century Scotland. One other place to consider is Dundee, quite close to St Andrews, where Alexander Moncur is recorded as working in 1517, and where plate was marked, more regularly than elsewhere, with a two-handled pot of lilies flanked by the maker's mark on either side, as there was no deacon. Certainly, the standard of such Scottish craftsmen's work was high, and who knows that it did not pre-date records, for an Act of 1457 setting a standard of 11oz for Scottish plate would seem to indicate clearly that goldsmiths were already following their craft in many parts of the country.

It had been fairly usual for craftsmen to adulterate the gold or silver provided by customers requiring plate with base metal. Now this Act, the first to show Edinburgh as an organised body, decreed that both the maker and a deacon of the craft, 'a cunning man of gude conscience', should stamp their marks on all plate, life being forfeit for any infringement of the rule. This standard remained until 1720, for although they were unaffected by the Britannia Act of 1696, Scottish silversmiths took the sterling standard of 11oz, 2dwt when England reverted to it that same year.

The Edinburgh town mark of a triple-towered castle was added in

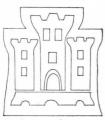

Edinburgh castle

1485, possibly the year the city formed its own goldsmiths' guild, though their first minute book did not begin until 1525. Date letters did not appear before 1681, when responsibility for the fourth mark was transferred from the deacon to an assay master, but dating of earlier silver is possible to a narrow margin by reference to records of both men. A thistle was adopted as standard mark in place of the assay master's initials in 1759, and the sovereign's head duty mark appeared in 1784, common throughout England but not apparent on Scottish provincial except in the more formal Glasgow.

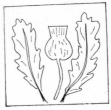

Thistle

Silver had always been mined in Scotland but James V developed gold mines, coveted by Queen Elizabeth, from which John Mosman obtained 56oz of gold in 1540, to remake and enlarge the royal crown of Scotland, the oldest in the British regalia. It is a marvellous piece of work by a very fine craftsman who also made a crown for the queen, weighing 35oz, and enlarged other pieces of the regalia, including the queen's sceptre, all with native metal. Another mine at Wanlockhead produced the gold to make a basin, capable of holding an English gallon, and this, filled with golden coins, was presented to the King of France, no doubt suitably impressing him with the wealth of the mine. This basin was made in Canongate, now the part of Edinburgh that

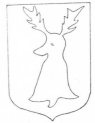

Stag's head erased

includes the royal palace of Holyrood, but then a separate burgh and close enough for constant bickering with the capital. The first mark of Canongate was a stag lodged, although the majority of Canongate work bears the later punch of the stag's head erased, sometimes with the addition of a wreathed anchor.

Amongst the most important silver ever made in Scotland were lovely sixteenth-century standing mazers, their wooden bowls beautifully decorated and set on an interesting stem. With the exception of one made for St Mary's College, St Andrews, these were all commissioned for private family use, two of the finest being made in Canongate. The St Mary's mazer, c 1561, is, however, the oldest hallmarked piece from Edinburgh, and bears the punch of the maker, Alexander Auchinleck, always to the left, the triple-towered castle, and the deacon's mark on its right. On ceremonial occasions, this mazer was passed as a loving cup, known as a grace cup in Scotland because, in about 1070, Margaret, wife of King Malcolm Canmore, effectively stopped the rush from table before grace had been said by letting it be known that the finest wine would be saved until after thanks had been given, when all could drink their fill.

The Watson mazer, unmarked and possibly composite, is beautifully decorated in repoussé on its fine trumpet stem and on the boss, found inside all mazers, there is an inscription in difficult old Scots, meaning 'Lose wealth, lose little; lose honour, lose much; lose heart, lose all'. Interesting and fine though it is, it none the less pales into insignificance beside the Tulloch and Galloway mazers made by James Gray of Canongate in 1557 and 1569 respectively. The Craigievar mazer by James Crawfuird of Edinburgh, 1591, is a trifle larger but of much the same style, basically a wide champagne glass shape on a baluster stem and foot. The elegance of these mazers is matched by superlative workmanship, shown again in all that survives of Gray's work. Nor does the great merit of these almost identical mazers lie only in the exquisite engraving on the deep lip band, the finely cut foliate border, the chased acanthus leaves of the stem, or the embossed foot with its oval lobes. It is their symmetry above all; the perfect balance and the delicacy of touch. The market for such magnificent silver, alas, passed when the court left Scotland for London in 1603.

Just seven of these mazers are known, and sixteenth-century spoons are equally rare but most distinctively Scottish. One of these, made by George Cunningham senior in 1589, is marked with the stag lodged of Canongate and the shake-fork device, basically a 'Y', of the Cunningham family, together with the normal ownership initials and a lightly engraved leaf design on the stem. These are very similar to a set made in Edinburgh in the late sixteenth century, all having a flat, rounded disc end with a small projection lacking on the Canongate spoon, and a flat stem joined to a round bowl by a very short rat tail, little more than a projecting V joint. On the back of the Edinburgh spoons the continental zig-zag assay groove, such as we saw in Elizabethan Norwich, although more distinctively Scottish, is also clear. In the early seventeenth century, similarly shaped spoons with bowls only a little longer also had the typically Scots design lightly engraved on the flat stem; a spoon by Alexander Galloway, of Aberdeen, 1672-8, with this pattern on its trifid-type top, also has it drawn to simulate a rat tail on the back of the bowl.

This thin, flat stem appears again on a cross between a seal top and a Puritan spoon made in Dundee and clearly marked with the pot of lilies. It is totally unlike anything English, its bowl, rounder than the fig shape of the times, being joined to the stem with the same stubby rat tail, while its tiny 'seal' top, although separately cast, is barely wider than the stem and joined with a diagonal cut across, unlike any English joint. There are other spoons more closely resembling the English Puritan which the late Commander G. E. P. How considered were introduced to England from Scotland; but the stem of one, c 1665, dug up at Haddington, East Lothian, has a leaf decoration unacceptable in Puritan England, while the bowl and stem are beaten together without any visible join. The round bowl of an Ayr spoon, c 1687, by Matthew Colquhoun, is also beaten out from the stem.

The initials on the Dundee spoon are of particular interest because of their connection with the Fergusson mazer. This elegant bowl, made in 1576 by Adam Craige of Edinburgh, has a tall, plain trumpet stem, spreading into a rolled and moulded foot, richly decorated with pots of lilies, and an unadorned, beautifully everted lip band finished off by a fine notched leaf fringe. Its boss, engraved with the arms of Fergusson impaling Durham, and the initials 'DF' and 'ID', commemorate the marriage of David Fergusson, who had been tutor to King James VI, its donor, and Alice Durham, who set up their home in Dundee. The spoon, bearing identical initials and said never to have been parted from the mazer, must have been another wedding present made at the same time.

Nothing survives of church plate before the Reformation, 1560 in Scotland, but old inventories show cathedrals and kirks to have been well endowed, and one must assume a similar standard in view of the history of church patronage. Yet the austerity of early days in the new kirk seems to have caused no resentment. Even in 1070 Margaret, wife of King Malcolm Canmore, found it necessary to teach the Roman faith to a people adhering to the old Celtic church in considerable numbers, and in 1560 they still preferred a more simple form of worship.

All that had belonged to the old faith was handed over to civic authorities, melted down and the money used for the common benefit. No hidden plate has come to light, and the inevitable conclusion is that this was done willingly, even though it meant having to start again with nothing but an empty church, the congregation even bringing their own stools to sit on. It is not surprising, therefore, that drinking-vessels were also brought from home for use in communion, which took place only four times a year in towns, and twice in country districts. The Sacrament was restricted to those who had passed theological examinations, a ruling which did much to stimulate the tradition for learning in Scotland.

Before 1617, when an Act required all kirks to be provided with communion cups in addition to lavers and basins for baptism, on pain of the minister losing his miserable stipend for a whole year, very few churches possessed their own plate at all. Yet a few exist of varying types made before that date. Because wealthy families still surrounded the court at Holyrood, and most, if not all, post-Reformation sixteenth-century cups were made in Edinburgh, it is most probable that they were originally intended for the home. A tazza-type cup on a fine baluster stem is the oldest of these, its bowl, at least, having been made by Henry Thompsone in 1563, when James Cok was deacon. Under the lip of the bowl, an inscription in clear lettering declares that it was given to the kirk of Forgue by James Crichton of Frendraught, and the date 1633 appears below. It seems probable that Frendraught had a new base made for a cup already in his possession and paired it with a newly made companion for presentation to Forgue church in thanksgiving, after being acquitted of the murder of two friends who had died in a fire at his home in 1630.

All cups do not display such evidence. A pair of tall, wineglass cups on exquisite slender stems, decorated only on the border of the foot, were made by John Mosman in 1585, and now belong to Rosneath in Dunbarton. They were probably given to the kirk in the seventeenth century, but lack of the usual inscription shrouds this in mystery. Another tazza-type cup with a plain, shallow bowl, baluster stem and enriched, domical foot, made by Hugh Lindsay between 1596 and 1600 when David Heriot was deacon, tells its story a little more clearly, for the inscription around the foot reads 'FOR X THE X KIRK X OF X CURRIE X 1657'. Obviously, one would say, a cup made for home use and presented that year. But was it? Its companion was made to match during the rush of 1617, and however near to the capital now, Currie would surely not have needed two cups then. A possible answer is that the maker copied an existing secular cup he admired. Conjecture in such matters adds interest to the intrinsic merits of a piece.

Only one sixteenth-century baptismal basin survives, but no ewer. The liturgy simply decreed that the minister should sprinkle water on the child's forehead and then give thanks, and so long as no font was used any basin would do. This magnificent parcel gilt platter, 18in wide made by David Gilbert between 1591 and 1594, was clearly originally intended for home use, for no ewer would have covered its finely decorated central boss. It is inscribed around the rim 'FOR THE KIRK OF PERTHE 1649', inside a moulded edge with a fine vandyke border.

Any jug could be taken to church to carry water to the basin, yet Queen Elizabeth is said to have presented the strange piece of rock crystal known as the Erskine ewer for the baptism of one of the Regent Mar's children. This was mounted in silver by James Cok, 1565–7, and is chiefly notable for its large, beak-like spout.

Scottish goldsmiths obviously prospered between 1617 and 1619, when every kirk in the country required new communion cups, lavers and basins, but poverty dictated that these be as light and simple as possible. Considering the quantity made, remarkably few survive, and it is hardly surprising to find that the majority were made by the better-class goldsmith. Most of those that survive were the work of Gilbert Kirkwood of Edinburgh, who turned out a great number in many varied forms. Bowls were conical-, bell-, or tazza-shaped; stems tall and slender or baluster, while bases took many forms. Each one contrived to be different, for even within the prescribed shapes of the day Kirkwood varied line with perfect balance, setting and charming decoration. Some of these cups were donated by wealthy patrons, which probably gave him more scope, and nearly all were inscribed, usually below the rim. These range from the stark 'CARSTAIRS KIRK', on a V-shaped bowl decorated only with an ovolo enriched base moulding, to 'FOR THE VAST KIRK OUTVITH EDINBRVGHE' and 'I·WIL·TAK·THE·COVP· OF·SALVATIOVNE·AND·CAL·VPON·THE·NAME·OF·THE·LORD·' with '116TH PSLM' in the centre and the date 1619. The 'Vast' kirk was able to afford more, and because of its larger congregation usually required bigger cups than the village kirk. Lavers and basins were largely adapted from, or modelled on existing rosewater ewers and dishes. Nothing surviving from that date is of particular interest, and later examples are severely plain.

The complete renewal of all church plate between 1616 and 1619 left the goldsmith short of work immediately afterwards, and troubles throughout the century gave him only brief opportunities to show his skills. Charles I drove the Presbyterian church underground, so that it

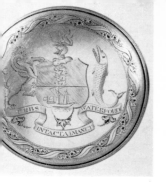

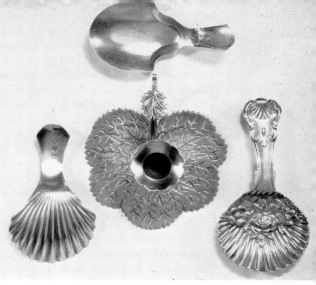

(*above left*) Irish freedom box by James Keating, Dublin, 1800; (*above right*) unusual perstick by Joseph Willmore, Birmingham, who made the caddy spoon [*right*] chased with owers, in 1824; the shell [*left*] 1796 and hoof [*above*] 1795, were both by Joseph Taylor, Birmingham; (*centre left*) 'Huntsman' snuff box by Nathaniel Mills, Birmingham, 1840; (*centre right*) 'Battle bbey' snuff box by Matthew Linwood, Birmingham, 1810; (*below*) five wine labels by Matthew Boulton and John Fothergill, Birmingham, 1775

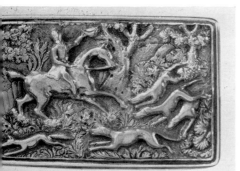

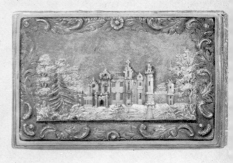

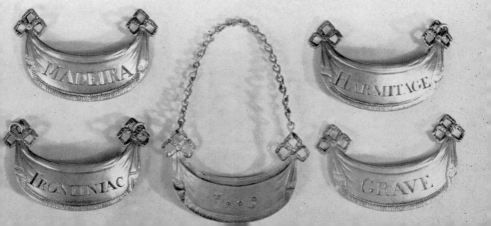

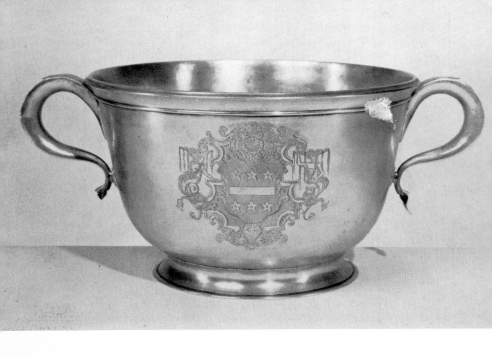

Page 208   (above) Bowl by Thomas Partis, Newcastle, 1728; (below) a typical Irish strawberry dish by Philip Kinnersley, Dublin, 1724, together with a pair of early George II tapersticks, by James Gould, London, 1730

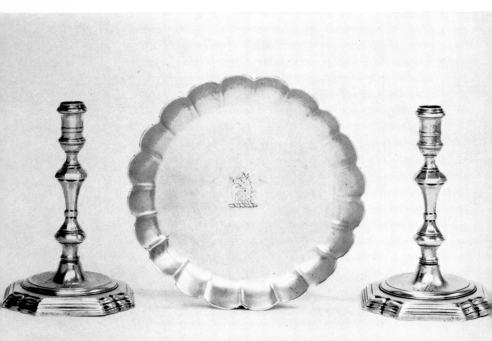

was the act of worship which then mattered more than the utensils used. Before the ʲional Covenant was signed in 1638 it is surprising that any church plate was made at all, and the four cups at Dunfermline, by George Robertsone, 1628 and 1629, or the four for Inveresk by George Crawford in particular, arouse curiosity. How came it that so much could be spent on silver at that time? Private citizens with a conscience or a thankful heart must have accounted for some. Thomas Kirkwood, possibly less imaginative than his father, was another to make church plate during this period, including a laver for Tron Kirk, Edinburgh, 1633–5. This would have been a high-class piece of work in any circumstances, and bears an interesting picture engraved centrally surrounded by inscriptions.

There was even less secular silver, for few followed the king and times were hard, so that there was more melting of plate to make coin than vice versa. There is a pretty wine cup by Thomas Cleghorne, c 1630, decorated all over with flowers emanating from a vase, and a few simply mounted coconut cups, made roughly between 1600 and 1637, but these hardly begin to compare with the Sinclair cup, inscribed 1588 on its elegant sloping rim, with two coats of arms and a lovely foliate border. This most attractive coconut is set on a short baluster stem and plain domed foot, and is inscribed 'Forss 1608'. A nautilus shell, c 1611–13, is interesting in that its silver mounts were possibly cast from a German prototype, an Edinburgh practice of the time, and a really attractive mazer by James Denneistoune, 1617, also deserves mention. This was made entirely of silver in the old wooden form, and is decorated only with arms on its widely sloping rim, with a deeply notched lower border, and on the inner boss. Only a handful of survivors—and there were not many more—to afford us a glimpse into the work of a vanished age; simple, because the court had left for London; miserably few, because the majority of families were forced to sell 'capital' to live, silver being their currency.

Nor did times really ease before 1690, when Parliament finally passed an Act agreeing to a Presbyterian Church of Scotland. During that period, when the Civil War and Commonwealth had come and gone in England, the fortunes of Scotland were tossed on a bumpy see-saw, both church and government being involved in continual friction with English rule, hard on the purse and rarely effective. Freedom at last to worship in their own way could not fill empty coffers overnight, but the Act of Union in 1707, necessary but unpopular with an independent race, saw the beginning of prosperity.

Despite all this, the production of silver increased during the second half of the seventeenth century when communion cups were generally heavier than those of 1617, and rather more regional. Those in the counties bordering the Firth of Forth, with Edinburgh at their centre, have larger, rather clumsy tazza-shaped bowls, the foot and stem lacking the old grace, some with a waist and flattened knop in place of the bulging baluster stem. There are, of course, exceptions, four cups at St Giles Cathedral and four at Linlithgow, by John and Alexander Scott respectively, c 1660, have hexagonal, diminishing stems, those at St Giles also having engraved panels and fine gilding.

Silversmiths in the country districts, facing the same difficulties, may have benefited from the inability of customers to afford Edinburgh craftsmen, and some produced church silver in the most distinctive styles. Beautifully proportioned cups were made in the Dundee workshops of the Gairdine family, responsible earlier for the Fergusson spoon, and Alexander Lindsay made others with nice, bell-shaped bowls on rather heavy stems.

There were two separate Incorporations of Hammermen in Aberdeen, the new town recording its earliest goldsmith before 1460, the old in 1699, but as the craft continued well into the nineteenth century without any apparent supervision, Aberdeen's marking system was exceptionally irregular. Basically both old and new towns used an 'AB' or 'ABD' in Roman capitals, and the maker's mark once, or sometimes twice, but there was a greater variety of additional devices than anywhere else in Scotland, presumably according to individual whim. Lack of deacons naturally led to abuses, and even Walter Melvil used inferior metal for his beautiful mace for King's College, Aberdeen. During the seventeenth century, much could be explained by the fact that this district remained Episcopal, so avoiding the wrath of England, but this cannot be the whole story. Aberdeen was an important port and university town, and may even have felt superior to the rules imposed on others.

Walter Melvil, who copied a Dutch beaker in 1642, was admitted to the Incorporation of Hammermen in 1650, and showed his own ability and originality of design on the fine, facetted stem of a wineglass type of communion cup in 1653. Nevertheless, the typical communion cup in north-east Scotland was the beaker, brought in originally by Dutch students to the University of Aberdeen, or by Scotsmen returning from studying at Leyden University. These circumstances, coupled with the style of decoration, clearly show the beakers to have been intended for secular use, but of the ninety or so now known the majority were made by Scottish craftsmen, who continued to use this very attractive form of decoration for a long time, even, as in the case of Walter Melvil's, when they were being made expressly for the church.

The kirk at Ellon possessed a beaker hallmarked in Amsterdam in 1634, and inscribed there. Melvil copied its delicate overall pattern of strapwork, foliage, fruit and flowers, below which there is an inscription recording its gift to the kirk in Ellon in 1642. Under this again and enclosing arms is a double circle containing the words 'I REJOICE IN THE LORD FOR THE LORD IS ONELY MY SVPPORT'.

These beakers were quite unlike those made in Norwich, also under strong Dutch influence, being taller proportionately and much more lavishly decorated, with lovely slender lines. When need came they were converted to church use, but while all bar one, at Biggar in Lanarkshire, belong to kirks north of the Tay, some came from Edinburgh workshops, including the oldest surviving, made by the versatile Gilbert Kirkwood, 1608–11, and given to a little kirk near Arbroath in 1633. It is possible that beakers were used in Scotland before the sixteenth century, but a set of four by George Walker were not made much before 1691, when they were given to the kirk at Monymusk. These were extraordinarily pleasing in shape and still decorated all over, a feature that lessened with the years as the plain surface was considered more suitable for the kirk.

The beaker had originated in Scandinavia, the name deriving from the old Norse word 'bikarr'. Peg tankards, the most positive Scandinavian form made in Britain, are less common in Scotland than in the north of England, where beer drinking was more usual, but there are a few to remind us of the strong connection between these countries, more pronounced from a Scottish viewpoint, perhaps, in Norwegian words such as 'kirke' and 'ghillie'.

The beaker also played an important part in the communion service of Colonial America, spiritually close to the Scottish kirk. Two of the earliest, more typical of the Norwich type, were made by Hull & Sanderson, who set up shop in Boston in 1634. An even stronger tie between the church in America and Scotland, however, occurred when the first bishop of America, Samuel Seabury, was consecrated at Aberdeen in November 1784. He was in a difficult position, for bishops were essential to this service, and though America had none, England would not help out a rebel.

Many more burghs in Scotland made silver than were listed by Jackson, and the majority produced communion cups. The elder William Lindsay of Montrose created some of the finest ever seen in Scotland, remarkable for their extraordinary grace and quality rather than any special form. His cup at Craig, for instance, has a beautifully proportioned bell-shaped bowl on a fine baluster stem, its foot slightly domed, with a repoussé border including winged angel's heads. The rest of the foot and stem are plain, but the bowl has a crest showing a stag's head so engraved that its cartouche covers the cup in exquisite decoration. Even the inscription below the rim contrives to be different, for it appears between zig-zag lines, rather like the continental assay groove. There is no known history of Lindsay having studied abroad, but such artistic talent, particularly north of the Tay, was surely not derived from fellow Scotsmen.

Lindsay's cups were made between 1671 and 1683, when he died, and anything later ascribed to him will have been made by his son, who qualified in 1688. Both used the double rose of Montrose, stamped twice, with their own mark between. This work was in a class by itself, but spoons marked with a single rose, with a thistle or some other device added, may be found up until 1838.

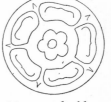

Montrose double rose

The quaich was entirely Scottish, and was made in many parts of the country, occasionally being used for the church. These shallow bowls with two projecting handles, or lugs, were originally made of wood, the staves hooped together, a long time before the goldsmith reproduced them in silver. Their use was then positively secular, generally for a short convivial dram, small quaichs being carried around like spoons. Larger quaichs, with each stave of a different coloured wood, were used as loving cups and were most important to formal Highland functions. It is generally agreed that they were first mounted in silver soon after the turn of the century, with rims, feet, and mounts for the lugs, and that copies entirely in silver appeared soon after 1660. Yet a quaich, bearing the initials 'MK' conjoined and the town mark of Inverness, 'INS', was dated c 1640 by Jackson, because the Forres communion cup with the same maker's mark was donated in 1643 and inscribed to that effect. Simon Mackenzie the elder worked in Inverness from 1643 to 1676, and this fits, but since no other quaich anywhere near this date is known and the Forres cup could have been remade from a 1643 gift, repeating the same inscription, it seems reasonable to suppose that it was made later in Mackenzie's career. Quaichs were produced in Inverness until about 1800, the last, by Charles Jamieson, also being stamped with a dromedary, an additional Inverness mark, but wherever made they deepened and degenerated into bowls with lugs on in later years.

The early silver quaich had incised lines, representing the old wooden staves, and very frequently a Tudor rose alternating with a tulip was engraved in every second panel, the blank space between enhancing the light effect. Thistles, which would appear more likely, have been found only on one from Aberdeen, c 1700, which is different in many ways, although some fine miniatures were made there in the early eighteenth century. The decoration was not invariable. An Edinburgh example by Charles Blair, 1736, in the Royal Scottish Museum, has a central hoop of three incised lines with chevrons below pointing downwards, while on an unmarked quaich, c 1680, recently for sale, the chevrons are set above four well-separated lines, giving less impression of a hoop. One from Banff, which mostly marked its work 'BANF', c 1680, is beautifully engraved with flowers and birds, and other forms of decorations occur. The lugs almost invariably bear the initials of the original owner—two sets in the case of marriage cups—but an Edinburgh quaich by Edward Cleghorne, 1663–84, belonging to the kirk at Alvah in Aberdeenshire, has a honeycomb design on its handles.

Edinburgh, which abandoned the quaich in the 1730s, made the majority of those given to the church. These were occasionally used for communion, but more often as baptismal basins or alms dishes, four in Ayr by Charles Dickson, 1722, being the only ones still used for communion. The greatest output of these fascinating bowls, however, was from Glasgow, although none appear in that city's churches.

The history of silver in Glasgow is somewhat mysterious, for no early plate survives. Though of less importance than Aberdeen, Glasgow was a cathedral and university city long before her goldsmiths were incorporated with other hammermen in 1536, and her first minute book runs from 1616–1717. The Glasgow town mark of a fish, tree and bell, had been adopted before the earliest piece of surviving silver was made. This was a fine quaich by Thomas Moncur, c 1670, a member of one of the city's finest goldsmithing families, all of whom were concerned with other industries.

This, possibly, is the clue to Glasgow's casual attitude towards the craft. Prosperity started with the Act of Union in 1707, when the city opened up trade with America, and this soon became successful enough, particularly in tobacco, to warrant dredging the Clyde, so founding Glasgow's ship-building history. Industry was all important and gold-smiths, however talented, were apt to look upon their craft almost as a spare-time occupation, each one stamping his own version of the town punch, which varied enormously within limits of a basic salmon, oak tree (usually with a bird perching on top), and a handbell. A date letter cycle was begun in 1681, but used regularly only until 1705 or 1709, four marks being pro- 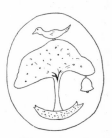 duced by the maker stamping his own punch twice on either side of the town mark. An official assay office was opened in 1819, when the lion rampant was adopted as standard mark to the left of the town punch, now regularised, the date letter, in definite shields for each cycle, the sovereign's head, and maker's mark. The queen's head was dropped with the duty in 1890, a thistle    Glasgow mark appearing in that fourth position from 1914 until the office closed in 1964. Between about 1730 and 1800, some makers apparently tried to indicate standard by the addition of an 'S' for sterling where the date letter should have been.

Church plate continued to be made in Glasgow, as elsewhere, throughout the eighteenth century, particularly the first half, but im-proved communications gradually reduced the role of the burgh crafts-man, who was further hit by the opening of Glasgow's assay office in 1819. Glasgow silver never had the character of some of those little places; no new styles were evolved, and while much that was good emerged, particularly from the Luke family, it largely followed Edinburgh, continuing with a form long after the capital had abandoned it. Yet while others struggled, Glasgow thrived.

One of the most delightful purely Scottish forms was the thistle cup, diminishing from a large teacup in size. Obviously such cups were not really practical as their strongly everted lips made drinking difficult without spilling. Their life was therefore limited, roughly from 1682 to 1700 in Edinburgh, though the burgh craftsmen carried on a few years longer, with Samuel Telfer of Glasgow making one as late as 1750. These cups had an 'S' scroll handle, usually beaded, and a waist, sometimes with a raised punched band, encircled by a fillet. The bowl below it was very slightly bulging and decorated with a calyx of applique lobes rising from the foot to the waist, giving them a thistle-like appearance. The only variation, beyond ability in creating exquisite grace of line, was a double waist fillet with a narrow band of plain silver between; they are rare, but one by James Sympsone of Edinburgh, 1694, was shown at the London Antiques Dealers' Fair in 1970. Thistle cups were also made in Inverness, notably tiny ones, as well as in Aberdeen, Canongate and Banff, where in about 1695 William Scott made one for that year's running of the Huntley Cup, a small horse race in Aberdeenshire. Few prizes would be more worth winning today, except perhaps the gold teapot by James Ker, 1736, with an engraving of the mare Legacy, winner of a race worth £100 at Leith, which was sold for an astronomical figure in 1967 and is now in the United States.

Racing trophies and presentation pieces were as much a part of the goldsmith's work in Scotland as elsewhere, and were generally in the form of bowls or two-handled cups, commemorating races and occasions that seemed important at the time. Searching out their story now can add an interest to collecting such silver, although some were for well-known events. After the Battle of Culloden, for instance, in 1746, George Kepple sailed to bring George II news of his victory over the Highlanders, and the Duke of Cumberland presented him with a travelling canteen to commemorate the occasion. This had been made by Ebenezer Oliphant in 1740, and consisted of beakers, all fitted neatly together, forks, spoons, and—most important—a corkscrew, all contained in a silver box chased with 'Cs' and 'Ss' and engraved with the Prince of Wales feathers and a coronet. A presentation piece to surpass all.

Secular silver was necessarily simple and exceptions, mostly before

1707, were rare, for the Scottish people disliked clutter. The idea of montieth bowls originated in Scotland in the 1680s when a 'fantastical Scotsman', by the name of Monteigh, wore his cloak notched, or just plain ragged, at the hem. Although few were made north of the border, Colin McKenzie produced an ugly great thing in 1698, and William Ged appeared to do even worse, for gold medals were hung in rows all over the bowl he made for the Royal Company of Archers in 1722. Hardly his fault, but such clutter could only have occurred in Scotland, where archery medals were a unique feature.

Montieth bowls were well made in themselves, and one by James Cockburn, 1702, sold at Christies in 1966 is really pleasant, with a scalloped moulded border capped with acanthus foliage and shells. There is no detachable rim to spoil its lines, only arms breaking the plain surface of the bowl below, lions mask drop ring handles at either side, and a fine gadrooned foot. All these bowls were made in Edinburgh, but this one is more typically Scots for at the time English bowls had a heavy appearance, with hollow fluting and embossed cartouches surrounding arms.

Punch bowls were also rare, for the wealthier Scot preferred claret, and most were made in the early nineteenth century, at least fifty years after other goldsmiths had given them up. In that ornate age these are distinctively Scottish for their good, simple lines, with a nice thick rim; Phillip Grierson produced one in 1825 adorned only with a single crest, and Robert Gray & Sons, Edinburgh 1810, used a pleasing chased and embossed leaf decoration and a gadrooned border. But another of 1825 was more heavily embossed on its upper half, its scrolls, foliage and flowers enhanced by the plain surface between it and the similar decoration on the foot.

It is hardly surprising, therefore, that punch ladles were extremely rare, a few being made in Perth, whereas toddy ladles were made in virtually every burgh in the early nineteenth century, after whisky had become important to Scotland—and to toddy, which mixed it with hot water and lemon. This was a warming drink to take before retiring to unheated bedrooms at night, and innocuous by comparison with the potent Hindu drink from which the word derives, which was distilled from the sap of several types of palm trees.

Other bowls took a variety of forms, some possibly for porridge, or mixing toddy, but many for uses that seem strange to us now. A delightfully plain bowl by Dougal Ged of Edinburgh, 1736, is like a small punch bowl with the addition of leaf-capped scroll handles, and one of the loveliest of all, an eight-panelled, circular bowl only 3in high set on a low-stepped base, was made by Patrick Inglis of Canongate, c 1715. It has deeply incised lines running down its flaring sides from the broad, graceful scallops of an inverted rim, with half-length lines in between, breaking the lower surface.

By the second half of the century Canongate had largely lost importance, and was mostly producing spoons, though one delightful exception was an oval sugar basket, c 1755, marked 'I.R.', probably for John Rankine, although John Robertson also stakes a claim. It is like a broad pear with the top sliced off, standing on a pedestal base with an interesting swing handle of twisted silver, including a distinctly different centrepiece; the upper part of the bowl is delicately engraved with sprays of foliage and flowers. This has the rare cross fitcheé added to the stag's head mark of Canongate. Two communion cups, dated 1763, at Auchtertool, by William Craw, were the last major pieces to come from Canongate.

As beer was never popular in Scotland, tankards were comparatively few, but John Luke of Glasgow made one almost before the city had founded its new prosperity in 1707, and a 1725 tankard by another member of that family, Robert Luke, was shown at the 1966 Scottish Antiques Fair. This has a plain cylindrical body, a bold, scroll handle, and a high domed lid with a tall acorn knop, found again on an earlier tankard, 1709, by Colin McKenzie of Edinburgh, more important for its slightly baluster body which preceded the form in England by many years.

The very few peg tankards made in Scotland were of the same distinctive form as those of York and Newcastle, although the one by Edward Cleghorne, 1663–81, with heavy embossing on the lower half, is nearer to the original Scandinavian. A large tankard by James Sympsone, 1702, is more typical of Edinburgh's superior work, the deep gadrooning of base and flange, with cut-card work on the flat top of its stepped lid and handle, showing off the lovely patina of its otherwise plain surface. (Illustration, p 85.) A pair by James Cockburn, 1685, are even finer, with their rope borders, two at the skirted base and one below the flat lid, crowned by a fine lion couchant, unique in Scotland.

Thomas Ker made tankards, among other good, simple objects. Admitted in 1694, he was the first of a family of six to bring honour to Edinburgh, Daniel Ker, the last, being admitted in 1764. While Glasgow was roaring away on a tide of prosperity after 1707, the bankers of Edinburgh found life difficult; the poor impossible. Coin was scarce and largely valueless; wealth was better invested in silver, and the goldsmith of the capital produced it in solid pieces that could be used, reflecting the 'no nonsense' character of the people. A barber's bowl by Thomas Ker, 1702, is typical of this attitude, being utterly plain except for arms engraved on the rim opposite a deep indent for the neck. A similar oval dish made by him in the same year is in the Metropolitan Museum of Art, New York, accompanied by a rather pleasing shaving-jug, oval in shape and slightly bulging below.

Quality of workmanship and elegance of line reached its heights in the first part of the century, when it was not sufficient merely to produce massive pieces, investing silver for the customer in bulk; it also had to be superbly made. Artistic pride may have demanded this, but the Edinburgh goldsmith was also a Scot and, like his customer, sought solid worth; so, to obtain this, the Britannia standard of silver was occasionally used, although it had never been enforced.

Objects peculiar to Scotland went out with the quaich, and the majority of domestic wares then followed basic English lines, without decoration other than engraved arms of exceptional quality. Even when the Edinburgh craftsman did try his hand at rococo, considerably later than in England, roughly between 1730 and 1760, it was of a restrained form, generally lacking both the excesses of the worst and the vigour of the best. Robert Adam was a Scot, and his neo-classic form was quietly used on larger pieces but without any distinctively Scottish mannerisms. Bright cutting was never used outside Edinburgh, Dundee and Perth, where the greatest exponent of the art in Britain, James Cornfute, 1772–1805, used it to perfection. His pupil, the elder Robert Keay, also employed it most beautifully but far more sparingly.

Exceptions to all generalisations exist, of course, but in a search for the typical, it is quality of workmanship and line rather than decoration that proclaims Edinburgh work. Yet at the same time Highland brooches in the Celtic tradition, mostly made in the north-east regions, and magnificent sword hilts and pistols, were minutely and elaborately decorated, particularly in Stirling. Despite the Turnpike Act of 1751 which largely opened up the country, the burgh craftsman continued along his individual way, caring nothing for London and little for Edinburgh.

From the start, Scottish sugar castors were notable for well-cut, simple piercing, seen later in cake and sweetmeat baskets, sometimes in rococo or Adam styles. A set of three by Andrew Law of Edinburgh, 1693, unique because they normally appeared singly in Scotland at that time, also show the fine quality of engraving which reached its heights early in the next century. (Illustration, p 34.) Such lighthouse castors normally had a gadrooned base, as they did in England, but once this form had passed at the turn of the century the Scots evolved their own shapes, one of the most elegant being globular on top, with a waist just above the base. James Sympsone improved this with cut-card work over the shoulders on an octagonal set of 1702; the octagonal castor did not appear in England until about 1715, and then slimmed towards the top. Another typical form had a bulbous lower half, cylindrical and tapering above, but Scottish castors have not survived in any quantity.

The teapot, on the other hand, was made prolifically and superbly well in Scotland. The habit of drinking tea supplanted claret with difficulty about forty years later than in England, but when its delights were finally discovered it changed social history. It was essentially a drink for the home, something to be savoured at leisure, but the upper classes had been in the habit of eating at the local hostelry. Tea changed all that and, one would imagine, created considerable work for the goldsmith in supplying the needs of the table, although the amount of surviving silver does not bear out the theory. Hash spoons appear in plenty throughout the century, made in many places, one of the finest being by John Luke of Glasgow, 1705. But they cannot have lived on hash alone. William Ged of Edinburgh made a set of three-pronged table forks in 1710, engraved with a crest and motto; a few plain standing tazze, or fruit dishes, also survive from the period, together with some soup ladles and various spoons.

The Scots must have drunk copious quantities of tea, for their pots are considerably larger than those of England. From the very beginning, early in the century, they made the bullet shape their own while holding no monopoly, and even Paul de Lamerie, with a superb example dated 1717, cannot take it from them. De Lamerie, of course, added refinements at a time when Scottish pots, their tops a little less rounded than later, were unadorned except for engraved arms. These spherical pots sat on an almost invisible moulded base, while another variety, taller and with a more oval curve to their sides, had a flat base and top. These are very rare, but a superb example by Harry Beathune, 1716, was sold recently. All had a short, straight spout with only a slight taper, a well-hinged lid fitting flush, and a thick wooden handle with a fine curve. Most teapots were made with their own stand, and while these occasionally turn up for sale alone a pot with its original base is worth a king's ransom today.

Colin McKenzie was the greatest early maker, but Thomas Ker, who made his first pot in about 1724, was the master by the 1730s when the shape had become a complete sphere or skittle ball, either word deriving from the French game of 'boule'. Things did not change overnight, but Ker's gold 'Legacy' pot of 1736 was typical. Set on a much higher circular foot than the English equivalent, with only a small part of the bowl touching its tightly waisted centre, the same straight spout emerges from the body without moulding. Lightly engraved decoration on the lid, which is an integral part of the sphere, spills over on to the body, below which the mare 'Legacy' is engraved with her jockey, with the royal arms on the other side. Ker made another gold race teapot in 1737, won by Lord Roseberry. Such teapots are not for the small collector, but the racing history traceable through them applies equally to lesser trophies. The Roseberry teapot, 1737, is more elaborately decorated, chased in the same positions with rococo scrolls, shells and flowers in a deeper cut—a beautiful, and for Scotland, very early interpretation of the form. The best of these teapots keep one of their finest points hidden from all but those who look inside and see that the spout strainer is most beautifully pierced. This really distinctive feature is found only on Scottish teapots.

Some makers, such as George Robertson, Aberdeen, 1708–30, or David Mitchell, Edinburgh, 1739, curved their spouts gently, adding fluting at the top. Teapots were made widely, the best including those by Robert Luke of Glasgow, c 1725, and Patrick Scott of Inverness, whose bullet teapot, c 1735, among other fine silver, is of the highest class. By mid-century the output of Banff and Dundee was dwindling, but Alexander Johnston maintained the respect associated with the pot of lilies mark, his teapot and stand being really outstanding among other good work. As forms evolved, Scotland did not lag behind, and a round, straight-sided, flat-topped Edinburgh teapot of 1758, totally lacking elegance, preceded the straight-sided, oval pot in England by some years. These were usually decorated in the Adam style, of which William Davie of Edinburgh used a delightful minimum in 1774, on a pot sold recently in New York.

A whole range of things followed the teapot, each one later than its equivalent in England. Cream jugs mostly copied English styles in heavier silver, but Mungo Yorstoune gave his baluster jugs, c 1719, a good scroll handle at a time when the English were mainly using the 'C'. His unusually high scroll handle, towering above the helmet form, was purely Scottish. Cream boats, like a long-lipped sauce boat, offered a good medium for the restrained rococo practised in Edinburgh, and William Aytoun, famous for teapots, used it on one he made in 1746. These cream boats had a leaf-capped, double scroll handle and three paw feet, the flared and wavy rim of one by Hugh Penman, 1743, being chased with flower heads, leaves, and scrolls. The hot milk jug, copying the skittle ball teapot on its high foot, was, however, the most distinctively Scottish form. One by Edward Lothian, 1735, was engraved lightly around the junction of body and cover, its short moulded spout alone changing the familiar outline.

Sugar bowls were extraordinarily pretty, with their round bowls set on a pedestal foot and a flat, everted rim with a shaped edge, often decorated like the cream boats. A delightful example of this type was made by Lothian & Robertson in 1753, but the normal covered circular bowl was also made, one by James Mitchellsone in 1719 having its spreading foot reversed on the cover to make a separate dish for replacing teaspoons, as there were no saucers.

All these objects were also made in the burghs, particularly Aberdeen, which also produced lovely little slop bowls on three feet. Tea caddies, always a rarity, were mostly made outside the capital, one of the few being by Robert Luke, 1735. Two plain, octagonal caddies belong to an Aberdeen tea service by George Cooper, c 1730, each having a domed detachable lid and well-engraved arms. This five-piece service has a covered sugar bowl, the taller type of early teapot, and a tall baluster cream jug with an unusually high scroll handle. The set is unadorned silver of high quality, but what makes it so outstanding is that matching tea services were not made in England before about 1785, except on rare occasions and then usually for royalty.

Another really early teaset, by William Aytoun, 1733, was sold at Christies in 1967; this had a lovely spherical teapot, complete with its circular stand, beautifully scalloped with a moulded rim, repeated on the everted rim of the open sugar basin, while the helmet cream jug had a moulded rib. These early services were not unique in Scotland, but the majority came later when kettles also appeared, sometimes as part of a set. Tea urns, or their smaller equivalent for coffee, were very rare, but two exist of the most extraordinary egg shape, each with three twisted serpent handles and scroll legs standing well out from the body. One by Hugh Gordon, 1729, has a spirit burner underneath and a nicely shaped spigot to its top, with well-engraved arms above it. At first sight the urn in the Royal Scottish Museum, by John Main, 1732, is identical, but in fact the bowl is more ovoid and the tap lacks character. Lids fit flush, an integral part of the egg, similar to those on the spherical teapot and just as Scottish.

Hot chocolate did not appeal to the Scots in early days, and coffee pots were also rare; nevertheless, Mr Ian Finlay describes an octagonal pot by Colin McKenzie, 1713, as one of the most beautiful in the United Kingdom. Every feature of it is eight-sided, even its dainty curved spout set opposite a good handle, while the body, tapering into its domed lid, is beautifully engraved with a crest. The majority of coffee pots were of much later date, when the temptation to emboss was rarely resisted, although decoration never went to the extremes found in England. There are good coffee pots to be found, but the majority from Glasgow and Edinburgh follow London styles.

The burghs, however, retained far more individuality, and a coffee pot made in Elgin by John P. Cruickshank, c 1760, is unique. The nearest equivalent might be the cylindrical coffee biggin made between about 1790 and 1810 in England, because they, like this, also rested on a spirit stand. But their sides were not quite as perpendicular, incurving at the top, while this just stops, the high-stepped lid fitting into it without hinge. Also totally different is its straight tubular spout, set at right angles to an outjutting wooden handle, fitted into a silver sleeve. A simple piece, yet its stand is exquisite, surmounted by a pierced gallery reminiscent of the work of Philadelphia craftsmen, set on classical legs with the spirit burner suspended by chains.

Perhaps it is the very remoteness of Elgin, away there in the north, that allowed such individual design. This burgh, with a ruined cathedral dating from the twelfth century, is one of many that research will show to have been more involved with the craft than had been thought. Five goldsmiths are now known to have worked there before 1700, but with the exception of a few beakers its marks have mainly been found on spoons. Some of these are marked 'ELGIN' in full, but variations are many, such as the 'E' on its back, looking somewhat like a castle, with 'N & L' fitted in below, found on this coffee pot. Some also bear the most

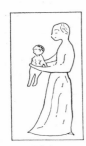

attractive stamp of a woman holding her child, said to be a widow of the Rebellion of 1715 who took refuge in the cathedral. It is a nice story, but the symbol was actually associated with Elgin from earliest Christian times and is also carved on the west door of the cathedral, ruined as a result of the Reformation, in about 1567.

Among the goldsmiths recorded in Elgin were William Scott and his son, previously seen in Banff, where they made the Huntley thistle cup. They also

Elgin

appeared in the records of Aberdeen and Perth, and may eventually be found to have worked in Wick and Tain, both of which marked silver with their town name in full. There was not sufficient work to keep a goldsmith fully employed in these remote spots, so that craftsmen like the Scotts, including Patrick, moved around, marking their work wherever they happened to be. There were many like them though not all of the same standard, the majority being mere tinkers, but Alexander Stuwart of Tain also worked in Inverness and Dingwall, another previously unknown place in the craft.

Spoons are the greatest surviving output of many of these little places, yet marking on spoons was lax all over Scotland and collectors find it a real challenge to discover representative examples. Nor were they apparently made in any great quantity, for even in Edinburgh the Georgian spoon is comparatively rare. These are closer to the Irish in character, flatter, with a more pointed tip, and made of softer silver. Bright-cut engraving was rare on spoons; the Scottish fiddle pattern omitted the wings of the English version, and other little differences are noticeable to expert spoon collectors.

In Tain, however, Hugh Ross made quantities of silver between 1751 and 1782, including coffee pots, teapots, candlesticks (rare in Scotland), a quaich, and many small wares including Luckenbooth brooches.

These love tokens, peculiar to Scotland, originated in Edinburgh, and took many forms involving a heart, often with initials, or a betrothal inscription, some of which were most touching. Hugh Ross recorded making forty-seven of these, and they were known also to have been made in Inverness in a distinctive form. These would make a most attractive subject for collection, again with the added interest of tracing their stories.

While on small wares, wine labels were usually severely plain and showed the Scottish preference for claret; but, as we saw in Birmingham, fascination is added by discovering the ingredients of the strange concoctions named on some of them. These were made in many burghs, but the most distinctive met with were made in Edinburgh by John MacDonald, 1817, representing pointer dogs, hung by chains, the wines named on the ground beneath them. Snuff boxes were also made, but the Scottish snuff mull was more distinctive. These again varied in form, but one from Aberdeen, c 1810, was typical of all they should be, for it had a full set of five accoutrements suspended on five chains from a ring, about $\frac{1}{2}$in below the silver top mounting of a short-cut ox horn. There was then far more ritual to the taking of snuff, and the use of forefinger and thumb did not suffice.

Aberdeen, one of the earliest in importance, had no bad period but was at its best in the first half of the eighteenth century. Output continued until well after the Act of 1836 should have stopped local production, the city's goldsmiths snapping their fingers at authority as they always had, while producing individual silver that owed nothing to Edinburgh, London, or anywhere else. A salver by George Robertson, c 1730, is sufficient to show that Aberdeen was not concerned with dull austerity. The silver was good, imaginative and cultured, and while the name of Coline Allan, a worthy apprentice of George Cooper, cannot be forgotten, a long purse would be necessary to collect the work of many others.

While Edinburgh and Glasgow continued to make silver distinguished for its solid worth and fine line, Perth and Inverness came second only to Aberdeen in keeping alive their native individuality. The whole subject of Scottish provincial silver is full of fascinating possibilities, wider by far than Jackson knew, and to mention all would read like a list. Equally, only a fraction of the things made have been able to find space here, although it does seem a pity to have left out bannock-racks, so evocative of good Scottish breakfasts and all that being in Scotland means.

Yet Edinburgh must have the last word, for during the Regency and the immediate succeeding years, a period hardly noticeable for good taste, the city continued to make good, solid silver which one can live with—and collect. Can anyone ask for more?

# Acknowledgements

The writing of this book would not have been possible without the kindness, co-operation and help of those who have given their time and experience to discuss with me the fascinating subject of silver made in their own particular region of the British Isles, its early history and the social customs involved. Many have also entered into the most helpful correspondence, while directors and curators of museums, town clerks and others have supplied invaluable lists of their treasures. The author is eternally grateful to all, most especially to those who have read individual chapters, giving expert advice, gladly incorporated, while bearing with my own conjecture and approach to the subject. These include Mr M. D. G. Clayton of Christies International; Mr John Abbey of W. H. Wilson Ltd; Mr A. P. W. Bruford of Exeter; Mr William Lee of York; Mr Brand Inglis of Spink & Son Ltd; Mr G. J. Levine of Norwich; Miss Sheenah Smith of the Castle Museum, Norwich; the Rev James Gilchrist; Canon Maurice H. Ridgway; Mr David Richards of Hawker Marras Ltd, Birmingham; Mr Peter Hughes, Assistant Keeper of Art, National Museum of Wales; Dr William O'Sullivan, Royal Irish Academy, Dublin; and Mr Henry Steuart Fothringham of Grantully, Perthshire. To Mandy, who has done the drawings and, with Judy, typed and retyped, coping with inconsistencies of spelling, and protecting a would-be author from a chaotic household, affectionate thanks are truly deserved.

# Bibliography

## General Books

Bannister, Judith. *An Introduction to Old English Silver*, Evans Bros (1965)

Buckley, J. J. *Irish Altar Plate*

Came, Richard. *Silver* (particularly for foreign and American influences)

Delieb, Eric. *Investing in Silver*, Barrie & Rockliff (1967)

Dickenson, H. W. *Matthew Boulton*

Evans, J. T. *The Church Plate of Breconshire* (1909)
  *The Church Plate of Cardiganshire* (1914)
  *The Church Plate of Carmarthenshire* (1907)
  *The Church Plate of Gowerland*, including full summary of the church plate in the Diocese of St Davids (1921)
  *The Church Plate of Pembrokeshire* (1905)
  *The Church Plate of Radnorshire* (1910)

Finlay, Ian. *Scottish Gold & Silver Work*, Chatto & Windus (1956)

Gilchrist, Rev James. *Anglican Church Plate*, 'The Connoisseur' and Michael Joseph (1967)

Harris, Ian. *The Price Guide to Antique Silver 1969/70*, The Antique Collector's Club (1969)

Hayden, Arthur. *Chats on Old Silver*

Hayward, John. *Huguenot Silver in England*, Faber & Faber (1959)

Jackson, Sir Charles J. *English Goldsmiths & Their Marks*, second edition, revised and enlarged; an unabridged and unaltered re-publication of the work first published by Macmillan & Co (1921) Dover, New York (1964)
  *An Illustrated History of English Plate*, 2 volumes (1911)

Jones, E. Alfred. *The Old Silver Sacramental Vessels of Foreign Protestant Churches in England* (1908)
*The Church Plate of the Diocese of Bangor* (1906)
Monson-Fitzjohn, G. J. *Drinking Vessels of Bygone Days*
Lewes, W. J. *Lead Mining in Wales,* University of Wales Press (1967)
Oman, Charles C. *English Domestic Silver,* A. & C. Black (1962), fifth edition
*English Church Plate* (1957)
*English Silversmith's Work, Civil & Domestic,* in the Victoria and Albert Museum, HMSO (1965) (mainly photographs)
Ridgway, Maurice H. *Chester Goldsmiths from Early Times to 1725,* John Sherratt & Sons (1968)
Scottowe, P. F. *The Leaf & The Tree* (1963)
Taylor, Gerald. *Silver,* Penguin Books (1956)
Wardle, Patricia. *Victorian Silver & Silver Plate*
Wenham, Edward. *Old Sheffield Plate,* G. Bell & Sons Ltd
Whitworth, Rev E. W. *Wine Labels*

## Society Proceedings

*Archaeologia Aeliana,* 'Goldsmiths of Newcastle' by J. R. Boyle (1894), and many isolated references in several other volumes
*Report and Transactions of the Devonshire Association* (1905). Rev J. Chanter on 'Devon church plate', vol 37, and on 'Barnstaple', vol 49. On 'Plymouth silver' (1936 and '37)
*Proceedings of Society of Antiquities of Scotland* (1935). Commander G. E. P. How, RN, on 'Early Scottish Spoons'
*Proceedings of Suffolk Institute of Archaeology,* vol 12. 'An Ipswich worker of Elizabethan Church Plate', by H. C. Casley
Yorkshire Archaeological Society, *Yorkshire Church Plate,* 2 vols by T. M. Fallow

## Articles from Periodicals

*Antique Collector*
Lee, William. 'Rare Yorkshire Church Plate', April/May/June (1967)
—— 'Civic & Other Silver Plate in York', October/November (1967)
Penzer, Dr N. M. 'The History of the Beaker', December (1965)

*Apollo*
Oman, Charles C. 'Plate and Prestige', January (1969)
*Burlington Magazine*
Jones, E. Alfred. 'Old English Plate at the Church Congress, Great Yarmouth, 1907' (1908)
*Collector's Guide*
Fothringham, H. S. 'Notes on Scottish Provincial Silver', August (1970)
Henderson, James. 'Scottish Silver', August (1970)
Hulbert, John. 'Scottish Standing Mazers', August (1968)
Ticher, Kurt. 'The Lion Rampant on Mid-18th Century Limerick Silver', August (1969)
*The Connoisseur*
Ball, Stanley. 'Ancient Chester Goldsmiths & Their Work', May (1932)
Gorman, M. J. 'An Internationally-known Hotelier and His Private Collection of Silver', June (1967)
Oman, Charles C. 'The Civic Plate & Insignia of the City of Norwich', vol 156 (1964) (also reproduced in pamphlet form)
—— 'Civic Plate & Insignia of York', October and November (1967)
*Country Life*
Hughes, G. Bernard. 'Hallmarks on British Provincial Silver', 9 April (1959)
Prattent, O. J. 'Marks of the Plymouth Goldsmiths', 20 October (1960)
*Newcastle & Gateshead Chamber of Commerce Journal*
Reid, C. Leo. 'Old Newcastle Goldsmiths', March (1928)

## Exhibition and other Catalogues

'The Connoisseur' Period Guides (edited by Ralph Edwards and L. G. G. Ramsay)
Church Treasure of West Suffolk at Ickworth, June 1967
Devon Festival, 1957. 'Exeter Silversmiths' Domestic Silver of the Sixteenth–Eighteenth Centuries', at the Royal Albert Memorial Museum, Exeter
Ellis catalogue of 'English Provincial Spoons', November 1935, with foreword by Commander G. E. P. How, RN
'English Silver of the Seventeenth Century'. Exhibition catalogue of Bowes Museum, Barnard Castle, compiled by J. W. Clark, 1961

Harlech Loan Collection of Silver by D. Kighley Baxendall, 1939, from National Museum of Wales

The Silver of the Holborne of Menstrie Museum, 1929

Norwich Silver 1563–1706. Loan exhibition at the Castle Museum, Norwich, with introduction by G. N. Barrett

Riley Smith catalogue, Christies, 23 April 1953

Society of Antiquaries of Newcastle Upon Tyne. Exhibition of silver plate of Newcastle manufacture: Black Gate Museum, 1897

Copies of accession sheets of Carlisle Museum & Durham Corporation Plate

Town, Church and Cathedral Guides to various places

Catalogues published annually: The Antiques Dealers' Fair; Irish Antiques Fair

Catalogues published frequently: Christie's, Manson & Woods; Sotheby & Co

## Miscellaneous

*A Guide to Irish Antiques, 1969*

Jackson, Robert Wyse. *Collecting Irish Silver Spoons*

# Index